History and Electronic Artefacts

History and Electronic Artefacts

EDITED BY

Edward Higgs

CLARENDON PRESS · OXFORD

1998

Oxford University Press, Great Clarendon Street, Oxford OX2 6DP

Oxford New York

Athens Auckland Bangkok Bogota Bombay
Buenos Aires Calcutta Cape Town Dar es Salaam
Delhi Florence Hong Kong Istanbul Karachi
Kuala Lumpur Madras Madrid Melbourne
Mexico City Nairobi Paris Singapore
Taipei Tokyo Toronto Warsaw

and associated companies in
Berlin Ibadan

Oxford is a registered trade mark of Oxford University Press

Published in the United States by
Oxford University Press Inc., New York

British Library Cataloguing in Publication Data
Data available

Library of Congress Cataloging in Publication Data
History and electronic artefacts/edited by Edward Higgs.
Includes bibliographical references (p.   ).
1. Documents in machine-readable form. 2. Documents in machine-readable
form—Conservation and restoration. 3. Documents in machine-readable form—Europe.
4. Documents in machine-readable form—Europe—Conservation and restoration.
5. History—Research.   I. Higgs, Edward, 1952–   .
CD974.4.H57 1997   025.06'001432—dc21   97–14790
ISBN 0–19–823633–6
ISBN 0–19–823634–4 (pbk)

1 3 5 7 9 10 8 6 4 2

Typeset by Pure Tech India Limited, Pondicherry
Printed in Great Britain on acid-free paper by
Biddles Ltd., Guildford and King's Lynn

CONTENTS

LIST OF FIGURES

ABBREVIATIONS

ACCIS	Advisory Committee for the Coordination of Information Systems
ACLIS	Australian Council of Libraries and Information Services
AHC	Association for History and Computing
AHDS	Arts and Humanities Data Service
AI	artificial intelligence
AIM	Advanced Informatics in Medicine
AMA	American Medical Association
ANA	Australian National Archives
ARA	Algemeen Rijksarchief
ASCII	American Standard Code for Information Interchange
ASU	automation systems of management
BIRON	Bibliographic Retrieval On-line
BL	British Library
BLOB	binary large object
bpi	bits per inch
CAD/CADD	computer-aided design/drafting
CAL	computer-aided learning
CBS	Central Bureau of Statistics
CCTA	Central Computer and Telecommunications Agency
CD	compact disc
CESSDA	Council of European Social Science Data Archives
COM	computer output microfilm
CPA	Commission on Preservation and Access
CP/M	Control Program for Microcomputers
CPSU	Communist Party of the Soviet Union
CRDA	computer-readable data archive
CSIRO	Commonwealth Scientific Industrial and Research Organization
CTI	Computers in Teaching Initiative
CURL	Consortium of Research Libraries
DAT	digital audio tape
DBMS	database management system

DDA	Danish Data Archives
DDP	data documention publication
DIAG	Datasets Inter-Agency Group
DIP	document image processing
DP	data-processing
DoH	Department of Health
DOS	Disk Operating System
DRO	departmental records officer
DSS	decision support system
DSS	Department of Social Services
EBCDIC	Extended Binary Coded Decimal Interchange Code
EDI	electronic data interchange
EDP	electronic data-processing
EIS	executive information systems
e-Lib	Electronic Libraries
e-mail	electronic mail
EMBASE	Excerpta Medica Database
ENIAC	Electronic Numerical Integrator and Computer
EPoSS	electronic point-of-sale scanning
EPR	electronic patient record
ESRC	Economic and Social Research Council
EU	European Union
FIGIT	Follett Implementation Group for Information Technology
GIS	geographical information system
GRAIL	GALEN Representation and Integration Language
GDR	German Democratic Republic
HBR	*Harvard Business Review*
HEFCE	Higher Education Funding Council for England
ICA	International Council on Archives
ICD	International Classification of Diseases
ICPSR	International Consortium for Political and Social Research
IFDO	International Federation of Data Organizations
IHR	Institute of Historical Research
IMOSA	Information Management and Office Systems Advancement
INION	Institute of Scientific Information on Social Sciences
ISC	Information Systems Committee
ISO	International Organization for Standardization
ISSC	Information Services Sub-Committee
IT	information technology
JISC	Joint Information Systems Committee

LAN	local area network
MAN	metropolitan area network
MBIT	International Bureau of Information and Telecommunications
mbps	million bits per second
MRDF	machine-readable data file
NAPA	National Academy of Public Administration
NARA	National Archives and Records Administration
NASA	National Aeronautics and Space Administration
NCBI	National Center for Biotechnology Information
NHDA	Netherlands Historical Data Archive
NHS	National Health Service
NLM	National Library of Medicine
NRPO	New Range Planning Organization
NSA	National Sound Archive
NSF	National Science Foundation
ODA	Office Document Architecture
OPAC	online public access catalogue
OSI	Open Systems Interconnection
PADI	Preserving Access to Digital Information
PC	personal computer
PRO	Public Record Office
RAD	Rijksarchiefdienst
RAM	random access memory
RDBMS	relational database management system
RLG	Research Libraries Group
RLIN	RLG information network
SAS	Statistical Analysis System
SD	study description
SGML	Standard Generalized Markup Language
SNOMED	Systematic Nomenclature of Medicine
SPSS	Statistical Package for the Social Services
SQL	Structured Query Language
STAR	Steinmetz Data Archive
TEAM	Tools for Electronic Archives Management
TEI	Text Encoding Initiative
TIFF	Tagged Image File Format
TLTP	Teaching and Learning Training Project
Unesco	United Nations Educational, Scientific, and Cultural Organization

UMLS	Unified Medical Language System
URL	Universal Resource Locator
VINITI	All-Russian Institute of Scientific and Technical Information
v-mail	voice mail
WAN	wide area network
WORM	write once read many

LIST OF CONTRIBUTORS

Lynne Brindley

Lynne Brindley is the Librarian of the British Library of Political and Economic Science at the London School of Economics. Her previous posts have included Director of Library and Information Services and Pro-Vice Chancellor for Information Technology at Aston University, and most recently she was a principal consultant with KPMG Management Consulting. She has written widely on the electronic campus and is a member of the HEFCE Libraries Review (as Chairman of its IT Sub-Group) and the JISC (Joint Information Systems Committee), which is responsible for policy and developments in UK academic networking, data sets, and other IT initiatives.

Martin Campbell-Kelly

Martin Campbell-Kelly is Reader in the Department of Computer Science at the University of Warwick. His research interests include the history of information-processing, the computer industry, and science/industrial policy. His publications include *ICL: A Business and Technical History* (1989). He is currently making a study of Victorian data-processing techniques.

Peter Doorn

Peter Doorn is a lecturer in historical computing at Leiden University and Director of the Netherlands Historical Data Archive (NHDA). He is co-director of a transnational postgraduate course in history and computing sponsored by the European Social Fund. His research interests focus on the settlement history of Central Greece.

Martin Gardner

Martin Gardner is a research fellow at the University of Glasgow. He has ten years' experience as a clinician in UK hospital medicine, chiefly in the specialities of anaesthesia and intensive care. Since obtaining a degree in computing science, he has concentrated on research in medical informatics, with interests in information retrieval, case-based reasoning, clinical decision support, and the World Wide Web.

Claes Gränström

Claes Gränström studied Latin, classical archaeology, and history at the University of Lund and wrote his thesis on sources in Swedish medieval history at the Regional Archives in Lund in 1968. In 1969 he moved to the National Archives in Stockholm, where he is now Deputy Director-General. In recent years he has worked on various aspects of the record life cycle, appraisal, cataloguing, availability, security, sensitivity, and integrity of electronic records. He has in various capacities taken part in the work of several government committees, which have dealt, amongst other things, with freedom of information, integrity and archival legislation, mainly concerning electronic information.

Daniel Greenstein

Daniel Greenstein is Director of the Arts and Humanities Data Service. Before taking up this post he was a Senior Lecturer in the Department of Modern History at Glasgow University. He completed his doctorate at Oxford and edited *Modelling Historical Data* (1991). Oxford University Press published his *A Historian's Guide to Computing in 1995*. He is also History Representative on the Text-Encoding Initiative.

Edward Higgs

Edward Higgs was originally trained as a social historian, with an interest in the quantitative analysis of historical data. He worked at the Public Record Office (the UK central government archives) for fifteen years from 1978 to 1993. He was the project manager for the establishment of a computer-readable data archive at the PRO. From 1993 to 1996 he was a research fellow at the Wellcome Unit for the History of Medicine, Oxford, and is now a lecturer in history at the University of Exeter.

Hans Hofman

Hans Hofman studied history, archival theory, and informatics at university, and has worked as an archivist in the Rijksarchiefdienst in the Netherlands for twenty years. He is currently the Director of the Electronic Records Project, which involves all the archival institutions in the Netherlands. This project, linking public authorities at all levels (central state, provincial, and municipal) in order to meet the challenge of electronic records, is under the joint guidance of the Home Office and the Ministry of Education, Science, and Culture.

Denise Lievesley

Denise Lievesley is Director of the Data Archive located at Essex University. A statistics graduate from University College London, she began her career in the government as a sampling statistician. She subsequently moved to the Survey Methods Centre, an ESRC-designated research centre, where she researched non-response and panel design. Together with colleagues, she established a Master's Degree in Survey Research. In early 1989 she took up the post of Director of the International Statistical Institute in the Hague and served in this post until she joined Essex University at the start of the 1992 academic year.

Hans-Jørgen Marker

Hans-Jørgen Marker completed his studies in history and mathematics at the University of Aarhus in 1982. Since 1984 he has been employed as one of three academics in the Danish Data Archive, where he serves as head of the department for historical studies and for technical development and support. His research has concentrated on Danish prices and wages in the sixteenth and seventeenth centuries, and studies concerned with the methodological aspects of representing historical sources in machine-readable form.

Tatyana Moiseenko

Tatyana Moiseenko currently works for the Inter Documentation Company in Leiden. Before taking up this post she was senior researcher at the Institute of Russian History at the Russian Academy of Sciences (Moscow) and senior lecturer in the Department of Information and Computer Sciences at the Russian State University of the Humanities. She is also a member of the Council of the Russian Association of History and Computing.

Jeffrey D. Morelli

Jeffrey Morelli is Director of J Morelli Consulting Ltd. Originally trained as a chemical engineer, he has spent more than fifteen years in data documentation and records management in a variety of industry sectors. For the last ten years he has been a consultant, specializing in the re-engineering of business processes and supporting information systems.

R. J. Morris

R. J. Morris is Professor of Economic and Social History at the University of Edinburgh, where he has taught since 1968. He was a founding member of the Association for History and Computing and edited *History and Computing* for the AHC. His research interests include the class and urban structure of nineteenth-century Britain. His recent case study *Class, Sect and Party: The Making of the British Middle Class* (1990) was based on a major record-linkage project.

Alice Prochaska

Alice Prochaska became Director of Special Collections in the British Library in July 1992. She has written on nineteenth- and twentieth-century British history, but her career to date has been spent mainly as an archivist and administrator, in the Public Record Office and the Institute of Historical Research. She is Chairman of the National Council on Archives.

W. Boyd Rayward

W. Boyd Rayward is Professor of Librarianship and Dean of the Faculty of Professional Studies at the University of New South Wales, Sydney. Before returning to Australia in 1986, he was Dean of the Graduate Library School at the University of Chicago. He is also a former editor of the *Library Quarterly*. His research has involved the historical study of attempts to organize information at the international level. Among his books is *The Universe of Information: The Work of Paul Otlet for Documentation and International Organisation* (1975), and he is the translator and editor of a selection of essays and papers of Paul Otlet published as *The International Organisation and Dissemination of Knowledge* (1991).

Seamus Ross

Seamus Ross is Director of Humanities Computing and Information Management at the University of Glasgow. Before taking up this post he worked for a company specializing in expert systems and software development, first as a software engineer and latterly as manager for European operations. He was then Assistant Secretary for Information

Technology at the British Academy until 1996. After completing an MA in medieval history at the University of Pennsylvania he took his doctorate at the University of Oxford. He co-edited *Computing for Archaeologists* (1991) and has published articles on various aspects of computing and history/archaeology. More recently he co-authored the report of the British Academy and British Library Research and Development Department entitled *Information Technology in Humanities Scholarship: British Achievements, Prospects, and Barriers* (1993).

Jean Samuel

Jean Samuel is Records Manager for Pfizer Central Research, a pharmaceutical company based in Kent. Prior to taking up this post in 1989 she was head of the BBC's Records Centre. After taking an undergraduate degree in classics at the University of Hull she earned an archival qualification from Liverpool University. She is an active member of informational professional groups, including AIOFI (Pharmaceutical) and the Records Management Society.

Kevin Schürer

Kevin Schürer is a lecturer in the History Department at the University of Essex. He is also seconded to the Cambridge Group for the History of Population and Social Structure, where he is currently working on a study of family structure and demographic change in the late nineteenth and early twentieth centuries. He was a founder member of the Association for History and Computing and currently serves as its Secretary. In 1990 he received a British Academy award to undertake a study on the feasibility of establishing a historical data archive in the UK. Until 1996 he was Assistant Director at the ESRC Data Archive, where he had special responsibility for data acquisition.

Helen Simpson

Helen Simpson is Information Systems Customer Support Manager with British Telecom. The role aims to maximize the value of information systems to the user community, including responsibility for IS education and training, helpdesk, and office systems support. After initial training as a historian and archivist, Helen spent the majority of her working life in the oil industry with British Petroleum. She moved between information management and information technology roles, heading teams within the IT field and planning corporate information management strategy.

Doron Swade

Doron Swade is Senior Curator of Computing and Data Processing at the National Museum of Science and Industry (Science Museum) London. He is an electronics/computer engineer and a historian of computing. He has published articles on the history of computing and curatorship and a study of *Charles Babbage and his Calculating Engines* (1991), and has co-authored *The Dream Machine: Exploring the Computer Age* (1991).

Dr Michael Wettengel

Michael Wettengel is the head of the machine-readable archives section of the Federal Archives (Bundesarchiv) in Koblenz, Germany, where he has worked since 1989. He is a trained historian and holds a Ph.D. on the history of nineteenth-century political and social movements from the University of Hamburg. He gives professional training courses for archivists on electronic records at the Archival Institute (Archivschule) in Marburg.

Ronald W. Zweig

Ronald Zweig is Senior Lecturer in Jewish History at Tel Aviv University and Chairman of the Humanities Faculty Computing Committee. He is currently editor of the journal *Studies in Zionism*, author of two books *Britain and Palestine during the Second World War* (1986) and *German Reparations and the Jewish World* (1987), and editor of a third, *David Ben-Gurion: Political Leadership in Israel* (1991). He is a graduate of the University of Sydney and received his doctorate at Cambridge.

Introduction

EDWARD HIGGS

The present work originated in a conference in London in June 1993 sponsored by the British Academy and the International Association for History and Computing. This brought together archivists, historians, librarians, museum curators, and record managers to discuss matters of mutual interest with respect to the management, storage, and dissemination of electronic records. Such an interdisciplinary approach was one which had previously been absent from the debates in this field. The proceedings of the conference were published in a limited print run (Ross and Higgs 1994), and the interest shown in that volume encouraged the editor to prepare this more polished work for wider circulation. The contributions to the original meeting which addressed wider issues have been published here in as revised and updated form as possible, and several newly commissioned chapters on related subjects have also been included.

After an initial introductory essay by Seamus Ross surveying the field as a whole, *History and Electronic Artefacts* is divided into four parts. In the first part, historians examine the implications which the spread of electronic information systems have for their discipline. Two historians (Morris and Zweig) express concern over the possible loss of societal memory inherent in the problems associated with the preservation of electronic artefacts, whilst another (Campbell-Kelly) takes a less pessimistic view. To some extent this difference of opinion may reflect the differing fields of research addressed—social as opposed to business history. The final contribution here (Greenstein) examines the professional issues for the historical community associated with information technology.

Part Two of *History and Electronic Artefacts* addresses the creation, use, and capture of electronic communications within various types of organization. These include commercial businesses (Simpson), British central government (Higgs), and the National Health Service (Gardner). Another contribution (Samuel) looks in more detail at the problems associated with the use of e-mail systems.

The chapters in Part Three examine various theoretical aspects of the preservation and dissemination of electronic artefacts. Schürer and Morelli raise some basic issues in this field, whilst others look at the impact of information technology on preservation policies in archives (Higgs) and museums (Swade). A final chapter (Rayward) considers whether the distinctions drawn between archives, libraries, and museums will retain their validity in the new Information Age.

In the final part of the book, a series of European authors describe the practical steps being taken in their institutions to address the problems described by earlier contributors. Three chapters discuss the situation in the United Kingdom, covering research libraries (Brindley), the British Library (Prochaska), and the Data Archive at the University of Essex (Lievesley). The markedly different treatment of the electronic records of defunct communist regimes in Germany (Wettengel) and Russia (Moiseenko) are then considered. Studies of the archiving of electronic data in Denmark (Marker), the Netherlands (Doorn), and Sweden (Gränström) reveal the differing approaches to the subject in these countries. The final chapter (Hofman) surveys the possibilities for an integrated approach to electronic preservation and dissemination amongst European national archives. The European perspective and the practical examples presented here are an important supplement to the theoretical literature in the field of electronic archives currently emanating from North America.

The contributions to the differing parts often take up themes raised in other sections, although discussing them from differing points of view and in a differing register. This is heartening, since it is an indication of the incipient formation of a unified field of study, to which this volume, and the differing disciplines represented here, can contribute. This does not mean, of course, that the authors represented here necessarily agree on the solutions to problems, or even their exact nature. This is to be expected in a multi-disciplinary project such as *History and Electronic Artefacts*, especially given the recent onset of many of the challenges discussed. Debate, and even disagreement, is, however, the first step towards synthesis and positive action.

Reference

Ross, S., and Higgs, E. (1993) (eds.), *Electronic Information Resources and Historians: European Perspectives* (St Katharinen).

The Expanding World of Electronic Information and the Past's Future

SEAMUS ROSS

ABSTRACT

Across the range of human activity contemporary society depends on digital information. The capture of increasing amounts of the record of our activities in digital form will provide future historians opportunities to study twentieth-century society in new ways. Such work will depend on these digital materials remaining accessible. This chapter examines the kinds of information which contemporary society is creating, the kinds of associated information which must be created if it is to be retained, and the obstacles to its survival.

From credit-card data to medical records, from airline databases to tax records, from electronic mail (e-mail) to digital film and sound, vast amounts of information about late-twentieth-century society exist in electronic form. This growing dependence of society upon digital information will change the fabric of the source material available to future historians. However, 94 per cent of all business information in Europe and the USA is currently in paper form, and the increasing use of personal computers (PCs) has continued to foster a dramatic rise in the production of paper-based records (*Network* 1993: 73). The demands made on electronically stored information by local and national governments, companies, charities, service providers (e.g. financial institutions), and individuals generated in 1993 in the USA alone an estimated one trillion sheets of printed matter. This reflects their need to satisfy customers, meet regulatory obligations, market services, and make the most advantageous decisions. While paper continues to play a crucial role in the provision and distribution of strategic management or executive information (Campbell-Kelly, Chapter 4, this volume), in many other areas of business and government electronic data have become the driving force.

Businesses from banking to transportation to retailing rely on the capture, use, exchange, and storage of operational information in digital form. Although most transactions involving operational information produce paper as their by-product (e.g. till receipts, credit-card vouchers, tickets, prescription forms, invoices, and statements), these paper records include only a fragment of the material captured in electronic form during a transaction. The sheer quantity, diversity, and rich quality of the electronic information resources from which these records have been derived indicate that their preservation in electronic form could provide historians with a better opportunity to understand our period than the paper records alone could ever do. Just as contemporary workers use operational information as the foundation for paper-based strategic and management reports, historians will want to have the opportunity to analyse the base data for themselves. They will wish to examine them in ways contemporary users do not need to and to analyse them in the context of other data sets. Digital information is a cultural product, e-facts, and it forms an essential fragment of the cultural record of contemporary society.

Awareness among historians of the changing character of contemporary information resources has until very recently been limited. Archivists, however, have been discussing the increasing prevalence of electronic records since the 1960s. Richard Cox's (1993) review of the literature on electronic records up to 1993 is a good starting-point, and more recent versions are available online (Universal Resource Locator (URL): http://www2.lis.pitt.edu/~nhprc/bibtc.html). The numbers of studies are increasing quickly, but the discussion is still very much driven by problems and activities in the USA, Canada, and Australia, although there is much work beginning in Europe. The focus has been mainly on government records at a national level, and the issues have been examined from the vantage of the archivist. Few studies approach the problems from the point of view of the historian; an issue of the journal *History and Computing* (1992) and *Electronic Information Resources and Historians* (Ross and Higgs 1993) are two notable exceptions. National governments and international organizations (e.g. United Nations, Unesco) were among the early users of computers to process large data sets (e.g. census data, tax records). Statutory obligations require that they retain their records in accessible form, and they have the financial resources necessary to experiment with the possible ways to undertake such preservation. In attempting to fulfil these duties, archivists have struggled to address such record-retention problems as hardware and software obsolescence, media degradation, and data documentation.

The work of archivists has established the remarkable size and complexity of the problem for governmental records (see NAPA 1991; Bikson and Frinking 1993). By the year 2000 an estimated 75 per cent of all US government transactions will be handled electronically (United States Congress, House Committee on Government Operations 1990: 2). The precise implications of this statement are not so clear (e.g. will these be transactions of significance in recording activities, processes, and decisions? how are transactions defined? how will they be documented? what manifestation of the transaction will be preserved?). What is evident is that the transition from paper to computer-based information collection and storage is occurring across a spectrum of human activity.

The increasingly significant role that the capture and manipulation of electronic information plays in contemporary day-to-day transactions becomes evident if we consider our last visit to a supermarket. At the checkout the cashier passes each item being purchased across a scanner which reads barcodes, on the pre-packaged items, which carry encoded information. Once the barcodes on the items have been scanned and the tabulated amount displayed, the purchaser may present a direct-debit card (or a charge card) to make payment. When the cashier passes the card through a reader, information held in a magnetic strip on its reverse is read. The cashier then initiates a sequence of automated steps to check a cardholder database to determine whether the card is legitimate (i.e. not stolen) and that the amount of the charge is within the cardholder's available credit limit. If these checks raise no anomalies, a charge for the cost of the items is allocated to the cardholder's account. This transaction results in the production of two paper outputs (one of which is in duplicate): a receipt listing the items purchased including the amount charged per item and a voucher signed by the cardholder authorizing the account debit or charge (one copy is kept by the store and the other by the purchaser). Tens of millions of similar electronically based transactions take place every day, all producing relatively similar paper outputs and 'electronic records'. Store computer systems use this barcoded data to locate pricing information, calculate automatically multi-buy discounts, collect data for sales and stock

accounting, perform inventory control and automated ordering, produce item-by-item profit-and-loss analysis, and identify the items that
have attracted greatest customer demand. For example, the grocery
retailer H. E. Butt Grocery Co. of San Antonio, Texas, provides its
staff with access to information in digital form about 275,000 items
by time and by store to provide them with the data to identify trends in
consumer behaviour. The individual paper by-products of each transaction may have particularist historical value, but their dispersed character makes it unlikely that their meaning could be reconstructed
without the aggregate data from which they were derived. The electronically captured information could be of remarkable historical value.
This is especially true for research into social history, the history of
consumerism, economic history, and ethnic/regional history. As Morris
explains (Chapter 2, this volume), not only will the transactions themselves provide a remarkable resource, but how they took place (i.e. their
context) will have historical significance.

Merely imagining the contexts in which we encounter electronic
systems offers some ideas about the diversity of electronically stored
information. Bank and credit-card details, airline reservations, medical
and genetic records, inland-revenue data, insurance files, mortgage
records, insurance records, satellite images, product manuals, and
maps are all examples of the variety of information encoded via a
range of input devices from keyboards to scanners on a daily basis. In
the commercial and the public sector, and even on a more private level,
astonishing amounts of data are being created as word-processed documents, some of which are printed out, but others, such as e-mail, are
sent over the wires and viewed only on screen by the recipient or data
user. In mid-1997 there are some fifty million users worldwide of the
most commonly used electronic network, Internet, a figure that is
growing at a rate of 10 per cent per month. Little of the information
available on the network is adequately archived and even less of it is
suitably documented (Ross 1995).

The amounts of information exchanged by participants in the Internet phenomena are small by comparison to the data which computers
automatically move across networks about financial transactions. It is
worth bearing in mind just how much data we are talking about. 'Visa
International, the biggest credit-card company, handles over 6 billion
electronic transactions a year—a figure that is expected to rise to 15
billion by 2000. To save itself from being swamped in data, Visa dumps
its records after only six months' (*The Economist*, 18 Sept. 1993: 90). By

the beginning of 1997 Visa International's services were marketed by 20,600 member financial institutions, and its 546 million cards were accepted at 13 million locations worldwide (URL: http://www. visa.com). So far the demographic and market data contained in these records have not been fully extracted before the data are disposed of. If the commercial benefits to Visa of retaining the data do not outweigh the costs of their retention, then there can be little hope that such data will be accessible to historians in the future. Historians would be likely to 'mine' this resource in different ways, examining it with change over time in mind and linking credit transaction data or travel information with, say, medical records or socio-economic groups. They will use the information to understand not the individual transactions recorded in the data, but the society(ies) that created them. In a study of the contemporary issues concerning the dichotomy between privacy and market value of information, Kenneth Laudon noted that in the USA:

The 400 million credit records maintained by the three largest credit agencies, the 700 million annual drug prescription records, the 100 million computerized medical records, the 600 million personal records estimated to be owned by the 200 largest superbureaus, and the 5 billion records maintained (and often sold) by the federal government, as well as the billions of records maintained and stored by state and local government, all have market value... (Laudon 1996: 96)

What is evident is that in post-industrial societies the collection of data sets is both diverse and comprehensive.

In the UK the three large credit reference agencies, Infolink, CCN, and Equifax, hold data on 100 million accounts. While much of their data relates to credit requests and fraud, an increasing amount of information details customer transactions. CCN, for instance, has a database of over forty-three million consumers in the UK which includes details of an individual's creditworthiness, lifestyle, gender, age, and purchasing habits. While this information is valuable as a contemporary business resource, it would be immensely valuable to historians studying the UK in the twentieth century. This would be true even if only bi-annual or annual 'snapshots' of it survived in electronic form. The credit agencies, data provide a detailed profile for only the top two-thirds of the social hierarchy. The Department of Social Security (DSS) in the UK, for instance, has a file on almost every person, and, from its 4,500 dumb terminals and 20,000 personal computers (PCs), its 4,200 staff and 800 contractors process fifteen million transactions every week (*Computing*

1994: 28). The great bulk of these transactions relate to the poorest one-third of society. The combined picture offered by the credit agency and DSS data sets would provide historians with the chance to examine the full cross section of the population.

Satellite imaging provides an important source to chart the impact of human activity on the environment and man's changing relationship with it. For example, material of this kind provides valuable information about the relationship between the built environment and the natural environment. Major new initiatives are being undertaken to collect data to improve contemporary understanding of these issues and to form a foundation for studies of change over time. The satellites in NASA's Earth Observing System are expected to collect data at rates of several terabytes a day by the year 2000 (Earth Observing System Data and Information System 1992; Kobler *et al.* 1996). These data can only be analysed in their digital form and increasingly sophisticated tools are being developed to assist in this task. Efforts being undertaken by the teams developing the data management systems show that they are aware of the issues of data preservation and access. But the evidence of what became of data collected by early earth-imaging campaigns is not promising. It is well known that many images taken of Brazil in the 1970s, which today could form a useful benchmark for the study of change over time in rainforest coverage and density, are no longer accessible (National Research Council 1995: 31).

This is, however, only one of many scientific research activities which are producing substantial quantities of data, and the study by the National Research Council in the USA indicates just how vulnerable these data are (1995). The commercial value of some information will make certain that it remains accessible. The Human Genome Project, which is generating a digital record of our genetic make-up and will eventually produce a database of billions of records, is a good example of a scientific project producing data which will be curated because of their commercial value. Scientific instruments can capture gigabytes of data every hour as they are used to monitor natural phenomena (e.g. seismic or metrological activity) or experiments. As a result, it is not uncommon for data sets to be as large as a terabyte, and it would not be impossible to collect a petabyte of data. In these data sets is a vast amount of information about bio-diversity, environmental conditions, and our genetic make-up. The modes of communication are changing and this will have implications for the historical record. Science is being reshaped by electronic communication and storage. In disciplines such as physics and medicine, e-mail plays a critical role in how the results of research are exchanged before formal publication (see Samuel, Chapter 7, this volume). Historians of science who want to understand the development of contemporary theories will need more than the printed journals, they will need access to the electronic resource. In order for this material to be available for the future, good records-management practices are essential. Retention of environmental data, experimental data, and other scientific information will provide valuable benchmarks for future scientists, and useful resources for historians. Curiously, while archivists have focused on issues of what makes adequate records (Duranti 1995), the issues surrounding the retention of scientific information and scientific metadata have received little attention.

Discussions of electronic information often focus on large numerical data sets and text files, but these represent a fraction of the uses and products of electronic information. Many architects and mechanical and electrical engineers use computer-aided design/drafting (CAD/CADD) systems. An increasing number of architects use virtual-reality systems to design and 'test' building schemes. Architectural historians will wish to have access to this material. If the information is preserved, it will be in an effort to guarantee its availability in case of legal dispute or product liability. Such preservation will be most likely where particular programs were run to determine the structural stability or the environmental efficiency of a building, or the individual or institution commissioning the structure was asked to accept a particular design after a 'virtual visit to or walk around' the planned building. Unlike numerical data which can fairly easily be migrated from one software/hardware environment to another, this material will be dependent upon access to specific software tools and its interpretation will depend upon the use of original hardware. If this is not possible, then the variation in presentation must be accounted for in some way. Where a geographic information system (GIS) has been used to assess proposals and display data in the course of evaluating road or building development plans, not only the data must be preserved, but also the software, any specialized graphics hardware, and even the virtual records that were created during the decision-making process (see Morelli, Chapter 11, this volume). Since a GIS involves the storage and manipulation of spatial data as well as the use of a graphical display system (two- or three-dimensional data display), it is feasible that the impression conveyed by the same data used in conjunction with a different display system might be distorted and might not permit future users to comprehend the meaning that it originally communicated. It will be crucial to know about the context(s) in which the system had been used. For example, was the end-user the decision-maker or not? Increasing amounts of film and sound are being created in digitial form. In 1996 the British Broadcasting Corporation was working on digitizing its collections. The retroconversion of this material will bring even more benefits, as the technologies to search images and sound achieve the same levels of discrimination as are possible with numerical and alphanumerical data sets.

The proliferation of more than 300 million PCs worldwide has contributed to a trend towards downsizing which has resulted in more and more information being held and analysed locally. Bikson and Frinking (1993: 20–1) have produced alarming evidence of the dangers that this trend poses to the preservation of information. Although many of these PCs are interconnected either locally or to wide area networks, they are used to generate electronic materials which are held and used locally. These computers have helped accelerate the propensity for independent users to generate text, keep spreadsheets (which might be laden with formulae that control calculations and are themselves based on discrete assumptions), and create private databases. Increasingly emphasis is being placed on cooperative work and file-sharing. The electronic versions of these documents might be crucial if historians wanted to understand how the documents were developed, especially in those environments where networks and cooperative work software ('groupware') had been used to enhance worker performance. The final records may exist in paper format, but, because the sources and the evidence for the process of document development are electronic, it will be impossible to understand how the documents evolved. Linked and embedded documents pose problems, as a change to one document effects a change in another. If the process of document generation is to be understood, a record of these links must be retained (see Gardner, Chapter 8, this volume, on linkages in relational databases). As document image processing (DIP), involving the use of optical scanners, mass storage devices, and networked computers, becomes a more common way to store paper information, new problems will arise, because even those strategic documents and the paper products derived from the operational data will exist only in digital form. Most large insurance companies hold the majority of policy and claims data in digital form, often as images of pages or sound recordings.

We must not imagine that such information is confined to large businesses. The majority of businesses have less than ten employees,

and an increasing number of them are turning to information technology (IT) as a low-cost way to improve productivity and record-keeping. Generally records of small traders have been lost to history, and
even with the transition to electronic media this is not likely to change.
Charities are also large users of data sets. The charity Oxfam processes
almost all its transactions electronically: orders for gifts from its catalogue, donations to its appeals, and even its own bills (e.g. telephones).
It also stores vast amounts of data about contributors, and uses this data
to target fund-raising campaigns. It is easy to imagine the uses to which
historians might put this information: from improving their understanding of the role of charities and giving, to providing material to
construct a profile of a twentieth-century charity. Marketing teams
analyse these data to produce profiles of those who give and then use
these profiles better to target fund-raising drives. Will the historian of
the future be adequately served if only the internal reports profiling
donors survive? Or would their understanding of charities be 'significantly' improved if all the data survived? (Compare the answer to this
question in Morris, Chapter 2; Zweig, Chapter 3; and Campbell-Kelly,
Chapter 4, this volume.)

E-mail is changing how we communicate, with whom we communicate, the kinds of material we can exchange as part of a message, and
the speed of communication. As a result, e-mail forms an important
historical source (Bikson and Law 1993). In the USA in the case of
Armstrong v. *Executive Office of the President*, known as the PROFS case,
the judge ruled that, since there was information contained in electronic
records (e.g. transmission and receipt data) that printouts did not
include, printed versions were not faithful to the original (Bearman
1994; Samuel, Chapter 7, this volume). He required, therefore, that
e-mail be preserved in electronic form. The premises underlying this
decision could eventually be extended to all US government electronic
information/data either by the courts or by legislation. More private
e-mail messages might be the electronic equivalent of the Paston letters
that so enliven social history of fifteenth-century England.

What is evident is that the *age of electronic records* opens numerous
possibilities that will enrich the understanding of contemporary culture.
But, on current evidence historians of the future will be left with a large
number of disconnected e-facts that will prove difficult to use. Would a
single airline reservation transaction have value to a future historian?
Would it be practical to retain all airline reservations for posterity?
Swamping future historians with vast amounts of digital information

may impede their research as they attempt to navigate through them. Faced with the vast quantities of surviving documents in conventional archives, few historians can be comprehensive, but, with an electronic archive and a toolchest filled with versatile software, historians could work with digital information more exhaustively (Zweig, Chapter 3, this volume). A combination of data-mining and data-visualization tools and neural networks is currently used in military, insurance, and retailing sectors to extract information from data (Snyder and Stromo 1993; Lee and Ong 1996; Simoudis 1996). These and numerous other software tools and IT methods will eventually be used by historians (see Greenstein, Chapter 5, this volume).

This assumes that most electronically stored information will survive. Perhaps an example would make the issue of the debate clearer. Digital switching systems allow telecommunications providers to record details of calls to justify charges made for the services provided. Would there be value to historians if a record consisting of number calling, number called, time, duration, and cost were retained for every call? Or does this example point up the absurdity of the assumption 'keep everything'? One view holds it might be worth preserving only information derived from the telecommunications record, but that it would make little sense to keep it all. Social historians might want to know that the average phone in the USA was used for twenty minutes a day in 1992, whereas the average phone in the UK was used for only four minutes. The retention of every minor detail might prove impractical, but there will be some historical study that would benefit from all the data being extant. There will be genealogists who will be fascinated to discover who their ancestors spoke to on 15 July 1996 or historical demographers who might wish to use these records to assess the role the telephone played in family communication (did the phone help to maintain family structure over extended distances?). Even if this information were to survive, it might pose significant challenges to future historians if sufficient documentation of the context of its creation and use did not also survive.

Contextual information will help historians answer such questions as: who read the document? what was the effect of its having been read? where was the document created? how was it created? what processes were involved? what was the purpose of its creation? who was it created for? who received it? what effect did its receipt have? why has it survived? (Duchein 1983). To work effectively with electronic resources, future researchers will need information about their form, format, medium, mode, content, context, and usage; even details of how they were originally distributed in society should be retained. We have already seen that in ruling on *Armstrong* v. *Executive Office of the President* the judge stated that, if only the message is retained, much valuable information is lost. Printed versions of electronic records are also made at the expense of opportunities offered by the records being electronic, such as ease of searching, comparing, and integrating with other electronic records (Zweig, Chapter 3, this volume). Not only must we keep the electronic resources but their context must also be retained. Of course, even for records preserved in electronic form a great deal of documentation is essential. Often the task of documentation fails to preserve remarkably important information, such as contextual information, or details of purpose. To understand a system adequately, the user requirements, functional specifications, user documentation as well as information about the behaviour of the organization that created the resource must be retained for as long as the data are kept.

In the case of images, for instance, metadata are needed about: how they were captured, how many times removed is the digital image from the original object, whether the digital image had been modified, how many different formats the digital image has been migrated through before it arrived in its current format, how was colour calibrated and recalibrated? Future historians may even wish to know how the image was originally distributed in society—on a stand-alone computer in a museum, on CD-ROM, or over networks. Metadata include information to allow the user to identify the resources; details of their content; terms of access; guidelines about how to open and read the material; assistance with the 'meaning' and details of how, why, and when the resource was created; information about functionality, technical requirements, and provenance—'the nature of the process that produced and/or maintains the source'. Metadata are expensive to create, but standards in this area are just beginning to evolve (Bearman 1994; Moen 1995; Weibel 1995).

The quantity and richness of knowledge of the cultural framework necessary to understand information or records increase as the time distance from the creation of records increases, so that what is suitable contextual information for contemporary data reuse may not be suitable for reuse of those data—say, climatic, pollution, or nuclear-waste-disposal records—100 years from now. In other words, over time increasing amounts of cultural, social, and linguistic information become essential to understand the context of a record. Metadata reflect current understandings of evidentiality and 'recordness', and will change over time. The effect of these factors on metadata encapsulation strategies cannot be ignored. This means that the question of 'what is the period of historical/record relevance?' must be asked.

Where governments retain electronic records, it is usually because national legislation requires their preservation. Even then, not all records are preserved. In the USA a survey conducted in 1989–90 by the National Academy of Public Administration (NAPA) for the National Archives found more than 9,000 databases in use throughout the agencies of the Federal Government. Of these, some 1,789 were considered major databases, but the NAPA team thought only 919 of them were worthy of examination by a panel of experts to determine whether or not they should be preserved. After this examination the panel of experts concluded that only 448 were worth transferring to the National Archives (NAPA 1991). Legal issues play a role in the preservation and destruction of the contemporary cultural heritage. These include rights of access, rights of privacy, statutory requirements covering record retention, and the need to secure records for use as evidence in the event of legal dispute (see Gränström, Chapter 22, this volume). Some laws, such as the UK's Data Protection Act, which states that data shall not be kept longer than is necessary for the purposes for which they were collected, encourage the destruction of data. Similar laws exist in other countries such as Norway (Thorvaldsen 1993: 203).

The survival of the historical record has always been subject to natural and man-made forces. Frequently in the past accident and some occasional planning (i.e. legal or administrative reasons) have preserved historical records. Electronic resources need to benefit from well-planned preservation campaigns, if they are to survive at all (Higgs, Chapter 9, this volume). Contemporary archivists and historians may not be the best prepared to select which records should be stored for posterity. In passing records of our culture to future historians we may pass an indication of our cultural myopia as certain types of records are selected for preservation at the expense of others. This is not to suggest that historians should not be involved in the process (see Higgs, Chapter 12, this volume). In addition to selection criteria used by the National Archives and Records Administration (NARA) (e.g. administrative, legal, and information value as well as long-term research potential), other important criteria which might be helpful if used when selecting records include technical issues such as the quality of data set/resource documentation and the uniqueness of the operating system, software, or hardware environment needed to access/use the information (NARA 1992). The problem is not so much that it is impossible to retain all information created in electronic form as a by-product of contemporary activity, but that it is not feasible to document it suitably. Because of the limited value of undocumented digital information, appraisal and selection will become increasingly important in the process of preserving information.

When electronic records are deposited in archives there are numerous difficulties associated with their cataloguing and documentation (Schürer, Chapter 10; Lievesley, Chapter 17; Wettengel, Chapter 18; Marker, Chapter 20; Doorn, Chapter 21; Hofman, Chapter 23, this volume). For all but the smallest data set these tasks take on average weeks rather than days (Doorn, Chapter 21, this volume). Often the task of documentation fails to preserve remarkably important information, such as contextual information, or details of purpose. To understand adequately a system, the user requirements, functional specifications, and user documentation must be retained for the life of the data. To this we need to add the details of the behaviour of the organization that created the resource. Some research archives such as the Data Archive have begun to approach the problem by shifting the responsibility for documenting the data sets to the depositor (Lievesley, Chapter 17, this volume). While this approach to the creation of documentation is feasible for research data, it may not prove as efficient for records created in the electronic office, business, or government department.

Preservation is associated with costs. Among the financial implications are the costs associated with overcoming the problems of hardware and software obsolescence, media degradation, support, and documentation. The economic costs of maintaining electronic information will not diminish with time. Electronic records or resources cannot be left to languish unattended; they require continual attention. Where there is economic advantage in reusing information, there will be an easy business case for the preservation of records. Visa records do not yet appear to have long-term reusable value, whereas 20th Century-Fox's Movietone film has taken on such value and the data collected as part of the Human Genome Project will have such value. Preservation of business data is likely to be limited because little of this information has a 'value-life' of more than five years. Banks typically save information only where legal or business requirements make the information necessary or useful. This is not a trend new to electronically based information; many businesses in the past disposed of paper records after they had served their useful life. Often it is only when their disposal did not go as planned that their existence or the fact that they once existed comes to the historian's attention.

Record retention will lead to a skewed vision of the contemporary world. Besides governments, it is likely that only the largest companies will engage in any kind of record retention and archive management (Simpson, Chapter 6, this volume). For most small firms, preservation of records beyond periods stipulated by statute will be impossible, but some might argue that this will not really matter, because, if sufficient quantities of government records survive in electronic form, there will be enough data for historians to build a picture of the economic and social history of small business in general. A new problem has become apparent in the evolution of the meaning of terms such as archiving. Computer back-ups are often described as archive copies and this can lead to the misleading belief that proper archival practices are in place within an organization. A similar problem exists with the new developments in the area of 'data warehousing'. Many organizations have latched onto data warehousing as a solution to the data-retention problem, but it is not. A data warehouse is a 'subjected-oriented, integrated, nonvolatile, and time variant' data store (Inmon 1996; Jones 1995). Whereas operational information is stored in structures that reflect business functions and processes, data stored in a warehouse reflect specific subject needs, such as customers, products, and accounts. In order to arrive at these data units, operational information is sifted and restructured to fit into the expected uses of the data warehouse. As a result, consistency is introduced across a diversity of information categories and operational units. Even though the information in a warehouse is never updated, it does not represent accurately the nature of operational information. It does not, therefore, provide an accurate record-retention strategy.

It would be very easy—and many of us have done so on occasion—to confuse data warehousing with archiving of data. Data warehousing is not an intermediate stage between operational systems and archives. Data warehouses often lose the relationship between the business process which created the records and the information in the records. Digital archives must retain this information if the data are to be used as a meaningful record of organizational activity and transaction. Archived materials must preserve the original order and structure, and this is not the case for data held in a data warehouse. In a similar way, the reuse expectations for archives are not set, and it is actually quite likely that the frequency of use will be low. The way in which users aggregate the data may not reflect the future needs of researchers either.

The variety of record categories (e.g. environmental records, electronic point-of-sale data, health records) is quite large. As the range of record types (e.g. e-mail, text files, databases, still images, moving images, and audio) expands, the dimensions of the problem are increased, together with the spectrum of material that archivists and librarians must preserve. Documentation is essential for those electronic resources that need to preserve the integral relationships within the discrete data units to provide the information resource. This difficulty is made worse by the variety of file formats in which the information is stored and encoding strategies which are used to mark up texts. In traditional parchment/paper document creation, standards of information provision and format arose naturally over time. Standards are essential in other areas, such as audio, image, video, and numerical data, but many of these areas are still in flux. Standardization is a complex, but essential process if data are to be preserved (Oksala *et al.* 1996). Currently hypermedia and multimedia standards pose seemingly insurmountable difficulties, and this only intensifies the already complex problems involved in archiving multimedia information. Even more seemingly intractable problems will be posed by attempts to store virtual reality. Here the maintenance of the peripheral devices used to access and present the information may be essential.

The accuracy of information in electronic resources poses an additional problem. A study of the quantities and types of information used by large corporations concluded that, even after checking, there is roughly 'one error for every four pages' of information. In the 258 million pages of information that are stored by a typical corporation, there would be some 64.5 million errors (Jones 1995: 85). These errors, which are as likely to exist in customer or personnel data as they are in product or supplier information, pose difficulties for future users because they may well go unidentified. Contemporary concerns with the dangers posed to the rights of individuals by incorrect information are reflected in the laws and institutions set up on national levels to protect individuals against incorrect data and the implications that might arise from any errors. Inaccuracies in the data abound and these will need to be considered by future historians. The problem of intellectual preservation can be met only if the twin questions of integrity and authenticity can be addressed. As Peter Graham eloquently explains, 'The need for intellectual preservation arises because the great asset of digital information is also its greatest liability: the ease with which an identical copy can be made, quickly and flawlessly, is parallelled by the ease with which an undetectable change may be made' (Graham 1994: 11). He noted three kinds of such change: accidental change, well-meaning intended change, and fraudulent change. A variety of techniques from encryption to digital watermarking could be used to protect against changes, but much contemporary data are not protected in such ways.

The distinction between privacy and confidentiality and the implications of both these concepts to electronic records must be considered. How long should records be kept confidential? Will we object in seventy-five years if our ancestors' medical records become publicly accessible? Should 'police records' enter the public domain? There are also issues of legal sensitivity.

Historians give different values to surviving documents, and in the future electronic records will be treated in a similar way. The worth of a set of documents or electronic information resource will depend upon numerous factors from prevailing scholarly attitudes to ease of use. One of the problems facing historians is gaining information about the sources that exist in electronic form (Lievesley, Chapter 17, this volume). This is even true for government records, as Moiseenko (Chapter 19, this volume) explains. In the Russian case, there is a lack of information about what electronic information was created during the Soviet period. No structure is in place for gathering the data, no information exists to assist with access, and there are no statutory bodies or even adequate laws to protect machine-readable records from loss. For the history of the Soviet people during the 1970s and 1980s, machine-readable data files are crucial, and Moiseenko argues that contemporary historians need to come to grips with the problem now. It would be foolhardy to believe that the Soviet case is unique. All over Eastern Europe similar cases could be found, and a similar state of affairs probably holds sway elsewhere (see Wettengel, Chapter 18, this volume). The Netherlands, Austria, and the UK all offer parallels involving the loss of vast amounts of machine-readable data. Registers of resources should be created. As electronic records represent a new resource, their location and the descriptions of the data they contain cannot easily be made accessible. So far the great bulk of archives set up to handle this material focus on collecting data sets created by research projects.

The majority of the discussion here has concentrated on data as a source for information about the past. Even where long-term access to the raw data can be guaranteed, such access is unlikely to be provided to future researchers in the same way as it has been supplied to contemporary users (Rothenberg 1995; Swade, Chapter 13, this volume). Valuable cultural data are contained in the record structures and the software that is used to access the resources: to sever the message from its medium of provision debases the message. This is particularly the case with virtual records. Without original software to process the data, it will be impossible to determine what kinds of (or specific) virtual records users might have created. A similar state of affairs holds for software-dependent data objects produced by GIS and CAD tools (see above). Future generations of cultural and social historians or anthropologists will be interested not only in the information held in the records, but in working practices and how social behaviour was conditioned by the available equipment and the working environment in which it had been used. Just as medievalists study the functioning of scriptoria and monastic libraries, future scholars will investigate digital libraries and twentieth-century work environments (see Rayward, Chapter 14; Brindley, Chapter 15; Prochaska, Chapter 16, this volume).

In many cases preservation of the data alone will not be sufficient. Since specialized software will have been used to store and access certain categories of data, this will also need to be retained (e.g. proprietary image formats). Whereas the loss over time of small amounts of data, through say media degradation, might not be disastrous under some circumstances, in other cases such as software and some graphics formats 'functional intactness' is essential (Swade, Chapter 13, this volume). Even if the software were to be retained, how would the hardware to run it be preserved? Since the 1950s hardware advances have become more frequent, and each one has given remarkable improvements to the processing, storage, and display capabilities of equipment. Image formats are often designed to reflect the available technology, such as video cards or storage media blocking factors. It is a utopian ideal to think that it would be possible to maintain computer hardware for use by future researchers. Doran Swade, of the Science Museum, argues (Chapter 13, this volume) that it will be possible to emulate current software on new generations of hardware (much as a team of his colleagues have emulated a 1958/9 Ferranti Pegasus computer on an IBM PC 486). This argument has also been pressed by J. Rothenberg of Rand Corporation (1995). This approach, although an exciting possibility, is expensive and unlikely to be effective in an environment where the range of hardware and software used to produce data sets and image banks is diverse. It will provide its most effective results in areas where we are examining terabytes of data.

Simulation does not provide the same level of understanding which can be provided by access to the original environment. While the simulation of the 1958/9 Ferranti Pegasus computer might demonstrate that such software emulation is possible, the experience of having seen the thirty-eight-year-old machine run and perform the same data-processing tasks provided an understanding of the process of work in the late 1950s which no simulation could ever have done. A similar example comes from the study of the Electronic Numerical Integrator and Computer (ENIAC) developed at the Moore School of Electrical Engineering at the University of Pennsylvania in 1946. The computer, which was constructed of 18,000 vacuum tubes and 170,000 resistors and measured 80 feet by 3 feet and weighed 30 tons, required a team of experts to run it. In celebration of the fiftieth anniversary of its development, researchers at the Moore School emulated the computer on a chip. An interface displays the instrument panel and includes programming and control switches, and material is displayed on the interface in the same way they were displayed on the original operational ENIAC. While the simulation demonstrates that it is possible to experience some of the aspects of the ENIAC and to comprehend the simplicity of the programmes it could actually handle, this simulation, like that of the Pegasus, lacks contextual relevance. It is the borderline where the accessibility of a facsimile does not compensate for working with the original. In a similar way, future scholars sitting *in* their virtual terminals and using visualization software to create interpretations of documentary evidence will be further removed from understanding text-based Internet communication than we are from clay-tablet archives.

Hardware, networks, and software are cultural artefacts and how they change tells researchers as much about the technological developments as it does about the interface between human and machine (Swade, Chapter 13, this volume). Current efforts to empower the end-user are typical of these—the qualities of current software document the transition to end-user computing. The growth in end-user computing will transform the way information is created and preserved. While the distribution of the creation and storage of information, whether text, data, or some other form (e.g. images, audio), complicates the process of preservation, the retention of software poses its own museological difficulties, and makes the creation of a software archive or museum complex essential. Huge cost factors would be involved in developing, organizing, and running such an archive, and major managerial and curatorial problems would need to be overcome.

A certain narrow-mindedness has pervaded studies of electronic information, as the focus has been predominately by national archives on the preservation of records about the national governments themselves. More attention needs to be focused on other records or information resources that document our culture and on a range of other institutions that produce them. Especially important are records that will allow us to give life to the many stories history can tell. I have drawn attention to the immense quantity, the rich variety, the problems posed by its retention, the difficulties with its analysis, and the opportunities that might be offered to future historians by contemporary electronic information resources. Writing the history of the electronic-information rich countries at the end of the millennium could be done with dynamic resources that would offer comprehensive profiles of political, economic, social, and cultural worlds. This information might be examined using an array of software tools. Alternatively, we may have fewer and poorer sources, as the vast amounts of electronic information are not accessible because hardware has become obsolete, software and data have not been migrated forward, and the media have degraded. The cost of maintaining information for the future is large, but it seems likely that the benefits will outweigh the costs. Historians should not be tricked into believing that the survival of vast quantities of data will alone provide the fertile soil for the writing of history. The quality of the data (whether texts, multimedia, databases, or audio), the training of historians, and the tools to investigate the data will each continue to influence the products of research.

What is clear is that a significant cultural artefact has become soft and ephemeral. The developing of links with record creators will be important if they are to be encouraged to exercise their moral responsibility to preserve these contemporary cultural artefacts, e-facts. Too great a focus has been placed on text and data. In recent decades historians have broadened the sources on which they rely, as they have widened their views of the past—to cover, oral history, archaeology, and art; in the future data and other electronically stored information will be included. Current records managers and archivists must not allow the limits of their imagination to constrain the kinds of information they preserve, because historians may wish to tap a wide range of possible sources to build up different views of the past. Just because information has been summarized about a data source may not justify the failure to retain the base data. Future historians would in all likelihood use the same data to help answer entirely different questions were the data accessible in their original form.

Researchers must be mindful of what information meant to its creator and how it was used in the past. The meaning and value of information contained in records will differ depending upon the user and the context of its use. Are we about to embark on an information explosion that historians could never handle, or are we about to dis-cover resources to make a historian's vision of our world fuller than the vision historians have of any other period? Historians need to be involved in the development of these regulations, because they under-stand documents, data, and information. Do we want to pass on our cultural heritage by accident or by design? Do we want legal and financial concerns to take precedence in the selection of resources for preservation? Clearly the shortcomings of electronic storage, software, and hardware require active intervention if a rich historical record of the late twentieth century is to survive. We need to preserve the past for the future in as great a variety as possible. The broader the array of surviving sources, the more likely future historians will be in a position to see the late twentieth century as the rich and diverse world that it really was.

References

Abukhanfusa, K., and Sydbeck, J. (1994) (eds.), *The Principle of Provenance* (Stockholm).

Bailey, C. (1990), 'Archival Theory and Electronic Records', *Archivaria*, 29: 180–96.

Bearman, D. (1994), *Electronic Evidence: Strategies for Managing Records in Contemporary Organizations* (Pittsburgh).

Bikson, T. K., and Frinking, E. J. (1993), *Het heden onthouden/Preserving the Present* (The Hague).

—— and Law, S. A. (1993), 'Electronic Mail Use at the World Bank: Messages from Users', *Information Society*, 9/2: 124–44.

Commission on Preservation and Access (1993), *Preserving the Intellectual Heritage: A Report of the Bellagio Conference, June 7–10, 1993* (Washington).

Computing (1994), 'Welfare Wellbeing' (20 Jan.), 28.

Conway, P. (1996), *Preservation in the Digital World* (Washington: Commission on Preservation and Access).

Cox, R. J. (1993), 'Readings in Archives and Electronic Records: Annotated Bibliography and Analysis of the Literature', in Hedstrom (1993), 99–156.

Díaz, R. A. (1994), 'The Principle of Provenance and the Problems of Authenticity', in Abukhanfusa and Sydbeck (1994), 139–69.

Dollar, C. M. (1971), 'Documentation of Machine Readable Records and Research: A Historian's View', *Prologue: The Journal of the National Archives,* 3: 27–31.

—— (1992), *Archival Theory and Information Technologies: The Impact of Information Technologies on Archival Principles and Methods* (Macerata, Italy).

—— (1993), 'New Developments and the Implication on Information Handling', in Menne-Haritz (1993), 56–66.

Doorn, P., Kluts, C., and Leenarts, E. (1992) (eds.), *Data, Computers and the Past* (Hilversum).

Duchien, M. (1983), 'Theoretical Problems and Practical Problems of "Respect des Fonds" in Archival Science', *Archivaria,* 16: 64–82.

Duranti, L. (1995), 'Reliability and Authenticity: The Concepts and their Implications', *Archivaria,* 39: 5–10

Earth Observing System Data and Information System (1992), *EOS Data and Information System* (Washington: National Aeronautics and Space Administration).

Fox, B. (1993), 'Old News Acquires Immortality on Computer Tapes', *New Scientist* (25 Sept.), 19.

Fresko, M. (1993), *British Library Research Delegation Study Visit to Paris* (British Library Research and Development Department, R&D Report, 6112; London).

Genet, J.-P. (1988), 'L'Informatique au service de la prosopographie: PROSOP', *Mélanges de l'École Française de Rome, Moyen Âge Temps Modernes,* 100: 247–63.

—— and Zampolli, A. (1992) (eds.), *Computers and the Humanities,* (Aldershot: Dartmouth [for the European Science Foundation]).

González, P. (1992), 'Computerisation Project for the Archivo General de Indias', in Doorn *et al.* (1992), 52–67.

Graham, P. S. (1994), *Intellectual Preservation: Electronic Preservation of the Third Kind* (Washington: Commission on Preservation and Access).

—— (1995), 'Requirements for the Digital Research Library', *College and Research Libraries* 56/4 (July), 331–9.

Hedstrom, M. (1991), 'Understanding Electronic Incunabula: A Framework for Research on Electronic Records', *American Archivist,* 54/3: 334–54.

—— (1993) (ed.), *Electronic Records Management Program Strategies* (Archives and Museum Informatics Technical Report, No. 18, Pittsburgh).

—— (1995), '*Electronic Archives: Integrity and Access in the Network Environment*', in Kenna and Ross (1995), 77–95.

History and Computing (1992), 4/3.

Hobby, J., (1993), 'The Computer that Came in from the Cold', *Computer Weekly* (14 Oct.), 48.

Horsman, P. (1994), 'Taming the Elephant: An Orthodox Approach to the Principle of Provenance', in Abukhanfusa and Sydbeck (1994), 51–63.

Information Infrastructure Task Force Committee on Applications and Technology (1994), *The Information Infrastructure: Reaching Society's Goals* (Washington).

Inmon, W. H. (1996), *Building the Data Warehouse* (Chichester).

Jones, C. (1995), 'What Goes into an Information Warehouse?', *Computer* (Aug.), 84–5.

Kenna, S., and Ross, S. (1995) (eds.), *Networking in the Humanities* (London).

Kiernan, K. (1994), 'Digital Preservation, Restoration, and Dissemination of Medieval Manuscripts', in Oakerson and Mogge (1994), 37–43.

Kobler, B., Berbert, J., Caulk, P., and Hariharan, P. C. (1996), 'Architecture and Design of Storage and Data Management for the NASA Earth Observing System Data and Information System (EOSDIS)', *Proceedings of the 14th IEEE Symposium on Mass Storage Systems* (Monterey, Calif.), 77–88.

Kurtz, D. (1993), 'The Beazley Archive Database', *Archeologia e Calcolatori*, 4: 49–51.

Laudon, K. C. (1996), 'Markets and Privacy', *Communications of the ACM*, 30/9: 92–104.

Lee, Hing-Yan, and Ong, Hwee-Leng (1996), 'Visualization Support for Data Mining', *IEEE Expert* (Oct.), 69–75.

Lesk, M. (1992), *Preservation of New Technology: A Report of the Technology Assessment Advisory Committee to the Commission on Preservation and Access* (Washington).

—— (1994), 'Electronic Libraries and Electronic Journals', *The Tenth British Library Research Lecture* (London).

Leslie, M. (1990), 'The Hartlib Papers Project: Text Retrieval with Large Data-sets', *Literary and Linguistic Computing*, 5/1: 58–69.

Lievesley, D. (1993), 'Increasing the Value of Data', in Ross and Higgs (1993), 205–17.

Marsden, P. (1991), 'Archival Processing of Electronic Records', *Machine Readable Records Bulletin*, 7/2: 2.

Menne-Haritz, A. (1993) (ed.), *Information Handling in Offices and Archives* (New York).

Michelson, A., and Rothenberg, J. (1992), 'Scholarly Communication and Information Technology: Exploring the Impact of Changes in the Research Process on Archives', *American Archivist*, 55: 236–315.

Moen, B. (1995), 'Metadata for Network Information Discovery and Retrieval', *Information Standards Quarterly*, 7/1: 1–4.

Mullings, C., Deegan, M., Ross, S., and Kenna, S. (1996) (eds.), *New Technologies for the Humanities* (London).

NAPA (1991): National Academy of Public Administration, *The Archives of the Future: Archival Strategies for the Treatment of Electronic Databases* (Washington).

NARA (1991): National Archives and Records Administration, *Report of the Optical Digital Image Storage System* (Washington).

—— (1992), 'Information about Electronic Records in the National Archives for Prospective Researchers', General Information Leaflet 37 (Washington).

National Research Council (1995), *Preserving Scientific Data on our Physical Universe: A New Strategy for Archiving the Nation's Scientific Information Resources* (Washington: National Academy Press).

Network (1993), Paper, Paper Everywhere' (May), 73–80.

Oakerson, A., and Mogge, D. (1994) (eds.), *Scholarly Publishing on the Electronic Networks: Gateways, Gatekeepers, and Roles in the Information Omniverse* (Washington).

Oksala, S., Rutkowski, A., Spring, M., and O'Donnell, J. (1996), 'The Structure of IT Standardization', *Standard View*, 4/1: 9–22.

Reed, B., and Roberts, D. (1991) (eds.), *Keeping Data: Papers from a Workshop on Appraising Computer-based Records* (Sydney).

Research Issues in Electronic Records (1991), Report of the Working Meeting (St Paul: Minnesota Historical Society for the National Historical Publications and Records Commission).

RLG/CPA (1996), Research Libraries Group and Commission on Preservation and Access, *Preserving Digital Information: Report of the Task Force on Archiving of Digital Information* (Washington: RLG/CPA).

Ross, S. (1995), 'Introduction: Networking and Humanities Scholarship', in Kenna and Ross (1995), pp. xi–xxiv.

—— and Higgs, E. (1993) (eds.), *Electronic Information Resources and Historians: European Perspectives* (St Katharinen).

Rothenberg, J. (1995), 'Ensuring the Longevity of Digital Documents', *Scientific American*, 272/1 (Jan.), 24–9.

Rundell, M. (1996), 'Computer Corpora and their Impact on Lexicography and Language Teaching', in Mullings *et al.* (1996) 198–216.

Simoudis, E. (1996), 'Reality Check for Data Mining', *IEEE Expert* (Oct.), 27–33.

Snyder, E. E., and Stromo, G. D. (1993), 'Identification of Coding Regions in Genomic DNA Sequences: An Application of Dynamic Programming and Neural Networks', *Nucleic Acids Research*, 21: 607–13.

Taylor-Munro, D. (1991), 'Acquiring Electronic Records of TNO', *Machine Readable Records Bulletin*, 7/2: 1–2.

Thorvaldsen, G. (1993), 'The Preservation of Computer Readable Records in Nordic Countries', *History and Computing*, 4/3: 201–5.

UN Advisory Committee for the Coordination of Information Systems (1990), *Management of Electronic Records: Issues and Guidelines*, (New York).

United States Congress, House Committee on Government Operations (1990), *Taking a Byte out of History: The Archival Presentation of Federal Computer Records,* House Report no. 101–987 (Washington).

Van Bogart, J. W. (1995), *Magnetic Tape Storage and Handling: A Guide for Libraries and Archives* (Washington).

Verity, J. W. (1994), 'The Internet: How it will Change the Way you Do Business', *Business Week* (Nov.), 38–46

Weibel, S. (1995), 'Metadata: The Foundations of Resource Description', *D-Lib Magazine* (July 1995) [URL:http://www.dlib.org/dlib/july95].

Wiederhold, G. (1995), 'Digital Libraries, Value and Productivity', *Communications of the ACM,* 38/4: 85–96.

PART ONE

The Historian in the Electronic Age

2

Electronic Documents and the History of the Late Twentieth Century: Black Holes or Warehouses

R. J. MORRIS

ABSTRACT

Electronically based information technology (IT) has and is making major changes in the manner in which human society creates the evidence which future historians will use to write the history of the late twentieth century. The large data sets used on the mainframe computers of the 1950s, 1960s and 1970s, like the assorted mass of disks created by the isolated personal computers of the 1970s, create technical problems for the archivist, but the data structures essentially mimic the world of paper. The 1980s and 1990s, with the growth of networked information systems, have created data structures of a very different kind. In many cases the use structure is quite different from the data-storage structure. Software, presentational environments, and knowledge bases have all become essential parts of the 'virtual' documents presented to the user. To comment on preservation strategies, historians need to know more about the types of data being created. Three examples are presented here, from a regional water authority, from retailing, and from airline booking systems. The quantity of information is vast, as is the potential for its rapid and total destruction. As always preservation will be related to legal requirements and institutional needs, but historians must create their own politics of information. They might anticipate that society will become more complex and more fragmented in a way which will require a variety of histories to be written. Any meaningful attempt to relate these histories will require well-stocked electronic warehouses, and historians with the skills required to interrogate the information they contain.

An increasing number of archivists and a few historians are coming to believe that a major change has taken place in the manner in which human society creates the evidence which will be used by the historians who, in the future, come to write about the late twentieth century (Morris 1992). The changes brought about by electronically based information technology (IT) are so fundamental that, for the historian at least, they must be equated with the invention and spread of printing or perhaps even the initial development of the written record. Each of us has a different way of trying to express this change. In June 1993 I brought home a letter from my daughter. It had been sent by electronic mail (e-mail) and transferred to a 3.5-inch floppy disk, and as a source of information it was useless without specific software and hardware. The medium was no longer the message. Accessing the letter required a technologically sophisticated method of intervention. It was no longer enough just to know how to read.

It would be wise to set out the nature of the problem, because it is not one problem but many. Electronically created data have been, and are being, produced in a number of different organizational and techno-logical environments. Each environment has its own qualities. The manner in which archivists and historians are dealing, and are ready to deal, with electronically produced data, and the adequacy of this response, and of potential responses, vary with the environment and nature of the data concerned. Since the 1950s there have been three major phases of electronic data creation. Each has set the archivist and the potential historian technical, organizational, and intellectual prob-lems of increasing complexity.

The 1950s initiated the age of the data sets. These were mounted on large mainframe computers for batch processing using a variety of packages and high-level languages, of which the Statistical Package for the Social Services and Fortran dominated the social-science world from which historians learnt so much. In the corporate and financial environment, numerically presented financial and survey data were subjected to increasingly sophisticated statistical and econometric ana-lysis. The available evidence suggests that archivists and historians have been fairly successful in tackling the problems of the data set and mainframe, although complacency would be misplaced (Lievesley, Chapter 17, this volume). One example of access to certain parts of the British census of 1971 (Schürer, Chapter 10, this volume) is a reminder of what can happen in the most favourable environments, whilst the situation of Soviet and Russian data indicates how dependent electronic data are upon organizational structures (Moiseenko, Chapter 19, this volume).

By the late 1970s, the world was full of PCs and word processing. This expanded dramatically in the 1980s. These machines were small in capacity, had primitive communicative abilities, but slowly increased in power and capability. All the while, in offices and homes everywhere, piles of floppy disks gathered in drawers, cupboards, and archives. Behind them stood the Big Brothers of the computing world, the Primes, Vax's, and assorted IBM mainframes. These were more powerful and versatile in their capabilities, and were developing slow and awkward means of communication and portability with a degree of interactive processing that still left time for coffee, and often for a three-course meal.

The age of the PC has left us with a messy, low-grade, grumbling crisis. There are technical problems of some complexity. There is no doubt that many disks will become degraded, and that the variety and rapid rate of technological obsolescence which has affected the hardware and software involved has created major problems of preservation and access. Much will be lost, but, even where disks become unreadable, they may well contain information which is ultimately recoverable. Within the next ten years, a small and élite band of e-palaeographers will emerge who will recover data signal by signal, probably using the pattern recognition capabilities of the new neural network procedures (Wilson and Blue 1992). Doran Swade has described the work being done at the Science Museum in London to decode 'unreadable' disks (Swade, pers. com.).

Intellectually, the problems from this phase are fairly easy to handle. It is true that we cannot see the crossings out in Tony Benn's diary diskuscript (Prochaska, Chapter 16, this volume), but the information structures on most disks from the PC era mimic document structures that are familiar from print and paper. For this reason, the most thorough and reliable long-term preservation procedure may well be to print out and preserve in microform (Morris 1992; Morelli, Chapter 11, this volume). One of the few things predictable about future input technology is that it will include an optical scan element which will be at its best handling the output from IT-related machines. For electronic documents the lessons of Text Encoding Initiative (TEI) provide an increasingly thoughtful guide. Documents have individual identities, and the constant prompting for information on document type, author, origin, version, and information elements within the document provided by the TEI guidelines that should find a ready response from potential users and archivists of material from this phase. True the archivist dealing with assorted disks from the 1970s office or even the politician's word processor will leave detailed mark-up to others, but the demands of producing simple headers seems very relevant here (Burnard 1993). It is true that, when historians come to the basic task of source evaluation and exploitation, they will not be able to examine the alterations and check the handwriting, but strategies of text analysis are already available which will allow researchers to evaluate authorship and even make judgements on changing style within an individual author's corpus of text (Holmes 1991).

By the late 1980s the world of networks and powerful applications had arrived. Databases, spreadsheets, windows, e-mail, and many more terms were added to the language. The desktop computer grew in power and user friendliness until it was increasingly hard to tell apart from the workstation. Indeed, by the time a modern PC 486 machine, or an SE or LC Macintosh, had been linked into a network, the distinction was almost meaningless. The age of the network is by far the most imposing of the problems faced. Not only are the technical and organizational problems huge, but it is not clear that we even have the intellectual concepts needed to talk about the issues we face. The meaning of simple ideas such as document, text, and context, of provenance and sequence, falls slowly and inelegantly apart (Hedstrom 1991; Michelson and Rothenberg 1992). It is not yet clear if the development of the Internet in the 1990s is simply an extension of this phase or a new development. The growth of gopher and World Wide Web sites as quasi-universal information providers, including bodies as varied as the US Census Bureau, the CIA, and the Scottish National Party, is now threatening concepts such as book, publication, copyright, and authorship.

Like the ages of flint, bronze, and iron, these phases were not exclusive. They overlapped but each new phase rapidly established dominance in the world of IT. Thus, the large data sets are still there, but those who manage them are more likely to place them on a file server with appropriate network access (Knight 1993). The PC, the Macintosh, and the rest continue to gobble up huge quantities of words and other information. Many still stand happily alone, but they all know that without an ethernet or some other network port, or at least a modem, they are very low technology in the world of the network. IT has become a central element in the bitter and disorderly competition of the postmodern world. There is a Darwinian struggle for survival between a wide variety of social, economic, and political systems, and that struggle is based upon the control of information. It is not simply enough to mass capital, military might, or political support. Those who go to war with a non-networked PC are likely to be on the wrong side of the line, or at least run out of tank spares first. Spend an afternoon with the gung ho capitalism of the *Harvard Business Review* and the message is clear. Those best placed regarding information systems survive. The capitalism of the Chicago meat yards has been replaced by that of the information system: 'organizations have shed more than one million managers and staff professionals since 1979 . . . technology will enable senior management to monitor and control large organizations more effectively' (Applegarth *et al.* 1988: 130).

In the face of all this, what is it that historians really want? There are two nightmares and my thoughts on these have been fuelled by discussions with Peter Burnhill and Donald Morse of the Edinburgh University Data Library. In the first, everything is saved. Storage is cheap, communication is easy, and every scrap of information from the information-rich *fin de siècle* is preserved for eternity in a series of great warehouses in the ethernet. The International Consortium for Political and Social Research (ICPSR) at Ann Arbor, the History Data Archive at the Data Archive in Essex, the Netherlands Historical Data Archive (NHDA) at Leiden, and the Jerusalem Social Sciences Data Archive (Israel) are on every desk (Doorn 1996). For each document, there are at once a single copy and a million copies. As the system is updated, nothing is lost, for storage is so cheap that it is always more cost effective to slap a primitive TEI-type header on each block of data and transfer it to the next store rather than sort out what is likely to be needed from what is not. The world will become a gopher's playground and those who navigate it best will command the earth (Southall 1993).

In the second nightmare, all is lost. Technological obsolescence means that information rapidly becomes unreadable. Punched card readers are already being sought by archivists. That Superbrain, with a quarter megabyte of memory, has only a finite life, and then any records and software dedicated to its operating system is material for the e-palaeographers. When Irish records were destroyed in 1922, it was because the Four Courts were shelled during the civil war. In late-twentieth-century Moscow, the danger appears to be that the collective record of the Russian and other Soviet peoples may simply ebb away electron by electron (Moiseenko, Chapter 19, this volume). We shall look back upon the nineteenth and early twentieth centuries as the golden age of the written word and printed page. A disaster begun by the telephone will be completed by the electronic network.

So what do historians really want? The archivists at least need some sort of a provisional answer. One barrier to giving even a provisional answer is the fact that we, as historians, have very little idea what is actually out there. One element of weakness in the debate is the need many of us have to take refuge in generality, anecdote, and the familiar. On this heady diet, discussion tends to move from intoxicating anticipation to deep despair. Discussion is easiest with reference to census and survey documents. Historians have encoded and used versions of these from the past they study and seek to understand. They learnt about such sources of information from their social-science colleagues. Diaries, diplomatic and intelligence records, the use of e-mail in the research process all come within the experience of historians, but after that what do historians really want? The honest answer is another question; well what is there? What happens once we get beyond the comforting world of the census and the diplomatic archive?

Let me do what historians should be able to do best: take examples, examine how they work, place them in context, and attempt to generalize. The first is from the Strathclyde Regional Water Authority in the west of Scotland. A wide range of information technologies are in use producing substantial amounts of data. They are not at the cutting edge of *Harvard Business Review* (*HBR*)-type networking but, it seems reasonable to suppose, are typical of many organizations (Davenport 1994). Active development has and is taking place. The overall strategy clearly involves creating an integrated network improving the efficiency and effectiveness of the Authority, but the current situation and day-to-day operations indicate an organization that is not yet fully into phase three, as described above. At the Water Department Headquarters is a geographical information system (GIS). This links via a wide area network (WAN) to the laboratory which processes water samples. The data from this is punched into the ORACLE database which physically resides at the lab (a mile or so away), and hence can be pulled down the line to map, say, aluminium levels and to check water quality against European Union (EU) regulations. At some point data entry will be done directly from the analysis process to the database. Meanwhile, at the twelve area offices customer complaints (e.g. poor water flow, dirty water, etc.) are received and put into a PC. These are collected and put into a PC database at the Headquarters, where the information can be used with the GIS to map the problem areas. In another part of the system are meter readers (customers such as industries, farms, and some shops pay by volume). The meter reader punches readings direct into a hand-held

Husky computer. This information is transferred directly to the Water Department Headquarters. Bills can be issued within two days rather than fifteen. When time is money, this can be a considerable saving, or, as the planning documents predicted, there was 'a considerable improvement in cash flow' (Janet Keddie of Strathclyde Water, pers. com.). From time to time, a van is sent down to the Regional Chief Executive's Department to get census data (on disk). The sampling frequency of water depends under regulations upon population density. Postcodes are used to link specific lists of addresses to areas of water supply—i.e. areas which are supplied from one asset (e.g. a storage tank, a reservoir, etc.). Digitizing boundaries of these areas was one of first GIS investments made. Elsewhere in the system is a computer based upon telemetry (e.g. electronic measures of flows, pressures, etc.), so that a complaint of water failure can be related to the supply network with accuracy, and relevant teams of engineers called out. This leads on to basic office systems and personnel records.

There are several lessons to be drawn from this. In theory, and in the planning documents, this can all be linked into a seamless network. In actual contemporary practice this is an intermediate technology. The WAN moves information around parts of the system. Elsewhere it is the disk in a van, whilst the paper document and punch operator still have much work to do. This is characteristic of a considerable amount of current practice. In theory the age of the seamless network and paperless office has arrived. In fact, hard copy and the four-drawer filing cabinet still play a major role in many 'information systems'. Indeed, there are those who consider that hard copy has a functionality which e-documents can never completely replace and it will always have a place in information systems.

Secondly, data structures are already beginning to come apart from use structures and GIS plays a central role in this. Thirdly, politics plays an important role. The potential privatization of water services in Scotland is a contentious political issue. The improvement in IT, with the efficiency gains involved, may be seen as a strategy which makes the Authority more attractive to a potential profit-seeking buyer, which enables the Authority to defend its current place in the state sector. Any judgement depends on political position, nationalist/unionist as well as left/right.

A sub-theme running through many of the chapters in this volume concerns the politics of data—data for sale, data for citizenship, data as power, data as a cost. Historians need to create their own politics of

data—to assemble interests which have a stake in the long-term retention of data. These include very specific interests groups such as those
concerned with contaminated land legislation, companies needing to
sustain reputations, and human societies which seek to explore their
own identities and pasts. For historians, the politics of information
involve creating and sustaining attitudes and values in society at large
which will support and demand the retention of the information
sources as the basis of writing history in the future. Some recent
literature seems to betray a tension between the need to service the
information-creating organization, and the need to serve the wider, and
harder to specify, requirements of a culture to preserve the record of its
own past. (Bearman 1992, 1993; Duranti 1995; Higgs, Chapter 12, this
volume)

In the case of the Water Authority information, preservation will
initially depend upon the compulsions of the organization. EU and
Scottish Office regulations, and public access to information requirements, will ensure the short-run retention of data, as will potential legal
and contractual disputes. Current legislation requires that customers
can view the water-quality record of their area for the past two or three
years, but the value of information to be derived from the water-quality
record may depend upon the access to several decades worth of data.
Legal requirements are double edged. Many organizations fear that
electronic data may be a potential source of evidence in legal action.
Product-reliability data, with their complex notion of probability, for
example, might become part of legal action regarding a product-related
accident. Thus a company may have motives for the regular destruction
of such data (Davenport 1994). The survival of documents has always
depended, and will substantially still depend, upon the needs and
compulsions of the document creators, as well as upon the survival of
the organizations that guard these documents. This is nothing new.

What would the historian want from the relatively simple records of
the Water Authority? There is a very obvious potential here for a history
of water supply, of a public service in the age of privatization. There is a
major source for the history of the environment in Scotland, which
would perhaps be linked with other archives when the 'green' generation writes the history of the 'greenhouse' world. Beyond that is the
history of the impact of IT itself on service delivery.

The second example comes from the growth of electronic point of
sale scanning (EPoSS) in retailing—in other words, the increasingly
common barcode which is passed over a scanning device linked to the

cash register. The accompanying bleep is now a familiar part of super-market shopping. The immediate and obvious impact of all this is an increase in speed and accuracy at the checkout. In Britain, Tesco, the grocery supermarket chain, estimated a 20 per cent increase in speed, enabling a 10 per cent reduction in the number of checkouts (Davison 1993). The implications for historians of business, of labour relations, of consumer habits, as well as of the impact of IT, go far deeper than this.

many retailers use EPoSS to replenish a perpetual inventory automatically. Linked into centralized buying structures, electronic sales and automatic order transmission to suppliers through EDI [electronic data interchange] networks, centralized distribution systems deliver goods into stores without branches being involved in day to day stock control.   (Davison 1993)

It takes little imagination to see that here is a huge resource for the study of consumer and retailing habits. Indeed, it is already a major resource for marketing policy-makers, raising major issues of privacy (Bessen 1993). If we follow the practice suggested recently by some archivists and take the network with its constituent data flows and data tables, software resources and analytical outputs, as a whole, as the document itself, this is a major site for examining the cultural effect of these systems. Each checkout contains a memory and a clock so that data are captured not just on sales but on the work rate of the checkout assistants. In 1990 it was assumed that each assistant would average twenty items a minute (Cutter and Rowe 1990). Thus, IT and its record has entered into the politics of the workplace. Some analysts claimed that the system intensified work discipline and stress; for supporters, EPoSS enabled management to identify staff who needed to be with-drawn for 'training'. In retailing as in many other environments, IT has a double-edged influence on power relationships and autonomy in the workplace which will be vital for those who study the perplexing topic of class relationships in the late twentieth century. Remember that class relationships are part of a wider structure of systems of domination, and that the tension between empowerment and surveillance inherent in IT is likely to be a major focus for studies of class structure in the 1990s (Morris 1979; Elliot and McCrone 1982). In the mass retailing of most grocery stores, EPoSS increases centralized surveillance and reduces the autonomy of store management. At the same time, other managements, notably in clothing and luxury goods, have realized that greater surveillance also means that subordinate management can be allowed greater autonomy. In 'craft' retailing, the store manager and staff can consult central databases of information, and back the 'hunches' which come from face-to-face contact with customers, rather than from postcodes and product-flow analysis. Why not let them? If they are right, profits increase. If they are wrong, central management will know within days (Smith 1988: 143). The clear lesson here is that not only is the IT archive, in whatever form it should take, the carrier of information which the future historian would want to use, but that the very form, structure, and dynamic of that archive as it is created and used will make a vital contribution to an understanding of the social relationships, the culture, and the power structures of the late twentieth century.

At their most fully developed, business information systems provide a formidable challenge to the creativity of archivists and historians alike. SABRE is an airline reservation system, developed by American Airlines in the 1960s but now generally available. The sheer quantity of information it contains is mind-boggling. In 1990, its database contained 45 million fares, handled 40 million fare changes per month, and created 500,000 passenger name records per day (Hopper 1990). Do we really want all this material (Campbell-Kelly, Chapter 4, this volume)? Before speculating on the value of such huge quantities of information, it is important to see this as part of larger systems of business information and decision-taking. In the 1980s management came to see its information system as part of a variety of decision support systems. In the 1960s such applications were dominated by financial-control, transaction, and personnel records. By the 1980s innovation was taking place in the recording and analysis of markets, transportation, and logistics (Eom and Lee 1990). Conference rooms were equipped at great expense and then torn out, as views on best practice changed (Lee *et al.* 1988).

Two important things happened in such systems. First, the use structure of information became even more detached from the data-storage structure of that information. In other words, the information as experienced by the user rarely took the forms in which it was held in the memories of the system or network. Not only has the written document lost its centrality in the historical record, but the electronic document as used in decision-making, as part of the historical actor's experience, is a virtual document. The metaphors of the page or the file are no longer adequate descriptions of such a document's relationships to its archive. This detachment of use structure and data storage, or archive structure, is being increased by the spread of client–server network architectures in many information systems. The client, say a desktop machine or conference-room workstation, may access information from a variety of data sources, many on physically different sites, and create virtual documents using software located on other parts of the network (McDowall 1993; Weissman 1994). In some sense the whole network has become a document (see Gränström, Chapter 22, this volume).

Secondly, the archive base became much more than the database (or rather its constituent tables). During the 1970s and 1980s there was an increasing layer of software intervention between the management conference or decision-maker and the data. These were much more complex than the statistical packages and linear-modelling applications of the 1960s. Two sorts of applications deserve attention here. The first are the rule-based, artificial intelligence (AI) knowledge systems which attempt to encapsulate past experience and collective expertise. The diplomatic or business historian may gaze at the e-text archive and ask who decided what, but, in situations which involve rule-based elements in a decision support system (DSS), the historian may well ask whose decision? Those who will seek to understand US policy on Kuwait, Somalia, and Bosnia in the 1990s will want to look not only at the personalities and style of presidents and advisers, but at the content of the knowledge base of their DSS, and above all at those who designed the system and created its rule base. The second software development is the increasing intervention of visual interfaces between data, complex statistical and rule-based manipulations, and the decision-taker. GIS is only the most familiar of these (Angehrn and Lüthi 1990). The old adage—garbage in garbage out—has been replaced by the new—garbage in pretty picture out—and it is dangerous.

Equally serious for the historian is the knowledge that the decision-takers are continually looking at virtual documents which are only infrequently captured for hard or electronic copy. For example, if one buys an air ticket to go to a conference, one would probably be involved in creating several virtual documents as one discussed travel arrangements with a booking agent. The full significance of this fleeting moment is only evident when the letter page of *HBR* reveals a bitter contest over screen design between American Airlines, the developers of the system, and transatlantic competitors: 'a chief legal officer of a major international airline... had just been involved in a long, rancorous struggle to get its non stop flight from Europe to the United States off the 23rd of SABRE's 23 possible screens' (*HBR* (July–Aug. 1990),

176). So anyone who wants to study competition, travel, and world capitalism in the 1980s for a Ph.D. programme in fifty years' time had better take a good look now. Recent literature has made it clear that in many industries size provides advantages because of the wide-ranging information systems which large companies can finance and sustain. Thus, despite deregulation, American Airlines is one of two dominant carriers in North America and, together with United, was the first to develop a successful integrated booking system. This was then used not just for steering information towards customers but for making rapid changes in marketing and fares policy (Bessen 1993).

The answer to one question raised in this volume is very clear. Software must be part of any archive strategy. Equal care must be taken with the knowledge systems that accompany such software. This does not just mean clever things like the expert system in the White House conference room, but simple things such as the UK postcodes for the early 1980s and the digitized boundaries of an old GIS. Software must be seen as capitalized technique. It is, as the AI evangelists say, a store of the skills and experience of its human creators and contributors. The data structures and information systems of large organizations are not just stores of information, they are evidence of the manner in which a business corporation or government department 'represents' the world to itself (Haeckel and Nolan 1993). As such, the nature of such structures and systems is essential to an understanding of the decisions taken in the late twentieth century. In the nineteenth-century account book, the data form and the content, the use structure and the data structure, are still closely related, but even in these documents the accounting manuals of the 1830s are important for interpretation. Software and its related manuals are equally important.

As one contributor to the present volume has suggested, the first intellectual task is to set on one side an archaeology of knowledge which has served us well for at least three centuries. The world of library, archive, and museum, of books, documents, and things, is breaking under the impact of IT (Rayward, Chapter 14, this volume). Simple notions such as document, sequence, and provenance are already gravely compromised.

There is no doubt that future historians will look to a more complex structure of data. The concepts they use may involve the following: data elements, data tables, databases, knowledge bases, software applications, interfaces. Some aspects of all these elements of our information systems will be essential to understanding the present in the future.

The outcome will be influenced by the needs of those who own and manage data. Already the information manager and the archivist are beginning to merge in a variety of business and government locations (see Higgs, Chapter 9, this volume). As has happened in the past, the information elements selected for preservation will be influenced by the needs of data owners. Social historians of the eighteenth and nineteenth centuries find more property deeds than grocery bills in the archives. Property deeds were needed in court. The need to preserve experience for knowledge-based systems, the need for verification in case of dispute over contract or other liabilities, legal requirements, and citizens' data access rights, will ensure the preservation of wide ranges of data. Organizations need to be able to attribute credit and responsibility just as historians do.

Bearing this in mind, software and expert systems are probably most at risk. To take a simple example, the Data Archive at the Essex University has a fine run of survey data from Family Expenditure Survey and General Household Survey well suited to the needs of those who want to create a time series as a part of current social-science analysis (Anderson 1992). Now a historian of welfare policy in the 1970s would want to access data and run them (i.e. view them), just as was done by the policy-makers and their advisers in the 1970s. This would require access to the data in the form they were used in the 1970s without 'cleaning', and ideally through the software/hardware environment of that period. Yet, it is possible to read the parliamentary reports of the nineteenth century at exactly the same speed and in exactly the same form as the policy-makers who used and created them. In an age when information is power, there are clear motives for archiving. *HBR* again; 'Information systems will maintain the corporate history, experience and expertise that long time employees now hold' (Applegate *et al.* 1988: 135). There is both comfort and danger in this. As in the past, preservation will be influenced not by what historians want but by the needs and fortunes of the social structures which created and guarded such information. Is this enough?

Thus, historians need to create an awareness amongst themselves of the shape and the nature of the information structures which will be used in the future for the history of the present. If they are to convince archivists and others that preservation should be driven by more than present need, then they need to consider how to answer the question, what are you going to do with it all? Long ago I went to a seminar of archivists who were confident that particular instance papers could be sampled by a variety of statistical methods and, if necessary, could be anonymized without damage. An account of nominal record linkage, I hope, changed several views on this (Morris 1985; Baskerville *et al.* 1992). Concepts such as privacy and confidentiality still threaten the long-term preservation of nominal records. If some of the more extreme versions of draft EU directives on this subject are allowed to dominate, then the possibility of capturing the individuality of ordinary people and their fortunes in the late twentieth century may well be lost. Historians who write about the late twentieth century in the late twenty-first century will read all the complaints about industrial society destroying individuality and identities. If concepts of privacy are allowed to operate in an uncritical manner, then such historians will look at the records and say, yes indeed, these people had no names, only fragmented unlinkable traces in the disparate records of courts, government, and business.

With this in mind, historians need to do three things. They must give greater publicity to the electronic methodologies which they are already using (Morris 1991, 1994). They must extend knowledge of, and training in, these techniques amongst themselves. They must plunder with much greater vigour the techniques of neighbouring disciplines. They must also enter the dangerous ground of anticipating the techniques which might be available in the future (Greenstein, Chapter 5, this volume). Only then can historians give even a sensible guess as to the potential of e-documents, and their associate structures and environments. It is in this context that the strictures on historians for their general lack of curiosity in text analysis need to be considered. At the same time, these strictures need to be put with much greater precision. Historians need to be convinced that prefixes such as 'literary' and 'linguistic' are an invitation and not a warning to keep out. Other forms of analysis of communication are likely to spread. Not just the use of the concept of 'noise' but dynamic forms of network analysis tracing power structures and patterns of social and intellectual interaction. The sheer quantity and complexity of information contained in these archives indicate that a variety of numerical, statistical, and symbolic forms of representation will be essential. With this in mind, the use of graphic and visual interfaces will be essential. Not all historians are numerate; still fewer are mathematicians of any sophistication. The same applies to their potential audience. All involved will need these interfaces for the same reasons as the political and business managers whose decisions are being studied. So far historians have made little use of AI and expert systems. This is likely to change. The world of neural networks and pattern recognition is likely to act as a major guide. The complex world of coding, the multiplicity of codes and of the non-coding structuring of data (Schürer and Diederiks 1993), together with the task of searching for patterns in data, are all likely to benefit as these techniques become more user friendly and offer shorter learning curves.

Conclusions must be provisional. They include practical matters such as the need for historians to be better informed about the nature of information creation in the present, and the need for archivists to be involved at the creation stage of 'documents' rather than thirty years afterwards. Preliminary conclusions must include the need for plural-ism in retention policy. Attention must be drawn to the value of the Internet as an access medium, the importance of software and know-ledge bases as well as data in the traditional 1960s sense. The training needs of historians need to be continually discussed in the context of IT.

But above all we need to finish by reasserting the 'politics' of doing history. Let us remind ourselves of the traditional skills and purposes of historians. It is not a matter of finding our way along career paths by seeking something 'new'. Their central task is not just to understand the past but also to relate the past to the present. For this reason each generation requires new stories, or the retelling of old stories. Some aspects of the historian's task will be constant. They should create an awareness of change over time, preserve an awareness of context, and prepare a critique of the nature of sources. They should plunder related sciences, especially the social sciences. The direction and detail of the manner in which historians of the future tell the story of the present will depend upon the nature of society in the next century. Historians will seek to understand the late twentieth century in order to relate it to the collective identities and experiences of their own period.

If the current analysis of 'postmodernism' is any guide to this, that experience will be complex and fragmented (Harvey 1989). The archives of IT, the e-data, will be one base from which that complexity and fragmentation can be recreated and interrogated. Even the current fragmentation of historical practice should warn us that historians will want to tell many stories. IT and e-data will be not only a source of these stories but part of the story itself. IT has been part of the creation of so-called postmodernism, through its ability to destroy the meaning of time and space. The ethernet at once has unity and no unity. Each document is at the same time unique and exists in a thousand places. Culture and experience have fragmented. Citizenship is access to your records in a database. The family that e-mails together stays together. Identity and cultural assurance will become a function of access to the e-data of your ancestors, or that of the cultures and social formations with which you identify. Individuals and communities will increasingly carry multiple identities and experience with them. The literature of the knowledge-based society already talks of organizational structures which are flatter. They mean that the work team has replaced the hierarchy, that knowledge has replaced capital, that working lives involve tasks not careers. The class structure is becoming dominated by the knowledge mercenaries who hire themselves out to the feudal barons of top management and state agencies, each of whom is as good as the last battle. This is an anarchy in which the tension between surveillance and empowerment will make and break individuals and social and economic organizations in rapid succession. Migrations, mixed marriage, the constant reformation of household and sexual alliances, and broken work patterns will mean that class, ethnicity, gender roles, and religion will not only divide communities but will also run through individuals. The meaning of age, gender, religion, and skill will shift with bewildering rapidity.

In such a heady and unstable environment, the historian must undertake two major tasks. Individuals must be able to understand and explore the multiple identities and experiences they, their families, and friends will carry with them. Communities must be taught to celebrate the complexity and diversity, the many stories, which the past has brought into the present. E-data are a means to addressing this complexity. If the e-data are allowed to disappear into the black hole of technical obsolescence, then the writing of history will fall into the hands of the ideological warlords of the company handout, the national curriculum, and the aggressive myths of ethnic purity and cultural uniformity. The historian must also struggle to see the future history of the present in terms of the unity of the human condition. If any sense of unity is to be preserved, it must be created by the historians who tell the story. The unity may be in data structures, in power structures, or in environmental trends. Meaningful debate will require well-stocked electronic warehouses, and historians and archivists able to search and manage their cargo of resources.

References

Anderson, S. (1992), 'The Future of the Present—The ESRC Data Archive as a Resource Centre of the Future', *History and Computing*, 4/3: 191–6.

Angehrn, A. and Lüthi, H. J. (1990), 'Intelligent Decision Support Systems: A Visual Interactive Approach', *Interfaces*, 17–22.

Applegarth, L. M., Cash, J. I., and Mills, D. Q. (1988), 'Information Technology and Tomorrow's Manager', *Harvard Business Review* (Nov.–Dec.), 129–36.

Baskerville, S. W., Hudson, P., and Morris, R. J. (1992) (eds.), *History and Computing*, Special Issue on Record Linkage, 4/1.

Bearman, D. (1992), 'Diplomatics, Weberian Bureaucracy and the Management of Electronic Records', *American Archivist*, 55: 168–80.

—— (1993), 'The Implications of *Armstrong* v. *Executive Office of the President* for the Archival Management of Electronic Records', *American Archivist*, 56: 674–89.

Bessen, J. (1993), 'Riding the Marketing Information Wave', *Harvard Business Review* (Sept.–Oct.), 150–60.

Burnard, L. (1993), 'The Text Encoding Initiative: Towards an Extensible Standard for the Encoding of Texts', in Ross and Higgs (1993), 105–18.

Cutter, K., and Rowe, C. (1990), 'Scanning in the Supermarket: For Better or for Worse . . . ?', *Behaviour and Information Technology*, 9: 157–69.

Davenport, T. H. (1994), 'Saving IT's Soul: Human-Centred Information Management', *Harvard Business Review* (Mar.–Apr.), 119–31

Davison, J. (1993), 'Electronic Point of Scale Scanning in Multiple Food Retailing', *Behaviour and Information Technology*, 12: 54–64.

Doorn, P. (1993), 'Electronic Records and Historians: The Case of the Netherlands', in Ross and Higgs (1993), 219–26.

—— (1996), 'Archives', in Mullings *et al.* (1996), 357–79.

Duranti, L. (1995), 'Reliability and Authenticity: The Concepts and their Implications', *Archivaria*, 39 (Spring), 5–10.

Elliott, B., and McCrone, D. (1982), *The City: Patterns of Domination and Conflict* (London).

Eom, H. B., and Lee, S. M. (1990), 'A Survey of Decision Support System Applications (1971–April 1988)', *Interfaces*, 20: 65–79.

Haeckel, S. H., and Nolan, R. L. (1993), 'Managing by Wire', *Harvard Business Review* (Sept.–Oct.), 122–32.

Harvey, D. (1989), *The Condition of Postmodernity* (Oxford).

Hedstrom, M. (1991), 'Understanding Electronic Incunabula: A Framework for Research on Electronic Records', *American Archivist*, 54/3: 334–54.

Holmes, D. I. (1991), 'A Multivariate Technique for Authorship Attribution and its Application to the Analysis of Mormon Scripture and Related Texts', *History and Computing*, 3: 12–22.

Hopper, M. D. (1990), 'Rattling SABRE—New Ways to Compete on Information', *Harvard Business Review* (May–June), 118–25.

Knight, V. (1993), 'The 1991 Census Data Sets and Social Historians', in Ross and Higgs (1993), 269–80.

Lee, R. M., McCosh, A. M., and Migliarese, P. (1988) (eds.), *Organisational Decision Support Systems* (New York).

McDowall, D. (1993), '"Wonderful Things": History, Business and Archives Look to the Future', *American Archivist*, 56: 348–57.

Michelson, A., and Rothenberg, J. (1992), 'Scholarly Communication and Information Technology: Exploring the Impact of Changes in the Research Process on Archives', *American Archivist*, 55: 236–315.

Morris, R. J. (1979), *Class and Class Consciousness in the Industrial Revolution, 1780–1850,* (London).

—— (1985), 'Does Nineteenth Century Nominal Record Linkage have Lessons for the Machine-Readable Century?', *Journal of the Society of Archivists*, 7: 503–12.

—— (1991), 'History and Computing: Expansion and Achievements', *Social Science Computer Review*, 9: 215–30

—— (1992), Editorial, *History and Computing*, 4/3: ii–v.

—— (1994), 'History and Computing', in A. Kent and J. G. Williams, *Encyclopaedia of Computer Science and Technology*, vol. 31, supp. 16 (New York).

Mullings, C., Deegan, M., Ross, S., and Kenna, S. (1996), *New Technologies for the Humanities* (London).

Ross, S. and Higgs, E. (1993) (eds.), *Electronic Information Resources and Historians: European Perspectives* (St Katharinen).

Schürer, K. and Diederiks, H. (1993) (eds.), *The Use of Occupations in Historical Analysis* (St Katharinen).

Smith, S. (1988), 'How Much Change at the Store...', in D. Knights and H. Wilmott (eds.), *New Technology and the Labour Process* (London), 143.

Southall, H. (1993), 'Getting into Gopherspace: Accessing Information Anywhere in the World at the Click of a Mouse', *History and Computing*, 512: 110–20.

Weissman, R. F. E. (1994), 'Archives and the New Information Architecture of the 1990s', *American Archivist*, 57: 20–34.

Wilson, C. L., and Blue, J. L. (1992), 'Neural Network Methods Applied to Character Recognition', *Social Science Computer Review*, 10: 173–94.

Beyond Content: Electronic Fingerprints and the Use of Documents

RONALD W. ZWEIG

ABSTRACT

Documents are generated within organizations. They record the process of decision-making, policy formation, and implementation which are also social events—things done by people acting together. The manner in which organizations are structured and function—that is, the social context in which documents are generated—is no less significant than the content of the documents stored in archives. Similarly, the significance of a document is often determined by the manner it which it is used as much as by its contents. Conventional archives are excellent repositories for documentary content, but retain meagre records of the way documents are generated and used. Electronic office systems create important information concerning the context in which documents were generated and the way in which they are used. This information can be a major resource for historians if it is retained. However, existing office systems mimic conventional office filing practices, and the evidence of the context in which they were generated and way they were used are lost.

The profession of history has a history of its own. The development of the vocation as an academic subject based on scientific scholarship has been due in large part to the preservation, organization, and availability of archival records. The evolution of the profession is closely linked to the history of the record-keeping practices of the institutions it studies. And, as archival practice has changed dramatically over the last decades, so too has the nature of historical writing. Modern history is now written in far closer detail, and historical explanation is based on documentary evidence of greater extent and depth than ever before.

In part this is a question of style. But it is also the result of the greater availability of records—because of the contemporaneity of the records open to research, because of the expansion of government and other social agencies that keep records, and because of the changing culture of governing that generates more records and preserves a larger proportion of them. This, in turn, can largely be attributed to the proliferation and ubiquitousness in even the lowliest offices of the inexpensive technologies needed to create and duplicate these records—typewriters, roneo or Gestetner stencil duplicating machines, and eventually also xerox machines. The proliferation of cheap office technologies has altered the way records are written, disseminated, and stored. This, in turn, has altered the way modern history is written, and transformed the nature of the profession.

The process of change described here is manifest, and it is hard to imagine any dissent from it. Even the most conservative and traditional historians will concede that something very significant has happened in the circumstances of historical research. Yet few academic historians are willing to pay attention to an even more momentous technological change—the advent of electronic records—that is beginning to transform the archives on which their future professional survival will depend. Computer-generated records will change the way historians work, and the way they use documents as evidence, far more dramatically than the spread of typewritten documents did in the past.

This chapter will attempt to outline the differences between electronic and conventional documents, and will suggest ways in which historians will be able to make use of these differences in the reconstruction and understanding of the past. The focus will be on the challenge to the customer of archival services (i.e. the historian) rather than the technical problems created by the new technologies for archivists themselves (Gavrel 1990; Hedstrom 1991). Previously, when historians adjusted to new office technologies, they themselves did not have to learn new skills. And the transformation of archival records was so gradual that the process of change was hardly noticed. This time, however, magnetic media and digital records require radically new skills from the users of archives.

Few historians have the necessary training, and even fewer are able to pass these skills on to their students. In general there is a huge unwillingness to acquire the ability to work with computer media at a level beyond word processing. Many historians are usually unwilling even to acknowledge the transformation of the archival record. It is widely felt that, if existing archival legislation remains in force, the thirty-year rule means that historians currently in the forefront of the profession will have no need to deal with records that are being generated electronically. The problem, many would like to believe, can safely be left to the generations of historians (their students) that will follow.

Such thinking is illusory. Vast amounts of machine-readable archival resources are already available. The online catalogue of the Center for Electronic Records at the National Archives in Washington, DC, includes over 30,000 record series or data sets. Many of these are numeric data that provided an input into the decision-making process rather than the record of how policy was formulated or implemented, and are supplementary to existing conventional paper files. However, the first collections of electronically generated documents that are the primary record of policy-making are already being deposited in archives. Leaving aside for the moment the immense technical problems that these tapes present to the keepers of public records around the world, the pace at which magnetic records are being accessioned by archives is growing at a geometric rate. If one measures the rate of introduction of electronic office systems in offices around the industrialized world—whether lone personal computers (PCs) or fully fledged systems with networked links throughout the organization and automatic archiving and document-tracking—it is clear that the proportion of records reaching archives that are computerized will soon expand even more dramatically. Electronic records are a tidal wave that will reach everyone's shores very soon.

In what ways are electronic records different from other records? There is no simple answer to this question. Many of the computerized office systems used to generate records simply mimic familiar office practices, which are in turn based on the technologies of the past. The proliferation of that easily recognizable icon of the filing cabinet in many computer operating systems and programs is not just an artifice. The computer files to which the iconized filing cabinet gives access are essentially the same (albeit in a different medium) as the paper documents they are masquerading as. There is little difference between records generated by millions of PCs and those generated by the typewriters that they replace. Records created on PCs used as typewriters are not going to change significantly the way historians will use those records when they are accessioned by archives and opened for research. If anything, because of the limitations of DOS file-name conventions, historians may well find it harder rather than easier to use these document files. How meaningful can 'eight-character' file titles be? How many variations on an eight-character title can there be? (Coombs *et al.* 1987). In all likelihood, what will be preserved for posterity from the records created in this early phase of using the new technology will be the paper copies of the original computer files. So the transformation of the historical record is not necessarily the direct result of the proliferation of PCs.

The real revolution in the nature of documentary evidence begins when records are generated by more sophisticated office software. When this happens, the meaning of the term 'document' will be transformed. Similarly, the way in which documents are used will change dramatically as well.

The printed page contains information at various levels. The words on the page convey meaning, and it is this meaning or content that is usually referred to when one relates to a document. However, the arrangement of the words on the page, the design of the page, the typography, the structure of the document—these factors also convey meaning. The computing world has found a way of translating this level of meaning together with the textual content. This is the purpose of the conventions of the various mark-up languages, about which much has been written (Coombs *et al.* 1987). Happily, historians will not have to get involved in the battles between the advocates of competing mark-up systems. Despite the continuing controversy over different mark-up systems, the basic principle is now widely accepted: that machine-readable versions of documents should not be simple files of ASCII (American Standard Code for Information Interchange) codes representing the text but also contain mark-up or tagging that conveys the 'document's' physical and structural attributes.

There is little here that is of special interest to the historian attempting to understand the past on the basis of documentary evidence. However, the more sophisticated electronic office systems record an additional level of information about documents, beyond their textual content, their appearance, and structure. These systems also record the organizational context in which documents were *generated*, how they are *used*. Office systems track the creation of a document, its evolution through various drafts by various authors, and its movement through the organizational hierarchy. One knows who received it, who read it, who annotated it. One can reconstruct how widely it was distributed amongst decision-makers. Its system priority, security level, and entire life cycle can be known in ways that can only rarely be reconstructed from the extant records of conventional documents. As any contemporary historian will appreciate, extraneous pieces of evidence such as distribution lists, and signed receipts for a document, can give valuable additional information about the significance of the documents to which they are attached, even when only a few such chits are attached to a small percentage of the records in archives. The electronic version of a document can be designed to retain these originating and usage attributes in a complete form.

Historians use archives not because they are interested in the documents *per se*. The study of an individual, isolated document is antiquarianism rather than history. Historians use archives because they are interested in the organizations which formulated and implemented policy, and in the processes by which this happened. Documents are the best evidence of these processes, recording how decisions were reached, policy was made and implemented. These, in turn, were social events—done by people acting together. The manner in which people interacted—that is, the social context in which documents were generated—is often lost to historians because of the paucity of the remaining archival evidence. Electronic records can retain as part of the 'systems-management' information tracking the fate of documents within the system exactly that type of information on usage that will make it possible to add an additional dimension to 'documents as evidence' in research. Figuratively, it is as if the fingerprints on all copies of a paper document were identified in a separate listing attached to it.

Clearly, this is a good thing. However, the potential of electronic office systems to retain additional dimensions of information concerning documents is no guarantee that this potential will be realized. As noted above, many such systems ignore the usage information, in favour of mimicking as closely as possible existing office practices. Other systems abandon the systems-management information on usage as soon as a copy of the document has been unaltered for a given period of time and it is archived. There are no agreed standards of what sort of usage information should be preserved, or how to do so.

All the users of archival records (amongst whom historians can be counted together with lawyers, journalists, and anyone interested in questions of precedent and accountability, and not just the historical past) should be bringing the combined weight of their opinions to the industrial manufacturers of the systems and the designers of the software that run them. In practice, only a few users of archives have even begun to think about the issues involved, and most lack the skills to make meaningful use of the technology or to articulate demands to ensure that the document-generating systems that are being built will be aware of their needs.

The new technology will change more than just the medium on which the documents are preserved, and the available levels of information concerning that document. Electronic records can be more comprehensive than any paper document, and modern documents will be compound things that cannot be expressed on paper. They will contain graphics, images, voice, video, animations. In these compound documents, text will be only one part of 'hypermedia'. Documents can contain links and pointers to many other (interlinked) files of 'documents' so that the hypertext links are part of the information that the document contains. Alternatively, the electronic document can be continually updated by links to databases. Historians will not work with documents that have traditional boundaries at all, but with 'entities' that are really pieces of links to other materials, which are stored throughout a computer network and are constantly being updated (Weissman 1990: 53).

The whole concept of a document as an integral and independent record will change. When records are 'virtual' items stored optically or magnetically, the physical limitations of paper and print will be overcome, and we will deal with information objects linked temporarily in order to focus human attention on a special array of information. The identification of these links will become more important than the particular conjunction of objects represented by any given document.

The easiest way to understand the ways in which the nature of records are changing (and not just the media on which they are stored) is to consider the role of the international networks and huge databases that now serve government agencies and multinational corporations. Information now flows, and officials interact, in ways that no paper transaction can accurately reflect.

The concept of 'document', based on the paper records stored in current archives, will soon be inappropriate as a metaphor for the electronic record generated by policy-makers. How is it possible to convert compound virtual documents into records? Current systems do not time-stamp the activation of links, and it is therefore not possible to reconstruct the chain of events that led to the creation of a virtual document in its given state. Furthermore, once a document has been updated through links to a series of pipelined events, it will be impossible to restore it to the state it was in before being automatically or manually changed (Weissman 1990: 54).

The communications revolution adds a further level of complexity. When compound electronic records are transmitted across networks, all traces of the linkages are lost. As Terry Cook points out,

if an electronic document has no physical existence, but rather is a 'virtual' composite of disparate information appearing but fleetingly on a terminal, how does the institution, let alone the archivist, preserve evidence of significant transactions, especially as they relate to important decisions regarding pro-gramme activity? Where is the 'evidence' or accountability of the transaction? Where is the context? What is provenance?   (Cook 1992: 206)

Despite these difficulties, historians will accommodate themselves to virtual documents in the same way that they have developed appropriate tools of analysis for inscriptions, scrolls, books, and other records. The problem is the preservation and later study of the logical, not the physical, evidentiary entity (Zweig 1992).

The emerging technology will allow historians to use entirely new approaches to archival research—approaches which they have barely begun to consider. The major difficulty facing modern historians in conventional archives is the vast quantity of records that survives. Very few serious archival research projects can claim to be truly exhaustive. There is never enough time available for the diligent researcher, and often one is left with the feeling that the pertinent records have been filed somewhere out of reach—but not in the obvious files where they should be. Whether owing to the quirks of the original filing clerk, or security considerations, or changing categories in the organization of subject matter, the most important files are often placed somewhere totally unexpected. Computerized records will make it possible to use sophisticated search-and-retrieval techniques. Simple search and retrieval can produce too much information. But, if the techniques are combined with an understanding of linguistic equivalences, proximity searches, Boolean logic, and other techniques of text retrieval, it will be possible to control the results of a search and to improve its quality. Historians will also benefit from the statistical techniques being developed for 'data mining' of large organizational databases.

The most widely used method of organizing archival collections is that of provenance. Records groups are formed on the principle of preserving together records generated by the same office, department, or other bureaucratic cell. While this is a logical way of organizing records, logistical considerations force the historian to plan his research in conventional paper records in the same manner, reading each record group or series separately. The chronological sequence of events is repeated, from beginning to end, for each separate group of records. The result is a tunnel vision on specific focuses of decision-making. Electronic records will make it possible to retrieve the documents pertaining to the subject of research across organizational boundaries. Although aware of the provenance of the documents, the researcher of electronic records will be able to pursue the documentary trail of evidence for any given moment across record groups, with the same facility as he will be able to pursue that trail across time for any given document-generating organizational centre.

Further, it will be possible to avoid tunnel vision in an additional sense. By focusing on the specific subject of a research project, one frequently loses the broader perspective. It is not always apparent in conventional records what other issues were occupying the attention of decision-makers at a particular time, or what was the overall agenda of government. Electronic archives will make it possible to examine the subject headings of other documents that crossed the desks of decision-makers in any defined period. Our understanding of the policy-making process can be enriched only if we are aware of the overall context of the subject being researched—to see as much as possible of the national agenda for any period, and not just the issue at the focus of a particular research project.

Governments and organizations are often large and widely dispersed bodies, in which the formulation and implementation of policy do not always follow any formal hierarchical pyramid. In the course of dealings with events, bodies of expertise, and vested interest, form at various nodes within the whole sprawling organism. It is not always immediately apparent, if it ever is from the hindsight of thirty years or more, where, when, and by whom decisions were being made. Electronic records will allow the historian to approach his subject with new tools that will help illuminate the flow of the decision-making process by studying how documents are generated and used. Ideally, it will be possible to map this process through the machinery of government.

Intelligence communities are aware that a sudden increase in activity, a sudden heightening of 'noise', indicates that something is occurring which merits closer inspection—regardless of the content of that 'noise'.

The mere increase in the flow of communication should attract the researcher's attention (Luttwark 1968: 145–6). It is not practical to pursue this concept in paper archives, but, if the emerging electronic office systems preserve information relating to document usage, then electronic archives will make it possible.

These are only a few possible approaches to the ways in which historians might conduct their archival research in electronic records. Of course, no technique or methodology will change the basic task of the historian—to read and understand the sources. But electronic archives do contain the potential for new, heuristic methods that may broaden understanding of the manner in which governments and organizations work.

Modern historians have a long and fruitful experience of working closely with archivists to identify the records relevant to the research of the former. Once the paper records have been produced, however, the historian generally requires no assistance in their use. This will no longer be true of electronic, virtual records. Unless historians address the issues discussed above, they will lose their ability independently to use the archival record of currently created documents. Historians will have to acquire new skills in order to retain their independence, or accept a new dependence on the archival and library professions not only to identify relevant sources of information but to interpret and analyse them as well.

The coming tidal wave of change in document-generating technology is leading many countries to re-examine existing records practices and current archival legislation. Historians have an unusual opportunity to contribute to the evolution of new policies. Records managers and archivists are not necessarily aware of the special needs of historians (see Higgs, Chapter 12, this volume), and it is up to the profession to define which attributes of electronic documents should be preserved to facilitate its work in reconstructing the past. This chapter has discussed briefly the concepts of document generation, usage, and hierarchy as meaningful document attributes that are worthy of preservation. There are certainly others which must be brought to the attention of the designers of office-systems software and the drafters of archival legislation. Archivists have already invested considerable effort in considering the challenges created by the new media for the preservation and storing of records. It is up to historians to make the same effort to define their own needs concerning the nature of the archival resources of the very near future.

References

Cook, T. (1992), 'Review Article: Easy to Byte, Harder to Chew: The Second Generation of Electronic Records Archives', *Archivaria*, 33 (Winter 1991–2), 206–16.

Coombs, J. H., Renear, A. H. and Rose, S. J. (1987), 'Markup Systems and the Future of Scholarly Text Processing,' *Communications of the ACM*, 30/11 (Nov.), 933–47.

Durance, C. J. (1990) (ed.), *Management and Recorded Information: Converging Disciplines: Proceedings of the International Council on Archives' Symposium on Current Records* (Munich).

Gavrel, K. (1990), *Conceptual Problems Posed by Electronic Records: A RAMP Study* (Paris: General Information Programme and UNISIST, Unesco).

Hedstrom, M. (1991), 'Understanding Electronic Incunabula: A Framework for Research on Electronic Records', *American Archivist*, 54/3: 334–54.

Luttwark, E. (1968), *Coup d'état* (London).

Orwell, G. (1983), *Animal Farm* (London).

Weissman, R. E. F. (1990), 'Virtual Documents on an Electronic Desktop: Hypermedia, Emerging Computing Environments and the Future of Information Management', in Durance (1990), 53–4.

Zweig, R. W. (1992), 'Virtual Records and Real History', *History and Computing*, 4/3: 174–82.

—— (1993), 'Electronically Generated Records and Twentieth Century History', *Computers and the Humanities*, 27: 73–85.

4

Information in the Business Enterprise

MARTIN CAMPBELL-KELLY

ABSTRACT

In this chapter, information in the business enterprise is classified as implicit, operational, or strategic. Implicit information is held in the organizational memory (for example, the description of office routine) and is rarely recorded or preserved. Operational data are used for day-to-day control of the business (for example, for the collection of customer payments) and are usually recorded but rarely preserved. Strategic information (for example, board papers and minutes, or research reports) is usually recorded and preserved. The impact of evolving technology on these forms of information is discussed using historical examples.

INTRODUCTION: A THREE-LAYER MODEL

Although the impact of new technology on business records is accelerating, it is not a new phenomenon. For example, in the 1890s new office machines such as typewriters and calculating machines had a major impact on the day-to-day operations of businesses (Cortada 1993). Again, in the 1930s the widespread introduction of punched-card machines had a dramatic impact on commerce, and helped to shape much of the accounting practice of today's businesses. In recent years there have been a small number of historical studies of information in business and large-scale organizations. Among the best are Yates (1989), Temin (1990), Bud-Frierman (1994), and McKenney *et al.* (1995). None of these books has included a general model of information in the firm, but most of the enterprises described would fit the simple three-layer model introduced in Fig. 4.1.

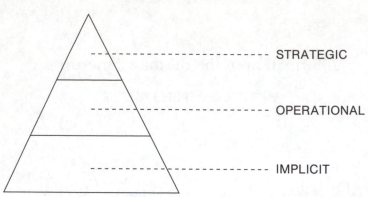

Fig. 4.1 Three-layer model of business information

In this model the top level represents *strategic information* used to govern the long-term behaviour of the organization. Examples of strategic information include board papers, product and marketing plans, financial reports, and so on. Strategic information is very high grade and of the highest utility to the business historian; it is usually manageable in quantity and readily accessible in hard-copy form. At the second level, *operational information* is the raw data which workers of the organization process to maintain operational control of the enterprise. The amount of operational data is usually vast—whether it be measured in information-theory terms (e.g. bits per second), or normal business measures (e.g. transactions per day). Operational information is generally low grade and of low utility for the business historian. It is rarely retained by the organization beyond its useful life. The bottom layer of the model represents the *implicit information* in the enterprise. This information is the intangible 'know-how' employed by information workers in the prosecution of their tasks. Implicit information is not generally codified or recorded, and is usually acquired by workers over several years of on-the-job experience. The economists Nelson and Winter (1982) describe this information as 'organizational routine', and have likened it to the information codified in computer programs.

To assess the likely impact of electronic media on the business historian, it is first necessary to understand which of the three layers of information is of most interest, which are tangible, and which are currently being preserved. To illustrate these points I offer two case studies. First, a nineteenth-century example based on the information-intensive insurance industry, and, secondly, a high-tech example from the late-twentieth-century computer industry.

Industrial assurance began in the 1850s as an entrepreneurial response to the need for working-class burial insurance. Put in its simplest terms, the function of the industrial-assurance enterprise was to use premium income to employ people to produce actuarially determined risk management (Campbell-Kelly 1992; Yates 1993).

The quantity of operational information in the industrial-assurance enterprise was vast. For example, the largest British industrial assurer, the Prudential, had some 2.5 million policies in force by the mid-1870s. At this date, in the first of three information 'revolutions', it abandoned traditional hard-bound ledgers in favour of handwritten manila cards. In the 1920s, a second revolution occurred when handwritten cards were replaced by punched cards. Finally, a third revolution took place when punched cards were replaced by electronic computer records in the 1960s. Because of the financial value attached to insurance policies, records were preserved with extreme care and existing records migrated to a new medium only when two criteria were met: first, that the technology was completely proven, and, second, that the number of policies in force made the transition practical. Generally, the operational data (that is the policy records) were destroyed within a few years of their fulfilment.

The knowledge workers in the insurance company were responsible for processing this mass of data to maintain operational control of the business. By the 1870s full specialization of function had been achieved and there were eleven functional clerical departments such as claims, correspondence, finance, lapse, policy registration, and so on. Clerks obtained their know-how by an apprenticeship system in which school-leavers learned on the job, beginning with low-level tasks and graduating to more complex ones. At this distance in time it is simply not possible to know in detail how the clerks did their jobs, for there were no manuals of office procedure, and the functional tasks gradually evolved so that they bore little resemblance to those of their forebears. The effect of new technology was to automate and deskill many of the clerical tasks, as more and more routine was taken over by punched-card machines and later by computers. In the case of the latter, the embedded knowledge is well documented in the formal requirements and specifications of computer programs, although I know of no active programs to preserve this information.

The second function of the knowledge workers was to process operational data to produce strategic information; this information then enabled board-level decision-making to achieve long-term strategic control. For example, one vital task undertaken by the clerks was a quinquennial valuation which ensured that the company's assets matched its actuarial liabilities. In the 1870s this was a mind-boggling task that took 300 clerks six weeks to complete. Later, punched-card and computer technology made this an entirely mechanical process. Regardless of how the data were processed, however, the resulting valuation report was always a short, printed, paper document. The same printed-report format was generally used for all other strategic information, such as new actuarial tables, investment performance reports, analysis of individual insurance products, annual reports, and so on.

Strategic information is generally modest in volume, of the highest importance to the business historian, and generally well preserved on paper media in corporate archives. The impact of electronic media on strategic information is likely to be slight, since the printed paper form will probably persist into the foreseeable future for both cultural and practical reasons.

CASE STUDY 2: ICL'S NEW RANGE PLANNING ORGANIZATION

ICL was created in 1968 as a 'national champion' computer firm in a government-inspired merger which brought together all of the then existing mainframe computer firms in the UK. As an inducement to the merger, the government provided a £13.5 million grant for the development of a new computer range to compete with the then best-selling System 360 computer family sold by IBM. Both the ICL New Range and the IBM 360 computer projects have been the subject of historical studies, the former at a strategic level (Campbell-Kelly 1989) and the latter in very much more detail (Pugh *et al.* 1991). These two examples illustrate the kinds of records that are produced in large high-technology projects, what records are preserved, and what records are actually of use to the historian. There have been several comparable studies of high-technology projects (e.g. Hounshell and Kenly Smith 1988).

The ICL New Range was by far the largest computer R&D project ever undertaken in the UK. Between 1969 and 1973 it was to cost approximately £100 million, and involve a design team of up to 100 people known as the New Range Planning Organization (NRPO). Later the New Range was to consume the largest part of ICL's 30,000-strong workforce in development, manufacture, and marketing. The NRPO was responsible for defining the 'architecture' of the New Range, determining the feasibility of development and manufacture, and establishing marketing plans.

Although the reporting process of the NRPO was highly formalized, its day-to-day activity was a chaotic mixture of formal and informal committees and networks, with a core of full-time planners and a larger number of people seconded part-time from within the company, and numerous consultants from outside. To take one example, at the beginning of the project seven committees were established, each consisting of about six people, to investigate one of a range of competing architectural possibilities. These committees met frequently, exchanged memoranda, wrote interim reports, made phone calls, met with external consultants, and consulted a wide spectrum of the published literature. Almost none of this information exchange has survived. However, because the New Range project is very recent in history, it was possible to interview key participants, who were able to elaborate on the minutiae of the planning process.

Clearly, the greatest impact of electronic media on the day-to-day interactions of an organization such as the NRPO would be the substitution of ephemeral electronic mail (e-mail) for slightly-less-ephemeral paper memoranda, and the use of teleconferencing for some face-to-face meetings. The scope for the retention of this kind of information exchange is not significantly better or worse today than it was then. In fact, the most significant change in the last twenty years of the twentieth century has been a cultural trend towards less formal minute-taking in meetings. This highlights the importance of active oral history programmes, not merely as a by-product of a celebratory history, but as a routine function of the pro-active corporate records manager. (In the information technology (IT) area, both IBM and AT&T are actively pursuing such programmes.)

The output of the two years' activity of the NRPO was a large number of technical and marketing reports, occupying several shelf-feet. This

constituted the formal, operational information produced by the organization, and it underpinned the subsequent R&D, manufacturing, and
marketing activity for the next decade. These reports included, for
example, seven reports evaluating the competing architectures referred
to above. There were also reports defining the necessary electronic,
electro-mechanical, and software requirements of the New Range; and
there were numerous marketing reports analysing the product requirements for ICL's specific market segments. All these reports were produced in a highly disciplined way and a catalogue was produced. There
was no active retention programme by ICL's corporate archives, but ICL's
Technical and Social Archive held a complete set of documentation,
which has recently been transferred to the National Archive for the
History of Computing at Manchester University. R&D is alive and well
in ICL today, but electronic media have had little impact on the operational information produced. It seems likely that the printed research
report will be the dominant genre of the research organization for the
foreseeable future.

Of course, the NRPO reports were simply the tip of an iceberg of
documentation generated by the New Range project. For example,
within the manufacturing and software development organizations
there was a corresponding, but much larger, networking activity and
related documentation. Virtually all of this information was routinely
destroyed as soon as it ceased to be useful (for example, once a set of
negotiations had been terminated or a product discontinued). For the
general business historian, this is a loss of little importance.

Yet another mass of documentation was generated for customers and
maintenance personnel. There was a manual for each hardware component and software product, the total running to perhaps a hundred
linear feet, not including the numerous multiple editions of manuals.
No attempt is made in ICL (or any other company I know of) to archive
product documentation once a product is no longer supported. Computer users, unfortunately, attach a singular importance to computer
manuals and they constitute much of the offerings that arrive at unwilling computer archives, which would soon drown in computer manuals
if the flood were not turned back. (By way of illustration, in the mid-
1980s the catalogue of IBM's mainframe-computer manuals occupied
about 300 pages with about fifty titles per page.) New technology
arrived for computer manuals in the late 1970s with the use of microfiche as an alternative to hard copy. While this has greatly reduced the
archival storage problem, it has probably made the access problem

worse. Much computer documentation has now made the transition to CD-ROM, which has eliminated the physical space problem, and greatly facilitated access, but it is not clear that the archiving of computer manuals will serve any useful purpose, other than to satisfy the cravings of the occasional computer buff with an obsessive interest in the technology.

However, returning to the NRPO documents themselves, they were far too discursive and voluminous to guide board-level strategic decision-making. Hence, the several dozen reports were reduced to a handful of summary reports for the three principal operational boards (R&D, manufacturing, and marketing) and a slim set of board papers for the main board. This strategic information was exceptionally rich, and, for the business historian seeking to understand the strategic behaviour of the firm, it contained almost all that one needed to know. Like all board papers and reports, they have been preserved indefinitely in the corporate archives. Given the cultural preference for the printed hard-copy format for board papers and reports, there appears to be little likely impact of new technology. Indeed, the chief difficulty I experienced researching ICL in the early 1980s was not the emergence of new office technologies, but the fad for making board 'presentations' unsupported by written papers. For these, the board minutes could record only highly abbreviated abstracts.

CONCLUSION

The impact of electronic media on records is one of the big issues facing historians and records managers in the late twentieth century for two reasons. First, there has been an explosion in the quantity of information, but no corresponding useful measure of quality. Secondly, there is uncertainty about what can be kept electronically, and what should be kept. To make these issues more tractable, it is helpful to consider the historical value of the three types of information produced by businesses, their usefulness to the business historian, and the best way of keeping and using them.

- *Implicit information* is by its nature intangible. Currently the best way to capture this information is through oral history programmes. The codification of knowledge into computer software does, however, suggest an intriguing new source for the future that is not yet being effectively captured and archived.

- *Operational information* has undergone several media revolutions in the last century. In principle, now that operational information is largely electronic, it could be preserved in electronic form in its totality. However, the volume would be simply huge (see Ross, Chapter 1, this volume). It is not clear that any useful purpose would be served by the indiscriminate archiving of operational information of this kind.
- *Strategic information* is the rich, top layer of information that is of primary interest to the business historian. It is in this layer that historians will discover answers to their key questions: how the firm responds to opportunities and threats; how it interacts with government, other firms, its employees, and its customers; how it establishes R&D programmes and marketing strategies; and so on.

Thus, the answers to the big questions are generally to be found in the top-level board papers of significant firms with professional records managers, and electronic media present little threat in the foreseeable future. Electronic media do however present very great opportunities for the enlightened corporate records manager to provide enhanced storage of strategic information and improved access for researchers.

Reference

Bud-Frierman, L. (1994) (ed.), *Information Acumen: Global Perspectives on the Information Revolution* (London).

Campbell-Kelly, M. (1989), *ICL: A Business and Technical History* (Oxford).

——(1992), 'Large-Scale Data Processing in the Prudential, 1850–1930', *Accounting, Business and Financial History*, 2: 117–39.

Cortada, J. W. (1993), *Before the Computer: IBM, NCR, Burroughs, and Remington Rand and the Industry they created, 1865–1956* (Princeton).

Hounshell, D. A., and Kenly Smith Jr., J. (1988), *Science and Corporate Strategy, Du Pont R and D, 1902–1980* (Cambridge).

McKenney, J. L., with Copeland, D. C., and Mason, R. O. (1995), *Waves of Change: Business Evolution through Information Technology* (Cambridge, Mass.).

Nelson, R. R., and Winter, S. G., (1982), *An Evolutionary Theory of Economic Change* (Cambridge, Mass.).

Pugh, E. W., Johnson, L. R., and Palmer, J. H. (1991), *IBM's 360 and Early 370 Systems* (Cambridge, Mass.).

Temin, P. (1991), *Inside the Business Enterprise: Historical Perspectives on the Use of Information*, (Chicago).

Yates, J. (1989), *Control through Communication: The Rise of System in American Management* (Baltimore).

—— (1993), 'Co-evolution of Information-Processing Technology and Use: Interaction between the Life Insurance and Tabulating Industries', *Business History Review,* 67 (Spring), 1–51.

Electronic Information Resources and Historians:
A Consumer's View

DANIEL GREENSTEIN

ABSTRACT

Standards for encoding and exchanging machine-readable texts, better training in the use of computers, institutional infrastructure, and more and better professional support—these are four key areas in which historians must make significant advances if they are to gain maximum advantage from the proliferation of electronic information resources. Yet advances in these critical areas are unlikely to be realized by historians acting alone. In order to harness information technology (IT) effectively to their teaching and research, historians must engage in more extensive cross-disciplinary collaboration with other humanities scholars. In short, this chapter argues that the future of historical computing relies essentially upon the relaxation of inhibiting disciplinary boundaries and the elaboration of humanities computing more generally.

INTRODUCTION

Historians do not so much develop computational solutions as adapt and apply those solutions developed elsewhere (Greenstein 1994*a*: ch. 1). Consequently, if historical computing is a discipline in its own right, it is a very eclectic one. The historian compiling a critical edition of a text requires an apparatus designed for textual analysis and thus tends to rely on software tools and computational methods which are on the whole developed by and for literary scholars. Those very few historians who are interested in linguistic-content analysis also borrow shamelessly from their colleagues in literary studies and likewise from the computational linguists. The vast majority of computer-literate historians are far less adventuresome and stick more closely to techniques taken from their cousins in the social and behavioural sciences. Most notable amongst them are methods of database management and statistical processing. But historians' needs hardly end at this classic trinity of processing aims: document preparation, linguistic content analysis, and categorical analysis. They rely increasingly for data exploration and delivery upon international networks, online data services, and hypertext and multimedia systems. Needless to say, few of these systems were developed by historians or with the historical user community particularly in view.

Given historians' truly catholic approach to computing and their reliance upon methods developed elsewhere, they may be unique among other computer-using humanities scholars. Historians' computational needs are distinctive owing to their extent and not, as some might claim, to the nature of historical data or their analysis. Why, then, are historians so adamant in developing their computational methods and resources in near complete isolation from other communities with which they have so much in common and from which they have borrowed so extensively? This 'splendid isolation' was explicable in the 1970s and even the 1980s, when the field of humanities computing was so wide open, and the methods appropriate to historical teaching and research so poorly developed (Thaller 1989). The climate in the late 1990s is very different, however. High-speed computer networks and the relative cost of producing machine-readable information have forced isolated communities and computer platforms to talk to one another; representatives from Apple and IBM have even been seen together around the same table.

So far historians have not responded to these changing circumstances. Consequently, it is impossible to address historians' needs with respect to electronic-information resources without being concerned over their relative seclusion. Historians are never going to take control over the direction of IT developments. They can, however, have a much greater influence than at present over how such developments impinge upon their professional practices. They can develop a proactive rather than simply a reactive approach to the development of IT resources. To do this, however, they need to alter fundamentally the 'departmental' mentality which has emerged amongst the computer-literate members of their profession and seek collaboration with other humanities scholars. Four areas in which collaborative ventures should be developed are discussed here: the development of inter-change standards, training, institutional infrastructure, and professional support.

First and foremost we need to recognize that individual historians will wish to process the same body of machine-readable data in different ways. Imagine what might be done with the collected works of American Founding Father, Alexander Hamilton, if they were to be published electronically on CD-ROM. Linguistic-content analysis would help illuminate debates about the extent of Hamilton's nationalism and elitist principles. Sophisticated database-style analyses would reveal the kinship and patronage networks in which Hamilton was involved. A text-critical edition replete with learned commentary would be developed and become a valuable reference tool. A multimedia system designed to instruct students in aspects of American history would be built by integrating a selection of Hamilton's works with other literary, visual, and audio materials.

In an ideal world, the one body of machine-readable data would support these four very different processing aims. The text-processing software used for the linguistic-content analysis would view the data as running prose interrupted with a heading and some rudimentary bib-liographic material wherever a new item in the corpus began. It might also recognize previously marked passages which dealt with nationalis-tic themes or with the nature of government. The database would see the same data differently—as a series of database tables comprising highly structured social profiles of the people with whom Hamilton came into contact and about whom he wrote. The desktop publishing system used by the text-critical scholar would have yet another view of the same data. The corpus would appear as a series of pages interrupted periodically by a heading and extensive bibliographic information. The package would also recognize footnotes (perhaps nested to several levels) and support variant readings of those texts which were originally found in heavily edited manuscript form. Finally, the multimedia sys-tem would have an altogether different view, this time of a body of text embedded throughout with handles linking text segments to one another and to a range of externally stored texts, images, and record-ings. Alas, this is not the ideal world. The works of Hamilton which would eventually appear on CD-ROM would probably be susceptible to basic text retrieval but that would be about all. Each of the projects outlined above would have to download the data and comprehensively re-edit them before further processing could get under way. In the case of the database project, it is doubtful that the published electronic text would be of any use whatsoever.

None of this is meant as a criticism of electronic publishing. On the contrary, electronic publishers provide valuable reference material and should be lauded for their novelty and foresight. The example is chosen simply to demonstrate how sadly lacking we are in the very facilities which historians require most—mechanisms for exchanging data between different processing environments. In a recent contribution to *Computing and the Humanities*, Greenstein and Burnard use a seventeenth-century sasine or record of landholding and transfer to demonstrate mechanisms which furnish these very facilities (Greenstein and Burnard 1995). The problem, they argue, is that, hitherto, data-processing aims have determined how information is modelled and managed in machine-readable form. Consequently, data which are collected for one particular analysis or processing application are unsuitable when they are required elsewhere for a different purpose. By devising and adopting standards for encoding machine-readable information, data exchange can take place independently of processing considerations. Such a standard, they claim, has been developed by the Text Encoding Initiative (TEI), which has provided guidelines and extensive documentation for the use of the markup language known as Standard Generalized Markup Language (SGML) in the creation of machine-readable text (Burnard 1993). The standard that they advocate is not a prescriptive one. It does not tell historians what to encode in a given source and thus impinge upon interpretation. Rather, it provides a set of very flexible solutions which enable historians to encode whatever they will, but in a manner which can be made generally recognizable.

The importance to historians of encoding standards that will facilitate data exchange cannot be overstated. Their impact on their data-creation practices is likely to be minimal. Anyone who has attempted to compile machine-readable data for either teaching or research purposes will agree that such an undertaking impinges so greatly on their time and resources as to minimize their interest in providing support for other scholars who might become interested in such data. It will, I suspect, be rather a long time before historians adopt SGML-authoring software as their own. At the same time historians need to recognize that machine-readable data created elsewhere will increasingly become the stock in trade of their research. The history of the late twentieth century, for example, will rely very heavily indeed on machine-readable information. It is an all too sobering thought that in the mid-1990s the mechanisms which would enable historians to index, search, and ana- lyse those data according to their very many and particular research interests had not been developed. Is it too much to ask that in 2023 the historian confronting a machine-readable run of the *Financial Times*, 1997–2007, should be able to perform serial calculations with the stock prices quoted therein, without having to re-enter or extensively edit the data? The interest of historians in standard mechanisms for data-encod- ing and exchange need not be driven, then, by altruistic considerations about the value of secondary analysis. It should be driven instead by their recognition that they have a vested interest in using the vast quantities of data that are currently being produced by government, publishing houses, banks, and information services.

How can historians support the development of encoding standards which will facilitate data exchange? First, by abandoning the notion that only historians can model and manage data in a way which facilit- ates their particular data-processing aims. Figuratively (literally in an increasing number of cases), machine-readable information is inher- ently in the public domain. The electronic collection of Alexander Hamilton's works will hold out as much interest to the linguist, philo- sopher, and the political scientist as it does to the historian. In a similar vein, the level of interest in machine-readable copies of the *Financial Times* or of any number of government records is not solely restricted to the historical community. To secure access to information which will not necessarily be created with the historical community in mind, historians must be willing to develop the common ground they share with other scholars and computer-using communities. Only this will ensure that in future all machine-readable data can be exchanged across disciplinary and professional boundaries.

Of course historians cannot expect linguists, text critics, or publishers to explain to them how best to interpret, mark, and process those classically ambiguous phrases which are now the stock in trade of historical data modelling exercises. Only a historically trained scholar will be able to identify the likely internal structure of the name 'Johnny Turner', of the ambiguous temporal expression 'a few days before the fair', or of the relative place name 'five minutes away from Foorler's house' (Thaller 1986). This does not mean that historians are alone faced with the problem of disambiguation. Anyone who is unconvinced of this need only speak with a linguist about how to interpret and mark up the expression 'wash sinks' (Sperberg-McQueen and Burnard 1990). Historians, too, must determine how to classify their data for analytical purposes. I for one would not trust a lexicographer or philologist to determine whether the socio-economic profiles of eighteenth-century Scottish immigrants to the American colonies should be represented in social-class terms or as indices of their pre- or post-industrial occupations. Once again, however, the process of coding data whose meaning are uncertain, disputed, or theoretically contingent is not unique to the historical profession. Here, the non-believer need only discuss with a literary scholar the identification of noun phrases in the works of Charles Dickens. Finally, they should recognize that historians are not the only computer-using community which has felt constrained by industry standard database packages and mark-up languages which simply could not cater for historical dates, currency measures, and time scales. The development of object-oriented processing techniques reflects the fact that such constraints are widespread. Why, then, are some historians so busily proliferating new historically specific 'data types' by implementing them in proprietary software while the computer-literate researchers in other disciplines are giving generic definition to their eccentric data so that they may be implemented on any platform which permits user-defined objects? Again, the historians' focus is too narrow. They need to recognize that, at some level, the processes of computer-aided historical research which involve the application of expert or subject-specific knowledge should be explicable in generic terms accessible to non-specialists. If the machine-readable data produced by other users are ever to become accessible to historians, and that produced by historians to other users, historians need to begin thinking about the research process in such generic terms.

Having adopted this generalists' view of data-processing and exchange, it might be prudent to secure the historical profession's involvement in the development, testing, and adoption of encoding standards. Only by making its processing needs known can the profession expect them to be catered for by the computer and data-creation industries. Whatever the ultimate fate of the TEI, it does seem as good a place to start as any in making these needs felt. It is not an alien commercial body. On the contrary, it is a consortium of humanities scholars with whom they need anyway to establish more and better contact. It has also produced very comprehensive Guidelines now in their third edition (Sperberg-McQueen and Burnard 1994). Thus, their participation in a rather advanced project minimizes the danger of reproducing work already completed elsewhere. At present, the Guidelines need to be reviewed by historians. They need to be read and commented upon by a wide audience. The Guidelines also require refinement and elaboration through application to real projects, including historical ones. It is also worth considering whether historians have a role to play in developing SGML-aware software and/or conversion utilities which will enable them to fulfil their favourite processing aims while reading and writing TEI-conformant files. In sum, it is probably time to transcend the politics of standardization—'standards are good so long as you adopt mine'. It is also worth transcending an approach to computer-aided historical research which assumes that the complexities inherent in disambiguating and interpreting fuzzy information and of representing idiosyncratic data types are unique to history. Overcoming this subject-centred narrowness, historians may not win a greater influence over the computing and electronic publishing industries. They may none the less ensure that the products of those industries will be more readily incorporated into their teaching and research.

TRAINING

More and better training also requires a priority place on this wish list. There is not much point in delivering information in a manageable and flexible format if the skills required to use it in even the most trivial analyses are not widely available. But who is to provide this training and of what should it consist? Two recent international meetings of computer-literate historians addressed these very questions and resolved to prepare a curriculum of instruction in computational methods and techniques which could be adopted at any number of institutions (Spaeth *et al.* 1992; Davis *et al.* 1993; Greenstein 1994*b*). This 'core' curriculum will make a useful contribution, but its elaboration pointed to trends which are as troublesome as the perception of a currently inadequate training provision.

First, who should deliver the training? Should it come from humanities-computing or computing-science departments, or from the history departments themselves? Different universities have opted for different strategies with interesting ramifications. Where training is provided by humanities-computing or computing-science departments, there are pressures to dress it up in formal scientific terms so as to legitimize it in the eyes of the surrounding scientific community. This is no easy task when one considers that what is required is some competence in a range of applications software and a degree of sensitivity to the data-modelling and analytical problems that historical source material and historical research involve.

The alternative strategy—historians providing computer training from within their own departments—is no less problematic. First, it is difficult to justify an expert in Italian Renaissance cities teaching students how to use a spreadsheet. Moreover, historians who are teaching computer methods are under the same pressures as their counterparts in humanities-computing departments to justify their activities. But, while the humanities-computing people dress up computer training in terms of bits and bytes, historians mystify it by talking about fuzzy data, source criticism, and subjectivity. The irony, of course, is that people involved in what is patently the same activity are increasingly pulling apart from one another as they pursue their own institutional and professional goals by drawing boundaries around the same very narrow patch. In the event, historians' needs, and thus the role that the computer should play in the classroom, are overlooked.

Indeed, defining the computer's role in the classroom was a second problematic area encountered at the international meetings. A large majority agreed a central role for the computer, and this underpinned the applications and methods approach ultimately adopted in the core curriculum. From this group emerged a curriculum made up of various modules—for example, about document preparation and text-processing, database management and data-modelling, and graphical and statistical analysis. A small rump felt that computers might be best employed to deliver information otherwise inaccessible to history students. In this guise, the computer's role was to elaborate some of the issues which emerged in a course which focused primarily on historical themes rather than on computer methods. Thus, a student studying eighteenth-century American history might be advised to query a database of American trade figures or perform basic content analysis on the *Federalist Papers*. In this guise, the computer's role was to deliver machine-readable information that would supplement that normally found by students in printed form or received by them in the shape of lectures and seminars.

Undoubtedly these rather different agenda reflected to a certain extent divisions between the needs of teachers operating out of humanities-computing and history departments, respectively. As significantly, however, they reflected very different conceptions of what training historians requires. The strategy which envisages the computer as a sophisticated delivery system for information similar in fundamental respects to the library is ideal for undergraduates. For such students, historical content remains the principal staple of their diet. The applications and methods course, on the other hand, seems more closely tailored to the needs of history postgraduates. This necessarily much smaller group needs to acquire the comprehensive training that such a course provides. But should historians assume the same training is also required by undergraduates who are not destined for academic careers? Surely, the answer is no. The bulk of history students need a kind of training which they can use to advantage at an interview or in a post with an accounting firm, commercial venture, publishing house, or wherever else they end up. In crassly materialistic terms, such students are unlikely to benefit from a training that rests on the principle that historical computing is distinctive owing to its scientific properties (as advocated by humanities-computing departments), or its especial role in subjective historical analysis (as advocated by history departments).

Hopefully what will emerge from the tensions which are apparent in the community interested in providing historians with computer training is a tripartite approach. Some training in computer methods and applications should be required for all university students, and this should be provided by a service teaching department. There is no reason why such a department cannot make the training accessible and relevant to liberal arts and science students alike. At the rather more advanced end, the small community of postgraduate history students requires training in the computer methods and applications that are appropriate to historical research. The departmental affiliation of such a course does not much matter, provided that it is taught by people with relevant research experience. Why not let local circumstances and relative departmental strengths be determinate? In addition, one should encourage colleagues to integrate machine-readable data and computer exercises into their more traditional thematic courses. Having filled their computer methods requirements outlined above, students will neither shrink from the challenge that such components hold forth, nor demand rudimentary applications training from their history teachers. On the contrary, the use of such materials will consolidate and extend students' familiarity with computational techniques, while introducing them to a range of important historical source materials not otherwise available in printed form.

Having settled the tripartite and integrated structure of history students' training needs, we should perhaps consider how best to provide for them. Training in advanced methods is already reasonably well catered for. There are any number of examples of such training schemes in the UK, the rest of Europe, and the USA, and the core curriculum developed in the mid-1990s is likely to consolidate and extend existing initiatives. There are numerous examples too of the more general training that might be offered by humanities-computing departments. The computing component of the thematic history course is more problematic. At present, the development of such components relies heavily on individual initiatives taken by historians whose own research involves some element of computation. Their data sets are familiar and close at hand and, in some circumstances, can be tailored for student use, perhaps with the aid of self-instructional documentation or workbooks. The present situation is unacceptable if this strand of computer-aided teaching is considered at all important. If the resources in question were printed ones, it would not be considered at all acceptable for teachers to be compiling course bibliographies solely from their own publications. University and college libraries enable the enquiring mind to range freely over a vast array of literature. Is it not time to consider the creation of a similar library where the data of computer-aided history are available for similarly free-ranging enquiry?

Clearly the computer-aided learning materials currently being produced by consortia of scholars, and by the electronic publishing industry, point a hopeful direction (Rosenzweig *et al.* 1993; Doyle 1994; and Wissenburg and Spaeth, forthcoming). I wonder whether data archivists might be encouraged to lend support as well by providing basic instructional materials for their most frequently requested data sets. Training and support for history teachers are as important as the provision of packaged data sets because they will enable the teachers to develop their own materials. There are other reasons to support initiatives for using the computer as a means of delivering subject-specific information. In the 1990s research and teaching libraries as we now know them will change fundamentally (Joint Funding Councils' Libraries Review Group 1993). An increasing number of journals, monographs, and reference materials will be available only in machine-readable form as high-speed computer networks enable hard-pressed university institutions to curtail drastically the escalating cost of their paper library provision. What delivery systems will be used by university libraries in the twenty-first century is not settled (see Brindley, Chapter 15, this volume). It is certain, however, that, by developing new ways of integrating machine-readable data into their thematic courses, historians will be contributing to (and thus perhaps influencing) a wider trend which will have a lasting impact on how we conduct teaching and research within the historical discipline.

In considering our training needs in the present, then, we need to anticipate the future, and here, too, there is every reason to encourage historians to abandon a rather narrow departmental mentality. Those few history students who require a highly specialized training in computer-aided research skills can and should be taught by historians, though the provision need not be available at every single university. The rest of the students need a general computer training organized perhaps especially for humanities students. There are also financial considerations. By organizing computer training for humanities students generally, significant economies of scale can be achieved. Finally, the use of machine-readable information in the traditional subject-specific theme course needs to be considered, but once again, in a general, not in a subject-specific way. In future an increasing amount of information will be available to history students and teachers only in machine-readable form. To ensure the best and most appropriate access to that information, historians might be advised once again to pursue collaborative initiatives with scholars in other disciplines who will also rely as heavily upon such materials.

INSTITUTIONAL SUPPORT

The need for cross-disciplinary collaboration is only reinforced by the logic of network technology. Simply put, academic departments in the arts which act in collaboration will provide a better infrastructure of network servers, computing laboratories, independent workstations, and technical and other support than any single department acting independently. Developments at Glasgow University illuminate such a trend and may serve as an example. In 1991 Glasgow University established a centre for humanities computing within its so-called Arts Technological Resource Unit. The Unit developed as the university distributed many of the computing services which had previously been focused on three mainframe computers operated and supported by a central computing service. One result of devolution was that the twenty-one humanities departments which had previously negotiated directly with the university and its computing service for the development of local (departmental) installations turned instead to their own Arts Faculty. Rather than mediate competing demands (thereby perpetuating the development of largely independent departmental computing installations), the Faculty established the Unit in order to coordinate them. The result was genuinely synergetic; the development of an integrated arts computing network delivered more services to more users than had hitherto been possible by all of the independent local installations put together.

Four departmentally based local area networks, which together served five student computing laboratories with sixteen to twenty personal computers (PCs) and one with sixteen Macs, a fifty-one NEXT multimedia installation, and hundreds of staff desktop computers, were initially networked into a more powerful open system. The gains to participating departments were immediate and substantial. Prior to integration, the departmental initiatives had required locally based file servers and on-site technical staff. More subject-specific expertise had been left to knowledgeable academic staff who 'volunteered' to take on extracurricular responsibilities. Further, users had by necessity been confined to the computing laboratories operated by their own departments, as they alone had housed the requisite data and software. As computer-based teaching had made increasing demands upon the departmental facilities, users had found it more difficult to schedule independent work around times when the labs were free. With the establishment of the more generalized arts network, file and application servers, technical support, and systems administration are provided commonly and more cost effectively by the Unit. The departmental initiatives have lost their network independence. They have enhanced their subject-specific profile, however, as on-site support staff who once spent most of their time providing technical and systems support now devote themselves to helping departmental staff and students use IT in a manner that is most appropriate in their disciplines. In addition, users are no longer tied to a single computer laboratory. The data and software applications appropriate to their work are available on all compatible platforms across the entire network.

The establishment of an interdisciplinary and collaborative arts computing environment has resulted in as many indirect gains. Network integration has lowered the start-up costs of departmentally based computer labs, and thus facilitated their extension into departments which had hitherto lacked either the expertise or the funding to consider them. Thus, the Department of Theatre Film and Television Studies has established a growing Mac laboratory whose workstations will, in future, provide students and staff with better and more flexible access to the department's large video library, as well as to basic print and file services. The History of Art Department is installing a small multimedia network through which students will access digitized images of art objects bound to brief commentaries which describe them. The Philosophy Department has developed a Mac laboratory which provides print and file services and houses a growing collection of machine-readable philosophical texts. Finally, the archaeologists have developed a PC laboratory which offers essential facilities for computed-aided-design (CAD) graphics in addition to the basic suite of word-processing, statistical, network, and database software. Students and teachers in the History and other departments have benefited from the increasing number of networked workstations which are available for laboratory-based teaching and for individuals' independent use. In the longer term, they can expect to gain from the expertise, teaching materials, and data sets that are developed and used in computer-assisted teaching and research in the newly equipped departments. Departmental developments in art history, in theatre, film, and television studies, in archaeology, and in philosophy, for example, promise historians network access to important electronic source materials which they would not have developed for themselves, and to software applications which would have been too costly to purchase independently. Historically, humanities disciplines have benefited directly by borrowing one another's source materials and analytical and conceptual methods. Where costly electronic resources and computer expertise are concerned, the interdisciplinary paradigm promises to work especially well to the humanities' collective advantage.

PROFESSIONAL SUPPORT

Finally, it is worth considering how historians can achieve some of the aims outlined above. First, we need to stop paying lip-service to the importance of IT in history and other humanities disciplines, and do something actively to take the lead in promoting its development. There is already an impressive array of humanities scholarship which actively employs computers in innovative and fruitful ways. Currently, nearly all of it is conducted on shoestring budgets (British Academy and British Library Research and Development Department 1993: 28). The intention here is not to turn this contribution into a diatribe against under-funding in the arts. Rather, it is to indicate that underfunding may, in this case, accurately reflect the second-class status that computer-assisted research and teaching have within the humanities. Why should government or industry consider funding the activities of scholars who are marginalized within their own professions and professional associa-tions? This is neither a bold nor an embittered question. It is merely one based upon observation. Generally speaking, the published products of historical scholarship, monographs, and articles in learned journals, are still the principal criteria upon which promotion and professional recognition are meted out within the humanities. Other contributions which absorb as much in the way of time and intellectual effort—new methodological or computational techniques, data sets which have some general usefulness—are only just beginning to be accorded academic value. In the UK, Europe, and North America, historians who are interested in harnessing the IT revolution have been forced to take refuge in their own Association for History and Computing (AHC) (for information see the AHC website at URL: http://www.let. rug.nl/ahc).

Altering an academic culture so intent on defining a boundary between the pure and the applied, the liberal and the vocational, is the real challenge which faces IT-aware historians and other humanities scholars. There may, however, be some short-term objectives that are worth pursuing. There are too few conduits between the methodologic-ally sophisticated humanities scholar and potential sources of funding. These must be developed. Take two examples. If they know nothing else, humanists know texts. The problems they encounter in creating and interpreting them are as sophisticated and as complex as they come. Accordingly, where humanities scholars have engaged the computer in text creation and analysis, they have done so in a sophisticated way. Are humanities scholars alone interested in applying computer technologies to texts? I think not. Accordingly, there must be any number of initiat-ives in which humanities scholars can fruitfully collaborate with pub-lishers as well as with the media and telecommunications industries. Similarly, one could argue that humanities scholars understand teach-ing. Consequently, they might make a significant contribution to the development of computer-aided instructional materials and delivery systems for machine-readable information which will be found increasingly in the commercial as well as in the academic worlds.

All that is left is a question about how historians might open up these and other conduits to more and better funding. First, form a cartel in the best eighteenth-century mercantile tradition. This will not be a shipping cartel, but an agreement amongst humanities scholars to develop IT applications generally and to put an end to territorial squabbling over who owns what encoding, interpretative, or processing problems. Secondly, bolster their corporate identity through recognition within their universities and established professional associations. Historians need not be apologetic any longer about their expertise. It is very much in demand and that demand is not likely to slacken. Thirdly, having overcome sectional tensions and established a corporate identity, they can perhaps enlist the support of their universities and professional associations to establish more and better access to the funding which, in relation to the sciences, has historically been denied to them.

References

British Academy and British Library Research and Development Department (1993), *Information Technology in Humanities Scholarship: British Achievements, Prospects, and Barriers* (London).

Burnard, L. D. (1993), 'The Text Encoding Initiative: Towards an Extensible Standard for the Encoding of Texts', in Ross and Higgs (1993), 105–18.

Davis, V., Denley, P. R., Spaeth, D., and Trainor, R. (1993) (eds.), *The Teaching of Historical Computing: An International Framework* (St Katharinen).

Denley, P., Hopkin, D., Fogelvik, S. (1989) (eds.), *History and Computing II* (Manchester).

Doyle W. (1994), *The French Revolution: The People Enter Politics* (version 1) (Hypermedia Teaching Materials, Glasgow: TLTP History Courseware Consortium).

Greenstein, D. I. (1994a), *A Historian's Guide to Computing* (Oxford).

—— (1994b), 'Four Courses in Search of a Discipline: European Approaches to Teaching History and Computing', in Oldervoll (1994), 3–18.

—— and Burnard, L. D. (1995), 'Speaking with One Voice: Encoding Standards and the Prospects for an Integrated Approach to Computing in History', *Computers and the Humanities*, 29/2: 137–48.

Joint Funding Councils' Libraries Review Group (1993), *Report* [Chairman: Sir Brian Follett] (HEFCE, Bristol).

Oldervoll, J. (1994) (ed.), *Historical Informatics: An Essential Tool for Historians? A Panel Convened by the Association for History and Computing at the Nine-*

teenth Annual Meeting of the Social Science History Association. Atlanta, Georgia, October 14th, 1994 (Association for History and Computing).

Ross, S., and Higgs, E. (1993) (eds.), *Electronic Information Resources and Historians: European Perspectives* (St Katharinen).

Rosenzweig, R., Brier, S., and Brown, J. (1993) (eds.), *Who Built America? From the Centennnial Celebration of 1876 to the Great War of 1914* (CD-ROM, New York).

Spaeth, D., Davis, V., Denley, P., and Trainor, R. H. (1992) (eds.), *Towards an International Curriculum for Historical Computing: A Workshop of the International Association for History and Computing, University of Glasgow, 15–17 May 1992* (St Katharinen).

Sperberg-McQueen, C. M., and Burnard, L. D. (1990) (eds.), *Guidelines for the Encoding and Interchange of Machine-Readable Texts* (edn. P1, Oxford).

—— —— (1994) (eds.), *Guidelines for the Encoding and Interchange of Machine-Readable Texts* (edn. P3, Oxford).

Thaller, M. (1986), 'A Draft Proposal for the Coding of Machine Readable Sources', *Historical Social Research*, 40: 3–46.

—— (1989), 'The Need for a Theory of Historical Computing', in Denley *et al.* (1989), 2–11.

Wissenburg, A. M., and Spaeth, D. A. (1995), 'In Search of a Metaphor for Hypermedia: The Enriched Lecture', in O. Boonstra, G. Collenteur, and B. van Elderen, *Structures and Contingencies in Computerized Historical Research. Proceedings of the IX International Conference for the Association for History and Computing. August 30–September 2 1994, Nijmegen, the Netherlands* (Hilversum, 1995).

PART TWO

Information Creation and Capture

The Management of Electronic Information Resources in a Corporate Environment

HELEN SIMPSON

ABSTRACT

Large multinational corporations produce and acquire vast volumes of information in the course of their business. Information-management strategies are being developed in many large organizations to manage this asset effectively, enabling the organization to achieve crucial business objectives, in addition to controlling costs. Electronic systems have long been used for data, but, as increasing volumes of information and records are also created and stored electronically, issues are raised about the management of this information. All information is shaped by its creating organization, so how do the culture, organization, and pace of change within the company affect the management of information, particularly its availability for use by third parties in the longer term?

INFORMATION AND CORPORATE ORGANIZATION

Large multinational corporations produce and acquire vast volumes of information in the course of carrying out their business activities. Over long periods methods and tools for handling paper-based records have evolved, but similar practices have not yet been developed for managing the ever-increasing quantities of electronic records that businesses create and use. The Hawley Committee in its report, *Information as an Asset*, argued that 'all significant information in an organization, regardless of its purpose, should be properly identified, even if not in an accounting sense for consideration as a business asset. The board of directors should address its responsibilities for information assets in the same way as for other assets—e.g. property, plant' (1995: 3). This outlook reflects both a growing concern with the problems of managing information and its impact on the performance of companies, and an increased realization that information has value. The report painted a remarkably accurate and timely picture of the business climate. As it tries to encourage board-level concern for the issues of information management, there is an increasing focus within large companies on the development of strategies to manage this asset effectively. It is widely accepted that well-managed information will assist the organization to achieve crucial business objectives, in addition to controlling costs. Electronic systems have long been used for data, but, as increasing volumes of information and records are also created and stored electronically, issues are raised about the management of this information. Since the culture, structure, and evolution of companies shape information and its management, how do these impact on the availability of information for use by external bodies in the long term?

Complex sizeable commercial organizations have certain characteristics and trends in common. These have implications for their approach to information management and more particularly to the management of electronic records. The sheer size of many large corporations creates an enormous diversity and volume of information. This is not new to the electronic environment, however. In its 1992 survey *Information Management: A Survey of Current Practices and Trends*, Touche Ross found that 'One organisation of 2,000 staff dealt with 45 tonnes of incoming mail last year and 48 tonnes of outgoing, equivalent to generating 25 kilos of paper per person every year' (Touche Ross Management Consultants 1992: 12). The two more recent surveys (for 1994 and 1996) indicate that, rather than diminishing, the paper problem is ever increasing. Two other worrying trends were encountered as well. While many respondents noted that their companies had strategies for management of paper records, few knew the policies for handling electronic records and nearly 66 per cent did not believe that their organization had any such strategies.

The range of information needs is equally varied and this reflects the spectrum of activities undertaken by the organization. By examining the process and priorities of a business, it is often possible to begin to understand its information-management needs. Many large organizations have a distinctive culture, a 'way we do things round here', which is informal, but powerful. This culture may include its own language and ways of communicating, and determines the way in which information is perceived and valued. The transnational dimension may contribute to the feeling that the corporate culture is a complete world in itself. The need to meet information needs across national boundaries raises telecommunications and linguistic issues. The wider 'family' may also provide expertise in new methods or technologies.

In the 1990s many large organizations have highlighted the ability to respond to a changing business environment rapidly as a factor critical to their survival. The ability to respond constructively to frequent reorganizations and a moving requirements target has become part of life. One tangible response to the need for improved responsiveness has been a change in approach to how organizational structures facilitate a company's mission. Traditionally, many organizations were structured as hierarchical pyramids, with several layers of junior and middle management. One function of these posts was to sift, summarize, and present information to the layers of management above them. These posts are often intensive users of information services of all types—'knowledge workers'. These workers were the means by which an organization synthesizes externally generated information with its internal information sources. This model can be represented as in Fig. 6.1.

Recent developments in organizational theory, currently in vogue with many large corporations, suggest that hierarchical organizations are slow to respond to change and can limit the optimization of staff potential. They also have high fixed costs. These realizations have led to the move towards networked organizations. Networked organizations operate as a fluid interrelationship of different teams. An individual may be part of several different teams, and teams are constituted and

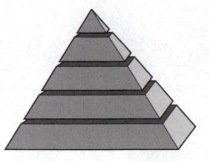

Fig. 6.1 Hierarchical organizations
© Clive Holthman 1992   *Source*: Holthman (1992).

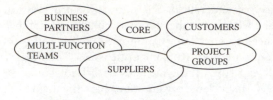

Fig. 6.2 Networked organizations
© Clive Holthman 1992   *Source*: Holthman (1992).

disbanded as the needs of the business require. Teams may be outside or cross the conventional boundaries of the business and encompass business partners, suppliers, or customers. Teams and individuals are encouraged to contribute effectively by empowerment. This pattern can be represented as in Fig. 6.2. This has a dramatic effect on the information-management strategy of the organization. The lack of continuity in team structure changes conventional patterns of information provision and can create problems in the custodial care of the resulting information early in the life cycle. The effective management of the information at the time of creation is vital to ensure both that the successive teams do not 'reinvent the wheel' and that the corporate memory does not suffer.

In reality, some business processes do not operate best as networked nodes, so many organizations actually operate to a hybrid model somewhere between Figs. 6.1 and 6.2. This in itself raises issues of how the information infrastructure can best serve two models at once. This mixed model can be represented as shown in Fig. 6.3. This snapshot

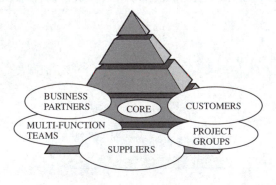

Fig. 6.3 Mixed organizations
© Clive Holthman 1992   *Source*: Holthman (1992).

of the corporate environment makes it possible to analyse the way in which such organizations approach the management of information resources.

Information management is increasingly emerging as a means to enable organizations to manage their information, of all types and in all media, as a corporate asset. This strategic approach aims to optimize information and technology as valuable resources to achieve the key business objectives of the corporation. If the long-term use of information resources by individuals beyond the corporation is included as a benefit at all, it is unlikely to be a major priority for funding and may even be viewed with caution. The justification will concentrate on business deliverables. Increasing numbers of large organizations are investing in information-management strategies. There is confusion as to what information management is. In its 1994 survey, Touche Ross reported: 'In our first survey on the topic in 1992, we were not surprised to find that the term was not well known . . . However, we were surprised to find that two years on the level of understanding is disappointingly low' (Touche Ross Consultants 1994: 5). Although the 1996 survey shows some broader understanding of the issues, it still indicates how alarmingly limited prespectives are on information management. Given the scale of such organizations, where an information-management strategy does exist, the development of strategy and the completion of particular projects may be handled by different parts of the organization, possibly with a coordinating or quality assurance role linking them.

The consequence of ongoing organizational change is to create constant upheaval in the structures which create information and the teams and procedures which underpin record-handling in all forms. The life cycle of many records will be a patchwork of different units creating, amending, utilizing, and determining disposition, possibly without knowledge of what has gone before. Records in all media are subject to the disruption or destruction of provenance that can result. But electronic records are particularly vulnerable, as a change in organization may result in automatic change of office systems which may or may not be compatible in differing ways with the system which created the record. Sudden changes in funding may also result in the withdrawal of systems, the sudden deletion of information by creation date alone to create space, or uncontrolled over-retention as the result of expenditure on new memory capacity.

It is important to understand something of the recent history of information technology (IT) departments. Where large organizations have historically had separate technology and information specialists, the organizational evolution and current relationship between these functions may determine the organization's ability to have a cohesive view on information-management strategy. In the 1990s many technology functions have moved from large electronic data-processing departments with substantial directly controlled funding to much smaller information systems/services teams who may be distributed across the business, deriving funding from client business functions. As the traditional technology powerbase became dispersed, some departments began to be more conscious of the 'I' in 'IT'. For example, 'Today, information technology must be conceived of broadly to encompass the information that businesses create and use as well as the wide spectrum of increasingly convergent and linked technologies that process the information' (Porter and Millar 1985: 149). Current concerns for many IT functions include the serious consideration being given to outsourcing many of their activities to third-party organizations.

Information-services functions (including records managers, librarians, information scientists, archivists, and others) have, in many organizations, been reorganized in and out of numerous different departments. There is no apparent consensus about their optimum position within the organization. A significant number of information teams are now elements within the IT departments, seen as a distinct but valued part. Alternatively, they may be subsumed within the department and treated as a poor relation. Sometimes the assumption is that information equates to 'filing', and 'filing' is low skill, low priority, and about to be replaced by technology. This may contribute to the organization missing major opportunities to manage the records element of the information resource strategically. In more enlightened organizations, interdisciplinary teams have enabled records managers to acquire sufficient knowledge of the technology to make significant contributions both to how particular technologies are used, and to the development of the wider information-management strategy.

The relationship of the end-user or client within the business to both technology and information professionals has evolved. External information provision has seen the advent of end-user searching of external hosts and the increased use of intranets within organizations. There is a greater openness to information-sharing. This trend has been under-girded by the pattern of technical evolution. The central functions required to service the large mainframes are no longer perceived to be necessary on the scale they once were with the development of distrib-uted end-user computing and communications, and a generation of users who are not only 'literate' but competent technically. Client areas may be keen to be at the leading edge in the use of emerging techno-logies, often for all the best reasons, but sometimes to keep up with the latest toy. From an environment that handled data alone, the electronic systems will now be used to handle not only data, but also information and records-based applications.

Clients have considerable expectations about the means of delivery and timeliness of information. The increasingly user-friendly nature of electronic systems means that end-users are brought into more direct contact with information. Information is increasingly distributed in electronic form either via an office system or, more basically, sent out on a disk. There has been a breaking-down of divisions both between internally and externally generated information and among the distinct professional disciplines which act as handmaidens to information.

This evolutionary pattern has affected how the ownership of infor-mation and technology is perceived. Information ownership is often a distinctive trait of the corporate culture and varies from 'it's mine and I'll decide if you can use it' to 'it's the corporation's and we can use it', even to 'it's not my problem, I never need information'. Business users may increasingly interpret custody of information as a localized responsibility, especially if charging mechanisms mean they pay directly for assistance from the wider organization. Flatter organizations and an emphasis on empowerment may encourage this trend.

This range of factors creates changes which result in the constant need to rethink and repackage information-management principles in the light of current business plan priorities and technical developments and to express them in a way which makes cultural sense within the organization. The cultural variable of costing and benefit management may require careful handling, although experience suggests that approaches to this are usually cyclic. The ways in which internal charges are weighted can encourage users to feel that storing everything is cheaper and altogether easier than managing it more actively. A change in the way the culture assigns worth to information may be required to resolve the benefit equation. The findings of the Hawley report are encouraging because they are an agenda for board-level activities to develop better information-management strategies.

One of the main elements of successful information management is to overcome the impression that 'information is free'. Encouraging staff to appreciate the cost of information goes some way towards helping them to quantify the value of information.   (Touche Ross Management Consultants 1992: 43)

Given the enormity of the subject of electronic record-keeping, it seems appropriate to use one type of system to exemplify the key issues. Office systems (also previously known as office automation or office information systems) provide a good vehicle to explore the major questions.

Office systems provide electronic tools to support a range of administrative functions which most desk-based staff will undertake in addition to their substantive business functions. Such systems are therefore used across the organization and often act as a form of corporate cultural glue, enabling and contributing to the issues discussed earlier. Informal and formal, professional and personal usage is likely to be intermingled. The functions they provide may include a selection of the following: electronic mail (e-mail), fax, telex, word processing, records storage and retrieval (both individual and shared), diary scheduling (people and facilities), internal reference information, spreadsheets, access to other applications, and the importing and repackaging of data from other applications.

Organizations are often quite casual in their approach to the information created and stored on office systems and this is explained in part by their origins. In the early 1980s e-mail facilities were often available only to users competent to cope with the basic and rather cryptic tools inherent in operating systems on mainframes or large minicomputers. Word processors were bulky specialist machines for dedicated producers of text, and operated independently with little or no ability to communicate. Records were managed in paper form and word processors were tools to create but not subsequently manage records. With the advent of increasingly powerful personal computers (PCs) and organization-wide communication networks, these originally distinct functions began to be related. Users' skills and expectations rose. The advantages of beating time-zone differences and 'telephone lag', easy sharing of information, and the avoidance of rekeying (to name but a few) ensured the office system remained with us.

The life cycle of a record on an office system can vary greatly depending on the hardware, software, implementation, and state of mind of the user. It may be helpful quickly to sketch a 'best' and 'worst' scenario, acknowledging that the truth may often lie in between. At best, our record will be created using a prestructured format which helps the user to ensure that the information needed to optimize the use of the information through its life cycle is captured as part of the creation process. For example, the classification given will relate this document to its virtual folder and series, its retention grouping, allow reference to the provisional duration of different phases of the life cycle, who has what access with what rights, authorship, organizational ownership, information architecture key, and potential archival status (to name but a selection!). These will be prompted and predetermined where possible to minimize the effort involved. It will be created using the word-processing tools, but may include extracts from other documents, other databases, graphics, or live links to spreadsheet data. During a period of active mailing and amendment (with the system providing version control and appropriate access and editing controls) the record will be referenced by authorized users utilizing both function-based and less-structured retrieval tools in the communal electronic record system. This may be provided within the office system itself, or by automatically dropping into an appropriate application tool. This stage may represent a blurring of the 'creation' and 'current' phases of a hard-copy life cycle. The record will have a defined relationship to the multiple printouts that will undoubtedly be produced, with the primacy managed for retention purposes. Ephemeral documents will be deleted in an organized process quite early. For documents with a more substantial information or evidential content, as the usage rates fall our record may be moved off-line, but the retrieval and control information about it will remain accessible on-line in summary form. Some records may be transferred to other appropriate media at this phase. The destruction or disposition of the record will follow the retention decisions made at its creation unless a change of purpose either changes or temporarily suspends its enactment. The reasons for these decisions are appropriately available and the completion of these stages are all documented. For potentially archival material, long-term plans on the maintenance of supporting documentation, storage media, and system documentation will be made and reviewed.

A 'worst' scenario could include the creation of our document, in individualistic form by a user who chooses to exercise his ability to keep the document 'personal', only accessible to those to whom it is directly mailed. There are no defined relationships to other records, as everything is handled at document level. Retention is at the whim of the user (often under threat from the system manager), who may delete his copy when the pressure on space forces a clear-out. (It is difficult for him—the incoming mail has become inaccessible until he frees up some of his allocated disk capacity). Recipients control retention of their copies in a similar way. Even when the last recipient deletes his access, it is possible that the text remains undeleted, but relatively useless. The lack of any classification and very basic retrieval tools make finding the document rather tricky, but you may find a more organized recipient to re-mail a copy which you could cannibalize to form the basis of your next report on a similar topic. When the systems manager is stressed by complaints about the slowing access times on the system, he may send out warning messages and then complete a tape dump of all documents last accessed before a certain date. After that your document still exists but it will get much harder and more time-consuming to track it down. Longer-term uses (either within or beyond the corporation) are not taken into account, after all, it's your document, isn't it?

Approaches that were fine for controlling informal e-mail with a status comparable to a telephone chat are often failing to manage substantial volumes of prime electronic records resources adequately (Samuel, Chapter 7, this volume). The professional input that can make an application 'best' rather than 'worst' is complex, time-consuming, and therefore expensive. Only where organizations appreciate the consequences for information resources which they perceive to be valuable is that investment likely to be made.

Given the reality of the current difficulties with the use of office systems as tools to manage large volumes of records (a task for which, on the whole, they were not originally designed), how can records managers contribute to improving the situation primarily for the creating organizations, and indirectly also for other potential users of the records? Involvement needs to begin early in the life cycle of the record, preferably before its creation. The whole life span of a record, including its creation, needs to be planned carefully. In the case of electronic records, this is often only possible before the creation of the record itself. It is difficult or often impossible to 'retrofit' records-management controls to a system. This is why it is crucial to have involvement early in the life cycle of the system. Increasingly, records managers are contributing to the system specification. There are significant differences between vendors' offerings, and future product development plans. When the product selection has been made, some options for managing records may have been made impossible by the operating environment or application software. Subsequent additions and amendments to software may be technically possible, but inadvisable because of subsequent upgrade issues.

Particularly with office systems and groupware applications, the information issues may be at least as complex as the technology. The lead times for evaluating, selecting, testing, implementing, and 'QAing' (quality assuring) the information elements of the project cannot be completed in small amounts of time around other responsibilities. It is important to commit appropriately trained and resourced professionals to the task and to structure the project in such a way that information specialists are enabled to contribute as equals with technical colleagues, as an integrated part of the team. Some issues are likely to be relevant to certain vendors' products or certain organizational situations, but experience suggests that certain issues occur across a range of technical and organizational contexts. Two issues are worth noting. First, many systems operate at 'document' level, rather than allowing folder- or series-level management of records. In addition to the extra effort involved in maintenance, this has serious implications for the preservation of the contextual or evidential value of the record. Secondly, early records managers managed the message by managing the medium. It is important to distinguish clearly between the features of the paper-based life cycle which were a product of the limitations of the media and can now be joyfully abandoned, and methods which have an ongoing role when reinterpreted into the electronic life cycle. It is clear that: '... the lack of a record *per se* is not the source of the problem with decentralised electronic technologies in general or e-mail in particular; rather, it is the lack of shared electronic classification, filing, storage and controlled access and retrieval capabilities' (Barry 1990: 7). As the media and the information that it carries are increasingly separate, so records managers need to master managing virtual records, learning to optimize the immense flexibility this can provide, whilst minimizing the potential chaos.

For example, while concepts relating to the forms, design, and control of paper documents may be used to assist in the design and control of input and display screens in a computer system, management of underlying information may require a radically different approach. In a paper system there is a one to one relationship between a paper form and the information on it. In an electronic database, information appears to be a single document, form or table, when in fact it may be spread over different files, databases or in a truly distributed application, over several organisations and dispersed locations...Therefore, some of the tools developed in paper-based records management need substantial rethinking and extensions if they are to be effective in the context of electronic records management.   (Ibid. 73).

Many office systems assume that traditional data-operations procedures will apply to the control of retention. This may have been fine for early disposable e-mail, but, as office systems of all kinds have developed into tools to create, store, retrieve, and delete the only copy of more substantial record types, it is necessary to institute more organized retention methods. This is often seen as overkill by old guard data-processing staff. Where products do make provision for active retention management (many do not), it is likely to be at document level alone. It is vital that ways are found for archivists to have some input into provisional appraisal of records which may not yet have been created. If the mature wisdom of hindsight takes too long coming, the record will no longer exist to preserve. In the area of vital records, standard operations back-up provisions may be perfectly adequate in the short term for the content of electronic records themselves. Particular attention may be needed in ensuring a good correlation with related records stored on other media.

Information-sharing, access, and security are in many ways the same issue viewed from different angles, with the emphasis varying according to how open an organization is. Many systems make background assumptions about enabling or preventing access. It is necessary to ensure that the access arrangements complement the strategy one is trying to achieve. Many detailed provisions to protect the integrity of the record lie in this area. The use of diplomatic form (including structure and layout) can be predefined to help users with the creation process (e.g. telex format) and act as a retrieval key (Duranti 1995). This could also contribute to retention validation. The evidential value of the record lies in part in its context both to other records and within the organization. For records with a longer-term value this information will need to travel with the record through its life cycle. Information about the creating system and subsequent storage will need to be added for electronic records to provide a complete record of their provenance.

The corporate information management strategy may provide a common means of defining information and structuring its interrelations. It is important that this works well for records to ensure retrieval across media and different sources and is not derived from data-management methodologies alone. It can potentially be used as a tool to ensure the effective utilization of information resources across information types and organizational peculiarities.

Depending on the literacy of the users and the nature of retrieval requirements, it may be necessary to provide consistency for users to retrieve information. This may be a technical interface which remains the same across several systems, or a common approach in indexing and use of terms. A major challenge in the management of electronic records is to bridge the technical divides in how the information is stored and to 'reintegrate' information to present users with the ability to search for information according to their own agenda, not the organization's technical architecture. Finding information also poses problems to organizations, and 75 per cent of those surveyed in Touche Ross's 1994 survey admitted that they eventually 'give up the search and reinvent the information on occasions' (Touche Ross Management Consultants 1994: 8). This is particularly an issue with emerging technologies which are not yet able to provide seamless integration into the corporation's wider electronic world and in the definition and subsequent management of the same record stored on several different media. The most obvious example is the relationship between the electronic record(s) and its hard-copy counterparts, but other, less conspicuous parallels will exist. The control of drafts and different versions of a document can be managed electronically. Relationships between the same document in different media may require some thought. The advent of live links raises interesting questions about which is the master copy.

A 1992 survey revealed that 39 per cent of large companies either fear or have already experienced litigation owing to lost or missing records. The issues relating to legal admissibility require careful thought about how a major case could be coordinated. This may be a particular area where the records manager's experience of other media and enabling litigation may be particularly valuable. Metadata required to enable a credible response to a discovery may well provide some of the information required for other secondary long-term users of the records. Electronic record-keeping presents many new challenges, but these often require a reinterpretation of principles and methods rather than an abandonment of professional expertise gained to date. Whilst these issues are particularly considered in the context of office systems, opportunities exist to improve the quality of electronic record-keeping in the following types of developments: groupware, optical imaging systems, executive information systems (EIS), text retrieval systems, electronic data interchange (EDI), compound document management, and work-flow management, amongst others.

There also seems to be a consensus among professionals from widely diverse backgrounds that the corporate memories of organizations are threatened by a lack of tools, techniques, and procedures to enable the effective management of electronic records.

It seems that the two sides of the information management equation are set to come together: the technology exists, and people want to use it. What tends to be missing is a more structured approach to information management, along with more convenient tools to facilitate it.   (Thom 1993: 77)

Now is the time to meet this challenge. What holds organizations back from that commitment? It may be a lack of understanding of the potential benefits of information management, or a lack of the skills to develop these tools, techniques, and procedures, or, more worryingly, a lack of concern for the consequences.

References

Barry, R. E. (1990) (ed.), *Management of Electronic Records: Issues and Guidelines* (New York: UN Advisory Committee for the Coordination of Information Systems (ACCIS)).

Duranti, L. (1995), 'Reliability and Authenticity: The Concepts and their Implications', *Archivaria*, 39: 5–10.

Hawley Committee (1995), *Information as an Asset, The Board Agenda* (London).

Holtham, C. (1992), *Improving the Performance of Workgroups through Information Technology* (Cambridge: Lotus Development (UK) Ltd).

McDonald, J. (1991), 'Information Management and Office Systems Advancement' (unpublished, June).

Porter, M. E., and Millar, V. E. (1985), 'How Information Gives you Competitive Advantage', *Harvard Business Review* (July–Aug.), 149–50.

Thom, B., (1993) 'How to Have Power at your Fingertips', *Management Consultancy* (Mar.), 77–8.

Touche Ross Management Consultants (1992), *Information Management: A Survey of Current Practices and Trends* (London).

—— (1994), *Information Management: A Survey of Current Practices and Trends* (London).

—— (1996), *Information Management: A Survey of Current Practices and Trends* (London).

Electronic Mail: Information Exchange or Information Loss?

JEAN SAMUEL

ABSTRACT

Electronic mail (e-mail) is used for communication between members of a small work group, within organizations, and internationally across shared interest groups via the Internet. E-mail communication is both supplementing and replacing more established methods such as paper and telephone. As well as being a powerful business tool, e-mail systems carry information of value to future researchers. What will these researchers find? Anodyne, filtered, official records? A partial jigsaw of messages only hinting at passionate debate? An overflowing jumble sale of information with the bargains hidden in the clutter? This chapter will describe what we can currently expect to find and will suggest approaches to improve matters. E-mail is here to stay.

INTRODUCTION

pervading daily life...

the telephone is dead...

It has increased the total amount of communications significantly...

an accessory to face to face discussion...

an addiction...

All this communication is going to be lost to the history of science forever. There are no letters anymore.

These quotes from Eric Almquist of Decision Research (Lexington, USA), taken from a paper given at the Faxon Institute Annual

Conference in 1992, are based on the exploratory findings of some thirty interviews he had conducted with radio astronomers and biologists. In response to the last quotation, I will argue that, although valuable information in e-mail systems is currently being lost to history, it need not and it should not be lost, and the time has come to prevent it.

Communication by electronic means is growing at a rapid rate throughout industry and government organizations. The growth is in terms of speed, medium, integration, numbers, and area. (For some useful historic data on rate and speed of use, see Bikson 1994.) It has now reached the point where those professions involved in the management of data must take serious action to prevent information exchange becoming information loss. Four obvious groups interested in management of these electronic messages are the legal profession, historians, records managers/archivists, and computing professionals. The first three groups have some experience of working with each other, aware of the various imperatives in the fight to manage records well. It is in informed cooperation with the last group, computing professionals, that the key to successful management of electronic records lies.

This chapter aims to identify changes that e-mail is having on the world of records. With that in mind there will be a brief explanation of the various types of e-mail and their different functions. The chapter will then look at the issues raised for the user, lawyer, historian, and records manager/archivist. This will include the wider issues which all organizations or companies will need to face regarding the status and role of e-mail records. The chapter will then focus, for each type of e-mail use, on e-mail records in the scientific arena to illustrate what impact there could be to historical research because of their electronic nature.

TYPES OF E-MAIL

E-mail is an electronic communications facility. It can be subdivided into three forms: e-mail as an internal business communications network, external bulletin boards/list servers, and voice mail (v-mail).

E-Mail as an Internal Business Communications Network

In this context, e-mail is used to send electronic mail messages to colleagues within a company/institution. It is seen as an effective means of business communication where relevant staff have access to a computer network. It is of particular value where international companies are working in different time zones and the telephone is not always a convenient method of communication. Like facsimile messages (fax), it has the advantage of being less expensive than the telephone, as an entire message can be composed before transmission, with only the time of transmission attracting an external cost. Its strength lies in the ability to transmit factual information without causing an interruption whereas a telephone call may disrupt a meeting or a colleague's thought processes, and it may not be possible to see if an office door is open or closed. E-mail is also a great time-saver when the same message has to be relayed to a group of people. A study of e-mail use at the World Bank indicated that 'only about half of all messages are sent to just one person' (Bikson and Law 1993). In some companies reading e-mail has become the first task of the morning. When employees come into the workplace, they no longer open the paper mail first but will turn on the computer and read what messages have been left overnight.

External Bulletin Boards and List Servers

Individuals with a common interest—for example, engineers—post open messages to other authorized members. This will be either directly, for list servers, or to a central holding area in the case of bulletin boards. The aim is to disseminate messages as widely as possible within a given community. Bulletin boards, for example, can be used to advertise conferences or seminars to people in the same profession or may contain data packages, open for use by anyone. A list server is more like internal e-mail. Open questions will often be addressed to all subscribers. Has anybody out there come across this problem? List servers may be used to raise issues for a particular discipline or to air thoughts and to stimulate discussion between a whole range of people who will never meet. For information on using list servers and for details of those of direct value to records management personnel, see McMurdo (1995) and Ryan and Murdock (1995).

V-Mail

In the mid-1990s the concept of the 'ansaphone' has been extended to incorporate the idea of v-mail. Such a system allows you to leave and receive messages on a telephone which is part of a computerized network (and which can therefore digitally store and then replay sounds). The same message may be sent to many people in the same system. It has the same time-saving benefit as typed e-mail in that one message can reach any number of receivers simultaneously. Received messages can be deleted or stored and even structured to link messages from the same person or about the same subject. Originally this v-mail was aimed at short-term retention and as one of the desktop conveniences of the electronic office. Recently, however, companies are demanding, and so suppliers are developing, systems for more effective retention of voice messages to make them truly voice records.

E-MAIL ISSUES

It is clear so far that e-mail both gives and demands more from users and records managers than paper records do. It complicates established approaches to the management of records and requires some completely new ones. The three different forms of e-mail described above raise different records-management issues.

Issues Raised by E-Mail as an Internal Business Communication Network

These issues apply to records managers, users, and lawyers, and, because implementing any solution will lie in their hands, to computing managers. An investigation undertaken by the UN found that 'in the majority of reporting agencies, computing staff... have chief responsibility for management policies relating to e-mail communications... Just three agencies reported that records management staff have a major role in setting policies' (Barry 1990: 15).

The report suggested that, because of this trend, the resulting policies reflected technology concerns and not information-management ones. Computing staff are likely soon to be asked to broaden their technology policies to support the life cycle of organizational records.

First let us look at the way e-mail would be used in almost any organization. Most systems incorporate some useful facilities:

- all incoming and outgoing messages can be automatically filed (e.g. key words or phrases will be recognized and the messages sent to appropriate electronic directories);

- individual mail messages can be marked for urgent action or later action;
- messages can be consciously filed into a structure, by subject or source;
- messages can be moved in and out of word-processing packages so that a message received in e-mail can be incorporated into a document which you wish to send or work on. Conversely, the links used to send e-mail into word-processing accounts can also be used to mail word-processing documents; and
- replies can be edited so that the original message can be returned to the sender or to some third person with a reply noted against the original content.

To my mind, the records-management issues raised by this type of internal e-mail fall into two categories—those raised by the e-mail system with its technical environment and constraints, and those raised by the attitudes of the users. By users I mean here both the people sending and receiving at the screen, and senior management who invest in e-mail systems and set expectations of their use.

Looking at systems-based issues first, a problem for ownership identification can occur when messages are forwarded or circulated to others. If the original heading (showing source, date, etc.) is removed from the message or if the body of the text is edited (both of which are easily done on most systems), then the original temper or content of the message can be radically or subtly altered. So what may appear as the forwarded message of *X* is, in fact, the forwarded message of *X* with additions and changes by *Y*. Likewise, a message from *X* may be forwarded, without the original heading, by *Y* to *Z*. To *Z* the message will appear as *Y*'s own thoughts and message.

E-mail is automatically date-stamped on receipt, so the order of responses or interaction between accounts on the network is indisputable. Ownership of the message (in terms of the receiving account) can also be established automatically. These factors are crucial in the commercial world of electronic data interchange (EDI), where orders are placed internationally by subscribing companies via an electronic network.

Perhaps because of the speed of receipt of e-mail messages, users are increasingly giving priority to their e-mail in-tray. This element of immediacy, almost urgency, is influencing the outcome of business decisions and the records supporting them. One study has shown that

10 per cent of replies are received within fifteen minutes of message transmission (Bikson 1994). What effect on quality of response does this speed imply? A record-content issue. Furthermore, the same study has also shown that delaying a response to a widely disseminated message often means it is not included in the decision-making process, as most replies are already in and have provided sufficient input for progress. A further factor is that senders can easily produce 'catch-all' distribution lists, lists that imply to future researchers that everyone on that list has had a chance to provide input for a decision. From the archivist's point of view, that distribution list, allied to 'late' responses, can blur the history of policy decisions.

The second category of issues for this type of e-mail concerns the attitudes of users. As they become comfortable with their e-mail system and able to use most of its facilities, the fact that e-mail is in use is affecting who does what work and, consequently, who creates what sorts of records. Some early studies have found that networks have a high proportion of 'personal' messages—e.g. organizing social functions with colleagues (Rice and Love 1987). This practice may be on the decline (Bikson and Law 1993). The records-management issue is one of volume. Paper notes and telephone calls would not previously have been retained, but such e-mail messages commonly are, and can severely clutter an electronic storage system.

Another form of misuse results in unlikely and clumsy records. This is where people overuse e-mail and/or use it for concepts too compli-cated for this medium—e.g. where a proper report or formal memo or even a meeting would be more appropriate than an e-mail message.

In the world of paper memos, secretaries have access, both for filing and for informational purposes, to their managers' mail. Use of e-mail in the World Bank has shown one interesting result in this context: that the secretaries are bypassed, all e-mail going straight direct to/from their bosses, thus denying them information vital to their job (Bikson and Law 1993). In records-management terms, this has a negative impact on filing, as few managers are as disciplined as secretaries in filing documents consistently. If the secretary is filing the hard-copy elements of a subject and the manager the e-mail element, the results could be most unhelpful. Such direct senior-level involvement in record-keeping practices also makes education in company filing sys-tems harder, as managers are less likely to attend such training.

Looking wider than the secretarial role, support staff in general are affected by the introduction of e-mail: 'organisations are pushing decision-making and responsibility to lower levels of the hierarchy...to take advantage of the speed, flexibility, customizability, and connectivity afforded by the new media' (Bikson 1994: 59). It seems that this is particularly so where e-mail is used to connect work teams. Meeting dynamics are absent, status becomes less relevant, and there is a general egalitarian effect. This and the secretarial factor could impact badly on the traditional government archives approach, where the formal filing system for Important Person *A* is earmarked for collection and preservation but that of Nobody *B* is not. In some cases, the use of e-mail may mean that the records series for *A* will be incomplete, with key records held on the individual's personal e-mail account or in *B*'s file.

The above issues have reflected a variety of attitudes affecting e-mail, but one perception that seems shared by all is the informal nature of e-mail. The status of e-mail messages (excluding mailed work-processing documents) in most organizations is somewhere higher than a telephone call or a handwritten note but lower than a formal memo or report. This, despite e-mail's directive and senior-level use. This one factor has raised the most difficult of records-management challenges, that of raising people's consciousness regarding the status of the e-mail message as a bona-fide record. Bikson and Law (1993) have some useful quotations, reflecting this ambivalence, from the study into the World Bank's use of e-mail.

not an official action medium...more quasi-official...

it's accepted as an action-causing document. It's slightly less official.

The delegation of authority always used to be done by memo. Now it sometimes just goes on electronic message.

For formal impact you need a signed memorandum.

Advocates of official e-mail status add safeguards such as automatic proof-of-receipt requests to their messages.

This ambivalent status gives e-mail users a major advantage. For example, where a meeting started out being fairly informal but raised some key issues, and a member of the meeting feels that a record of decisions taken should be made, he or she may feel uncomfortable or that it is inappropriate to write a memo or produce formal minutes of those decisions. An e-mail message back to the participants, however, can record those decisions 'in writing' without making a big issue of it. This can be extremely useful. In archival terms these may then constitute some interim 'minutes', filling in some gaps to a major series. But, written in an informal format, not as part of a formal series, the credentials of such mail messages rely heavily on their context and supporting data.

A recent, long-running discussion on a records-management list server centred on a hypothetical situation of an offer to extend a contract of employment communicated by e-mail. If the promise was not met, could the employee use the mail message as he or she would a postal mail letter to sue for breach of contract or to support other legal action? Records managers responding fell into two groups. The first suggested that the e-mail message had no legal status, since there was no signature and, because of the lack of control over people allowing their staff access to personal accounts via their own password, there was no proof that the sender was in fact the account holder from whom the message was logged. Indeed, if the situation was reversed and the message concerned notice of termination, could arrival into the receiver's account prove that the individual for whom it was meant had actually read it? The argument from the other camp, that the message could have record status, ran thus: lack of control over who uses personal accounts to send or read messages should be governed by strict and well-enforced organizational procedures. Very few institutions have such procedures in place regarding e-mail but that is no excuse. The standards that are developed to support the authenticity of a piece of information as an 'official record' require organizational commitment and formal recognition. Just as organizations develop a set of rules for documents that are delivered through the postal service, they will develop rules for documents delivered electronically. Thus, if an organization chooses not to recognize its e-mail messages as having formal record status and its procedures accurately reflect this, then they would not be records and vice versa.

The PROFS Case

This is where the debate stood until a court case in the USA formally addressed the issue in 1989. The case has direct relevance for the role of records managers and archivists, because it focused on the role and responsibility of the US Archivist in implementing organizational policy regarding electronic messaging, including defining them as records. The case, *Armstrong* v. *Executive office of the President*, is known informally as the PROFS case, from the IBM system serving the Executive Office of the President of the USA and the National Security Archive (Bearman 1993). Scott Armstrong, Executive Director of the National

Security Archive, filed a claim that the defendants were ignoring their duty to manage records created by electronic means. The core question of the case, as far as this chapter is concerned, was whether the defendants had failed to comply with statutory requirements and whether the guidelines were reasonable or sufficiently clear to provide adequate guidance to personnel employed by the defendants in their maintenance and preservation of federal records. The other issue was whether the United States Archivist had fulfilled his statutory duties.

The defendants argued that the information concerned, on their computerized systems, did not constitute records until they were printed out. The system in question sent e-mail messages, and documents, inter- and intra-agency and externally. They contained transmit and receipt logs indicating to whom messages and documents were sent and indication of date and time. The defendants had to prove these communications were not records because if they were deemed records then the records-management responsibility clearly stated that each agency should maintain an active, continuing programme for the economical and efficient management of the records of the agency, with safeguards against the removal or loss of records the agency head determined to be necessary and required by the Archivist. The Archivist, in turn, would be governed by a 1943 statute that records of historical value involving the public should be preserved, particularly where such material reflected the function, policies, procedures, operations or other activities of the department or because of their information value.

The defendants put forward a two-part argument:

- that none of the material on the agencies' computer systems (as described above) were records; and
- any record material on the systems had been saved by staff printing them out into paper copy, thus rendering the computer-held versions only reference copies in a convenient medium.

The plaintiffs argued:

- that some of the material on the computerized systems in question met the statutory definition of records and thus could not be destroyed without the approval of the Archivist. The definition in the relevant statute which supported their case uses the words 'regardless of physical form or characteristic';

- that the agencies' staff were not necessarily being advised to save all computer records on paper and that the process was unmanaged and selective; and
- that it cannot be assumed that a paper print-out of an electronic record from these systems is the same as the electronic version, on the grounds that the paper version does not bring with it the context that gives the information provenance and credibility.

Both parties agreed that not all the information on the systems constituted records.

The Court ruled that, even if the agencies' staff were instructed to print out what they deemed to be records, the electronic was quantitatively different from a copy printed out in paper form and, therefore the defendants' record-keeping system violated the statute because it did not save all the information contained in these electronic records. The Court had in mind the fact that information regarding when and by whom the information was received would be lost. Distribution lists were also maintained separately from the messages sent and so would not be printed out with the message unless specified.

The defendants' counter-argument, that this infrastructure information did not constitute a record either, was not allowed by the Court. It maintained that the two elements taken together constituted the record and the material must be retained in a way that includes all the pertinent information. The Court felt that such information could be of tremendous historical value in demonstrating what agency personnel were involved in making a particular policy decision and what officials knew and when they knew it. The Court also stressed that, without professional guidance, agency staff were inclined to dispose of records recording their mistakes or not to think of information retention at all. Thus the need for the Archivist to establish selection standards. The Court quoted the National Archives Records Management Handbook: 'only records officers should determine the record or non-record status of files. ... Such authority (given to others) weakens the disposition program by indiscriminate use of the non-record label and can result in the loss of valuable records' (URL: http//clio.nara.gov/00/managers/federal/publicat/dfr.text). The records-management staff had a duty to safeguard electronic records from inappropriate destruction.

The overall message for records managers from this case is that internal and external e-mail messages in context constitute records. The context can be in terms of receipt and transmit logs and distribution lists which may be held separately from the actual message. The PROFS case had a federal government context which defined various levels of record status. Other cases have also impacted on the record status of e-mail in the business world. Case history in the USA has established e-mail as an acceptable record for legal audit, and the lawyers are having a field-day (Himelstein 1995).

User perception of e-mail status is in direct contradiction to the legal perception and the matter of unguarded remarks in e-mail (made because the writer deems the message unofficial), and the non-management of e-mail messages, together constitute a growing problem for organizations and subsequently their legal and records-management personnel. If the response of organizations is to gag their staff and/or press for early deletion in preference to a properly thought-out creation and retention policy, then the researcher of the future will have very few e-mail records to look at.

E-Mail in Collaboration

This chapter will now focus on the use of internal e-mail in the scientific community—an academic environment where e-mail could well constitute an important source of scholarly correspondence. Of course scientists confer with their colleagues. Previously, this would have included chats at coffee breaks and in corridors, or writing rough notes for someone's consideration. This meant that a lot of the interchange would be verbal with no record, or a mentally inaccurate record. It meant a lot more handwriting with the usual challenge to the reader, but with the advantage that different handwriting clearly shows what was original thought and what was later input by colleagues. With the advent of internal e-mail, expectations are higher, and the sort of exchange subtly different.

Because of the element of 'non-disturbance', some scientists feel easier using e-mail instead of waiting for the corridor/coffee-break meeting. It means that the communication might be less opportunistic and more frequent, with the participants targeted rather than random. The work group will now regularly include colleagues on another site, a structure not always possible and definitely less frequent (and more expensive!) in the pre-e-mail days. Another factor is that, because e-mail means keyboards, the 'rough notes' take on more structure and formality. But are the standards of presentation becoming unnecessarily high? E-mail has established its own etiquette and norms (McMurdo 1995). Will this discourage use rather than encourage it? Some scientists feel the ease of access brings forward the point of communication, others that the typing element slows it. Age, and familiarity with technology, are factors here. I am sure the former view will prevail as people become more comfortable with the technology.

With the ease of editing, forwarding, and so on, it is potentially more difficult to identify, retrospectively, what are original thoughts and what are later additions by colleagues. Scientists could become exactly the copious 'self-copiers' (i.e. automatically copying themselves into their own message distribution) that their records managers are trying to discourage, merely to demonstrate the stage of their input. Sharing ideas via e-mail with work groups across a global scientific institution is generally held to have speeded up project progression. This is not just because of the technical aids (speed of message transmission, ease of draft circulation, etc.) but because the lack of location and time-zone constraints has allowed teams to be 'dynamically composed in response to situation-specific needs in a timely and effective way...teams supported by electronic media permit the just-in-time delivery of knowledge resources' (Bikson 1994: 56).

My guess is that, if business e-mail is managed and retained, it will provide a fuller account of the development of successful ideas. But a fuller account for whom? Whether handwritten, or e-mail typed, these records are informal, frequently out of context or mixed in with other subjects, and meant purely for internal consumption. Their retention could therefore be a liability in terms of legal discovery and regulatory authority investigations unless some strong discipline were imposed. This would run counter to the very informal information exchange that is the strength of e-mail in this internal context. In its present form it would be of some value to the company historian, but, in public institutions, its status as a record, and therefore its management, need to be decided before we can determine its retention. I have no doubt it would contain some valuable missing links and insights for the historian.

Issues Raised by Bulletin Boards and List Servers

At all levels, bulletin boards and list servers are making an impact. In the context of the Internet, however, this impact is dramatic and it is worth looking at it in some detail. The Internet is a large network of networks, in which regional networks are interconnected, facilitating communication at great speeds. Individual users from their humble personal computer (PC) can tap into a wealth of information, on an international scale. The Internet, to my mind, represents information exchange at its best. Because its roots lie in the USA, where the 'public-domain' character of the information means a liberal approach to information-sharing in general, the Internet has set standards that belated attempts at commercial payback or selfish information restriction cannot now erode. It is important to understand that no one organization or sub net 'owns' the Internet—it has an ethereal existence as its own 'domain' and applies controls within that domain. This could be a university, a company, or an individual.

Within information supplier domains one can find the following elements:

- a list server—a news group where the managers of the domain have been persuaded (e.g. by a list-server member vote) that there is a short-term or ongoing need for a subgroup to discuss a special project or specialism. This section could be highly managed and is a possible focal point for collecting academic interaction on a given subject. Usually the suggesters get the job of managing the news groups and would impose only their own standards of control. This can lead to some very home-grown records-management practices;
- databases accessed through that domain—private-exchange type, public domain, or commercial;
- 'working parties', e.g. setting standards for a common structure to e-mail messages and other documentation used across the Internet;
- mail servers—like a list server but messages are received on request only (there is a filter system, e.g. by subject, or never from x!);
- software archives for programs.

Access to participants is not completely open. Companies tend to use a 'firewall' along their route into the Internet so that individuals cannot be looked up in a directory of users—a sort of ex-directory. This would parallel any company policy on not giving out individual telephone numbers but instead routeing calls through the switchboard. Academic bodies tend not to have firewalls.

Why are people so willing to provide all this free information? Internet users fall into two camps, the information-providers and the information-gatherers. The benefit to the gatherers—the parasites of the system—is self-evident. Providers get their intellectual payback in the currency of more information. In the face of this huge information jamboree, some archivists and records managers have shown concern over the loss of correspondence between historically important people; others that bulletin boards and list servers encourage 'garbage', or that its tenor discourages sufficient development of ideas between contributors.

Bulletin boards and list servers can be structured like company e-mail, in that subsections can be used to follow up a particular discussion, or to follow through all the different accounts and editions so that one person can go back and read the whole story from the beginning to the last entry. It is very important in this environment that somebody administers each system, otherwise it becomes cluttered. If there is no deletion mechanism, a system may be overwhelmed by the volume of messages travelling through it. The administrator role also encompasses vetting, thus preventing objectionable messages, for example, being sent. Although e-mail messages are faceless, they are by no means characterless, and can provide insight into the personalities within a discipline and the way they personally developed. In this, e-mail is far more useful than traditional published works or letter pages. Academic list servers have been known to start useful theoretical discussions over important issues within a field. Thus, in a profession-orientated list server, messages may act as a record of the change in theory and practice, and, as such, deserve good records management and perhaps long-term retention.

Use of bulletin boards and list servers in the scientific community is profoundly affecting records. As in nearly every discipline, the work of scientists is carried out in two arenas: the laboratory, where the scientist is working towards the goals of the institute or company, and the academic backdrop, where novel work, properly presented, can lead to individual and institution/company credit, and personal career development. The two go hand in hand. Past a certain point, where ownership of the method or idea is registered and institution/company interests safeguarded, ideas are tested in the wider scientific community, using seminars, personal contacts, and so on. Finally the ideas will end up as useful product, and published papers.

What difference does electronic communication make to this process? Previously, at the informal academic exchange stage, scientists would commonly attend conferences, seminars, and poster sessions.

Seminar papers would represent work well on its way to formal publication, and posters a much earlier stage. Communication would be limited to the attendees and readers of the published proceedings, posters to attendees only. In the electronic environment, bulletin boards are paralleling the role of poster session and list servers that of seminar papers. This means that a far greater number of scientists can be involved at every stage and, because of the open nature of the Internet, more information is shared. A good example is the work on molecular biology and the Human Genome Project. Many groups around the world are working in these areas and the rate of data exchange using 'traditional' tapes or CD-ROM meant it could be two months before one group heard of another's ideas. Fast by the seminar and poster standards, this was unacceptably slow to the scientific community involved. User groups can now get updated information weekly, or even daily, as they require. This is because individuals on the Internet took action. An example among many is the National Center for Biotechnology Information (NCBI) at the National Library of Medicine (NLM) which makes available its own and other US and European 'public-domain' molecular biology databases, plus the programs to use them. It is hoped that other groups using these databases will submit their data in return, but this is not compulsory. There is peer-group pressure, however, to contribute the data. For example, no reputable journal will publish papers without the reference indicating that the data were accessioned onto one of these databases.

The formal publication stage is much the same in electronic form as it is in paper with regard to record content—peer and institution review will still be looking for the same things. What is notable in the electronic publishing age is the improvement in terms of access. The publications will be technology dependent but, for the historian looking at a particular subject, there is the advantage of key-word searching, text retrieval (to abstracts as well as full text), and all on a physically small source (CD-ROM). An interesting trend, not just in scientific work but in academia generally, is that radical ideas, challenging the established view on a subject and which may previously have had a tough time getting an airing, are bypassing the formal publication process completely. This could be beneficial for a discipline in that establishment figures cannot stifle creative thinking that happens to run counter to their own lifetime's work, but, on the down side, lightweight theories, lacking rigorous testing, may be disseminated imprudently.

International collaborations on a scale made possible by e-mail via the Internet have highlighted provenance and ownership questions for the records manager. International collaboration in science is on the increase as it pools the burden of expensive equipment and laboratory facilities. This can have a positive effect on records creation, since before e-mail physicists tended to use the telephone, a practice that normally leaves no paper trail, (Warnow-Blewett 1994). The international element forces a records trail into e-mail (and, consequently, some hope of structured retention), whereas collaboration on a local scale would not. But who will save the collaboration-wide records? Who owns them? Who created which records? Provenance is complicated in international collaborations. Bell Communications Research (Bellcore) asked, via the Internet, for help in a computing-intensive calculation. They duly got help and succeeded. On publication they had problems attributing work and hence provenance. Mark Manasse of Bellcore put out a further message, 'If you helped us ... send us your name as you like it to appear in ... the paper.'

Warnow-Blewett (1994: 74) maintains, 'If we are to document significant multi-institutional collaborations without undue duplication of effort, the community will need to develop a broader sense of responsibility and co-operation.' If such progress can be made in this scientific area where computing technology is at the cutting edge, it will need to include consensus about long-term migration, retention, and access management, and is likely to influence standard practice on a wider scale.

Issues Raised by V-Mail

Storing voice messages as records is not as simple as adding a cassette or tape and storing the messages. The sort of companies looking for voice-record storage are often in a highly regulated environment. Here, records on all media may be subject to the scrutiny and approval of a regulatory body, and have to be produced and retained as part of a validated system where dates and times, source and receipt, version control and audit of changes must be an integral part of the system, and that system approved by the regulatory body. Without all these controls integrated into a v-mail system, companies will still be committed to writing up minutes to record policy decisions, and making standard phone calls and writing them up afterwards into signed telephone logs. A voice message on a cassette with no context to support it cannot be complete as a record. V-mail will undoubtedly be tackled with the increased use of multimedia technology. Until that is commercially established—i.e. cheap enough to become commonplace in business—it will not have the same prominence as typed e-mail. This does not mean that records professionals can be complacent, we must be in the forefront of groups concerned with the introduction of new technologies into the workplace if we are to influence future records management.

SUGGESTED APPROACHES TO MANAGING E-MAIL

The approaches to e-mail management that I would suggest fall into three areas: systems, filing, and training.

By ingratiation, impressing, helping, socializing, learning, or sheer force of character, the records manager must become a recognized member of the e-mail system selection and implementation team. As David Bearman argued, it is only when archivists help to define the systems that capture and handle electronic information that solutions to their management will be found (Bearman 1993). This need not mean a technical role, but involvement in activities such as sitting in on the working parties, being copied into reports and inputting into their preparation, being aware of packages, voicing opinions on their records-management facilities, taking a quality assurance role for the project, and offering to be one of the pilot users. Whatever gets archivists and records managers on the inside. Clearly, the records manager cannot afford to sit back while an e-mail system is introduced or developed and bemoan the resultant records problems. He or she will merely become the hated technology 'wet blanket', leading to even greater exclusion in the future. The profession must also be openminded in providing solutions to the very problems it anticipates. Records-management input at this stage will include challenges such as helping to define which data are to be captured and 'stamped' at creation, and devising audit trails of use throughout the system so that the context elements will be there for e-mail messages to constitute authentic and reliable records. Practicality is vital; a system must be simple to use.

These controls are likely to be encompased in a formal e-mail policy and procedure. Such documents will address both systems and user issues. In 1990 a group of experts in the USA met in the wake of the

PROFS case to investigate whether it would be possible to arrive at a consensus as to how best to manage electronic records for archival purposes (Bearman 1990). They identified ten guidelines for records-management control, among these were: 'require program managers to establish guidelines for use of systems that are dictated by organizational policy interests; do not permit guidelines to be driven by the data centre or systems adminstrators based solely on system administration such as the reduction of storage loads' (Bearman 1990: 14).

Once a policy on managing e-mail records has been established, clear guidelines must be established on how to file e-mail records properly to ensure their appropriate disposition, such as common file structures and naming conventions. These are real challenges. System constraints often limit filename lengths to a degree that makes them useless for descriptive purposes. To have any real hope of success, e-mail filenaming will most probably need to be linked to word-processed document management systems, both of which are well supplied with word-searching, text retrieval, and so forth. In the absence of these, users should not, however, be left without guidance.

CONCLUSION

In terms of what records could now be accessed by a historian, the quality, the volume, and the completeness have improved dramatically with the advent of electronic communication. The records are not handwritten. They are more focused and less personal, owing to the wider audience. The variety of sources that can be input into a debate are world-wide and some avenues of thought will survive because of this, when formerly they would have withered in a smaller community. Response time is faster, and, confident in the formal date stamping and public manner of their input, people are more willing to share information earlier, and on a global scale. This confidence is growing with the advent of copyright conventions. (Ryan and Murdock 1995).

So, is electronic communication encouraging information loss or information exchange? Without records-management skills and principles, it has been and could continue to be the former. Given creative records management, firmly based on archival principles but delivered in a proactive style to the user community, and given the matching input from the technologists to save and migrate those records, then archivists and historians could be entering a golden age.

References

Almquist, E. (1992), 'The Impact of Electronic Media on Scientific Research: Communication' and Collaboration' (paper in the author's possession).

Barry, R. E. (1990) (ed.), *Management of Electronic Records: Issues and Guidelines* (New York: Advisory Committee for the Coordination of Information Systems (ACCIS)).

Bearman, D. (1990), 'Electronic Office Records: Report of a Meeting held at the Brookings Institution, January 11, 1990', *Archives and Museum Informatics*, 4/1: 12–15.

——(1993), 'The Implications of *Armstrong* v. *Executive Office of the President* for the Archival Management of Electronic Records', *American Archivist*, 56: 674–89.

Bikson, T. K. (1994), 'Organizational Trends and Electronic Media: Work in Progress', *American Archivist*, 57: 48–68.

——and Law, S. A. (1993), 'Electronic Mail Use at the World Bank: Messages from Users', *Information Society*, 9/2: 124–44.

Himelstein, L. (1995), 'Legal Affairs: The Snitch in the System', *Business Week* (17 Apr.).

Kehoe, B. P. (1992), *Zen and the Art of the Internet* (Chester, Pa.)

McMurdo, G. (1995), 'Electric Writing: Netiquettes for Networkers', *Journal of Information Science*, 21/4: 305–18.

Records Advisory Service, New York State Archives and Records Administration, (1995), *Managing Records in E-mail Systems* (Albany).

Rice, R., and Love, G. (1987), 'Electronic Emotion: A Content and Network Analysis of a Computer Mediated Communications Network', *Communication Research*, 14: 85–105.

Ryan, D., and Murdock, A. (1995), 'The Internet and You', *Records Management Journal*, 5: 35–47.

Warnow-Blewett, J. (1994), 'Organizational Trends: Commentary', *American Archivist*, 57: 70–4.

Secondary Use of Computerized Patient Records

MARTIN GARDNER

ABSTRACT

For many years it has been recognized that archives of medical records in conventional paper form contain information of utility to secondary users such as epidemiologists, geographers, and historians. However, the difficulties involved in exploiting such archives are also well known. In the near future computerized medical records will be used routinely for the documentation of health care. This will rapidly lead to the accumulation of large, very detailed information repositories. The purpose of this chapter is to address the question as to whether computer-based medical-record archives will be more amenable to secondary users than existing paper-based archives.

INTRODUCTION

In the 1990s some health-care institutions in the UK began to keep medical records exclusively on computer systems rather than on paper, and this practice is likely to spread very rapidly. The aim of this chapter is to explore the implications of this revolution for users of medical records for purposes other than immediate clinical care, users such as historians, social scientists, and geographers.

An enormous and ever-increasing volume of literature has been generated in relation to the advent of so-called 'electronic patient records' (EPRs), to which justice cannot possibly be done in a chapter such as this. Rather the intention is to provide a brief overview of the general issues involved. Particular attention is paid to the significance of relational database technology, since this is likely to be a key component of EPRs in the near and mid-term future. First, a simple categorization of medical-record utility, for reference in the body of the chapter, will be introduced. Then medical-record storage technologies will be compared and contrasted. It is very likely that, for the first two decades of the twenty-first century at least, most EPRs will have at their core a relational database management system (RDBMS). The features of this technology will then be outlined. Problems related to the retrospective use of EPRs will follow, and the chapter will end with some conclusions.

THE UTILITY OF MEDICAL RECORDS

For the purposes of further discussion, I wish to propose in this section a simple classification of the utility of medical records, with particular focus on the character of users in each category. An alternative taxonomy can be found in the work of the American Medical Association (AMA 1993).

Primary Utility

The term 'primary' will be applied to medical-record use in relation to a currently active episode of care in respect of a single, specified patient. Primary utility covers both clinical and administrative purposes. Typical primary-clinical users would be doctors or nurses with full or partial responsibility for a particular episode of care. Typical primary-administrative users would be personnel responsible for such activities as making appointments, scheduling resources, and invoicing. A patient might have several simultaneously active episodes of care of variable duration. For example, active clinical management of diabetes mellitus might continue for many years, whilst active clinical management of acute appendicitis might be limited to a period of only a few weeks.

Primary use might be further qualified as direct or indirect. Direct implies that the subject of the episode of care, and the subject of the consulted record, are one and the same, whereas indirect describes the situation in which the record of patient *Y* is consulted as part of the care of patient *X*. At present indirect use is relatively infrequent. An example might be where patient *Y* is a relative of patient *X*, who has a disease of potentially genetic aetiology. However, new computational techniques such as case-based reasoning make extensive use of primary-indirect record consultation.

Primary-direct users usually have an explicit contractual relationship to the patient whose records they consult. They not only extract information, but also insert information into medical records. Primary users have a relatively high degree of implicit contextual knowledge; about medicine; about the institution in which they are operating; and about the record system they are using, gained through either experience, or explicit training, or both. The design and implementation of EPRs is quite understandably targeted toward primary utility.

Secondary Utility

The term 'secondary' will be applied to medical-record use for all purposes other than the immediate care of a specified patient.

Comprehensive EPRs could potentially support a very wide range of secondary utility. It seems probable that the major categories of secondary use would be, first, clinical and resource management audit (i.e. monitoring the quality and efficiency of recently delivered care), and, secondly, education of health-care personnel. These categories of use are likely to involve accessing records which are contemporary, in the sense that they have been accessed by primary users in the recent past—say, within the previous five years.

However, there are also many potential categories of secondary use which relate to medical records which have not been subject to recent primary use. Such records may have been in long-term storage for fifty to 100 years or more. Examples related to health care might be:

- investigating the spread of infectious diseases;
- looking for associations between environmental exposure (e.g. radiation, chemicals) and subsequent disease;
- tracing ancestors of those with inherited diseases;
- assessing the long-term consequences of various therapies;
- assessing the long-term effects on health of such things as social deprivation or occupation.

In addition, however, medical records may be of great utility for research disciplines not directly related to health care, such as social, cultural, or political history; human geography; economics; and anthropology. Others interested in archived medical records might include lawyers and biographers.

Secondary users generally have no direct contractual relationship with the patients whose records they consult, though they may be subject to legal constraints through, for example, employment at an institution or membership of a professional body. They may have little contextual knowledge about medicine, or of the institutional circumstances in which the records were acquired, and, especially in the case of computerized records, no contextual knowledge whatever about the record system used. In particular, the primary user generally has accurate foreknowledge of what information exists in a given data set, and can thus formulate efficient queries. The secondary user, on the other hand, is commonly searching for information which can be recognized but not predefined, without the luxury of knowing in advance whether it is there to be found.

STORAGE TECHNOLOGIES FOR MEDICAL RECORDS

Memory Storage

Clearly, in prehistoric times, human memory would have been the only option for the storage of 'medical records'. It is perhaps worth noting that this strategy is of considerable, though diminishing, importance in modern times, since it is the justification for the UK system of each patient registering with an individual general practitioner. It is reasoned that the GP will have immediate access to a large store of important if subtle information which cannot otherwise be maintained.

Physical Object Storage

In the twentieth century medical records have been stored as physical objects, such as sheets of paper or photographic films. Early medical record systems were essentially the journals of particular health-care providers or locations—a doctor's case book, or a hospital ward logbook. Inadequacies in this form of documentation led to the introduction of the current system of unit patient files, where all the information about a patient at a given institution is stored in a single folder. A more detailed discussion of this transition can be found in Maxwell-Stewart, Tough, *et al.* (1994).

Consider the record of a typical patient in a modern UK district general hospital. In principle this contains all of the information relevant to the clinical management of the problems for which the patient has sought help. For example, Mrs P, a 50-year-old woman, has attended the hospital regularly, though infrequently, for the last five years in relation to her ongoing problems with high blood pressure. Two years ago she needed a minor operation for a broken arm sustained in a traffic accident. The record of the former, continuing, episode includes information about family history, lifestyle, previous investigation and treatment, diagnoses considered and/or excluded, and plans for future investigation and treatment. The record of the latter, completed, episode includes information about the accident (testimony), about the injury (examination and investigation findings), about the treatment (a surgical operation), and about the results (more examination and investigation findings).

The physical record consists of an A4-size folder divided into sections labelled, for example, letters; clinical notes; operation notes; blood-test results; X-ray report forms; etc. The clinical-notes section is subdivided according to the job description of the author, such as orthopaedic surgery, general medicine, or renal medicine. Within each section, or subsection, items are arranged in chronological order. The folder is marked with a hospital number and a patient name. The actual X-ray films are in a separate folder, probably labelled with a radiography number unrelated to the hospital number.

Thus the structure of (and therefore implicitly the index to) the medical record in no way reflects the nature, cause, or outcome of the patient's health problems but is determined by a combination of datatype, speciality, and chronology. The arm X-ray reports are intermingled with the chest X-ray reports for no other reason than that they are both of datatype 'X-ray report', and the two sets happen to have overlapping dates. Information relating to the blood-pressure problem is spread between two subdivisions of the clinical-notes section because care is shared between two departments which, contingently in this hospital, have inherited a tradition of so doing.

To a large extent, the predominance of datatype is a consequence of the fact that physical objects are involved. Biochemistry result forms are a particular size and shape and must be pasted to a special mount card. However, there are several advantages associated with this style of record-keeping. No equipment is required other than paper, pens, folders, and mount cards. All users are familiar with it, and the record of every patient within a given institution has the same structure. Long-term storage does not necessitate any form of 'processing' of the record. Perhaps crucially, since the structure of the record is independent of its clinical meaning, records can be maintained by non-clinicians—finding the correct location for filing a report is simply a matter of identifying its type and date.

In respect of secondary use, however, there are major problems. The bulk of records generated by a large hospital is such that long-term storage of all records would incur heavy costs for building upkeep and staff. Indexing by name and hospital number is sufficient for primary use, and it is difficult to justify the cost of indexing a set of records by any other attributes. This means that linkage of records between institutions is difficult. Whether in respect of primary or secondary use, concurrent access to files is impossible. Moving even a small set of records from one location to another can be a surprisingly troublesome activity. Perhaps more important than any of these, however, is the problem of information retrieval. In brief, since the record is effectively indexed by datatype rather than clinical content, finding records which are relevant to a particular interest is extremely difficult, even discounting the issue of legibility.

In practice, secondary use of physical records becomes tractable only when the volume of information is drastically reduced. This can be done either by abstraction or by sampling, or both. Abstraction involves manual summaries such as SMR1 returns. These are used to notify central government agencies of the cause of death of deceased persons, together with a few demographic details, chiefly age at death, sex, and address. This allows the comparison of mortality rates standardized for age and sex. Though acquisition is labour intensive, the systematic collection of this type of data is justified since it is of high value to secondary users. Sampling involves preserving complete patient files, but only a small subset of the collection, with the intention that the subset is representative of the whole (Maxwell-Stewart, Sheppard, and and Yeo 1996: 19–25).

Analogue Storage

An alternative to the storage of original physical records such as letters is to store a representation of the object in either analogue or digital form. In respect of medical records, the most commonly used analogue storage technology has been microfiche. This technique overcomes the bulk problems associated with storing medical records as physical objects, and has been used by a number of health-care institutions. It seems likely, however, that analogue technologies will be superseded by digital methods, for the reasons explained below.

Digital Storage

Modern information-processing is now dominated by binary digital technologies. The major advantage of this is that facilities for the storage, duplication, and transmission of information are entirely independent of the content or meaning of the information, as indeed are facilities for encryption, if required. There are now a number of different types of storage devices available, including random access memory (RAM), magnetic disks, magnetic tape, and compact (optical) discs. The capacity and performance of these devices is likely to increase over the next decade. In addition, efficient data-compression algorithms (Spyns, Renkens, *et al.* 1994) will further enhance capacity. Increasingly wide bandwidth networks will be available for the distribution of information (Smith 1995), and a dedicated National Health Service (NHS) data communications network is already under construction.

Although, once encoded as binary data, information can be manipulated efficiently regardless of its meaning, for the purposes of data capture and display it is necessary to have agreed protocols for encoding and decoding information. Different protocols are necessary for different types of information, and, to date, agreement on the adoption of protocols as standards has not proved easy. Thus, for example, there are many incompatible protocols for encoding images. Even though the binary data representing an image may easily be stored for many years, if encoded in an obsolete protocol, its content may be unrecoverable. Despite the problems of encoding, however, there is no doubt that, for the twenty-first century at least, binary digital storage technologies are likely to be the foundation for medical record-keeping.

RELATIONAL DATABASE TECHNOLOGY

As suggested by Smith (1995), there seems little doubt that in the near and mid-term future EPRs will be stored using database management systems (DBMSs), most of which will conform to the relational model (Darling 1992).

The relational model for data storage was developed by Codd (1970) in the 1970s, and achieved widespread commercial success in the 1980s, initially in the banking and finance sector, but subsequently in many other fields. The importance of the model is that it is based on a formal mathematical theory of relations. All data are held in the form of relations, and the result of any operation on the data (such as a query) is itself a relation. This means that, for example, the output of one query can be used as the input to another. Also, a given sequence of operations may be replaced by a more efficient sequence having the same outcome, which can be mathematically guaranteed within the model. The relational model offers a combination of versatility, robustness, and efficiency not previously available. The software architecture of contemporary EPRs typically consists of three basic components:

- a DBMS, probably provided by a commercial DBMS specialist;
- a suite of user interfaces;
- a suite of application programs written in a general purpose programming language such as 'C', which pass data between the database and the user interfaces.

A major part of the design of an EPR is the data model, which is a specification of how information about objects in the real world is to be mapped to the tables and columns in the relational database. Creating a data model is a highly skilled task, particularly in a complex domain such as medicine. In order for the data model to be efficient and maintainable, it is necessary to ensure various degrees of a property known as 'normalization', and this often requires a design which is not intuitively straightforward to users. Normalization refers to a method of designing database tables such that adding data to one table does not cause data in linked tables to become inconsistent.

Operations on data in the database of an EPR are specified using a data manipulation language. By far the most popular is a language known as SQL (Structured Query Language). It was originally envisaged that SQL would be used interactively by end-users (e.g. bank managers). However, in modern practice SQL commands are embedded within the application programs which link the EPR user interface and the database, so that primary users are completely isolated from it and the complexities of the data model. In principle the data retrieval features of SQL support the retrieval of any item of data from the database providing the programmer, or user, can provide a suitable query.

PROBLEMS FOR SECONDARY USERS

In conjunction with the developments in data-storage devices and compression algorithms mentioned above, the advent of EPRs based on DBMSs will have a profound effect on the long-term preservation of such records. With the possible exception of signal data, it is likely that all patient data collected in an EPR database at any given institution will be preserved in its entirety, over long periods of time.

The reason for this, perhaps somewhat paradoxically, is that all DBMSs are vulnerable to large volume data loss through accident, error, or malice. Since the 1980s many large financial organizations have been totally dependent on RDBMS technology, to the extent that the loss of even one or two day's data would be economically devastating. Accordingly very efficient and robust data-mirroring and off-line archiving facilities on media such as magnetic tape are a mature feature of DBMS technology. In the context of health care, such insurance against data loss will be seen as equally important. Thus comprehensive archiving facilities will be an integral part of electronic patient records systems, not because it might benefit future secondary users, but because it is considered vital by primary clinical and administrative users.

However, although very large and detailed medical record stores may accumulate, there may be formidable barriers to the exploitation of such information by secondary users. Some of these are outlined in the following subsections.

Proprietorship

In recent years the organization of UK health services has been revolutionized by the introduction of an 'internal market'. This means that health care is organized through contractual arrangements between purchasers, providers, insurers, and regulators. One effect of this is that the information contained in medical records becomes commercially sensitive. It is likely that hospital trusts (i.e. providers) will be the effective custodians of the most detailed medical record stores, and it is providers for whom the information is most commercially sensitive, since in principle they are in competition with each other.

The long-term implications of the introduction of the internal market for potential secondary users is not clear. The commercial sensitivity of information contained in medical records is likely to be short lived, such that this may not be a problem for secondary users. However, a more subtle effect may be that, since there is no incentive for providers to share information, they will be free to use heterogeneous information storage and processing practices, and it may be very difficult for secondary users to synthesize information from different source institutions.

Confidentiality

A major issue for all users of medical records is that of confidentiality. As discussed in Cross (1995), even in respect of existing physical records, establishing the responsibilities of the legal owner is far from straightforward; and the situation in respect of future electronic patient records is likely to be no less complex. In a European Union draft directive (SYN 287), it has been proposed that disclosure of documents containing personal information should require the explicit consent of the individuals involved (van der Leer 1994). Whilst this might be appropriate for documents containing personal information held by employers or banks (the primary target of the proposed legislation), if applied to medical records it would effectively render secondary use impossible.

A somewhat less restrictive arrangement would be for disclosure to be authorized not by individual patients but by local ethics committees. This is essentially the intention of proposals of the Department of Health (DoH 1994) and of the British Medical Association Multidiscip-clinary Professional Working Group (Beales 1994). However, Wald *et al.* argue that this arrangement would also prove too stifling (Wald, Law, *et al.* 1994). Much research using medical records, in its initial stages, is either of a speculative and unpredictable nature unlikely to impress an ethics committee, or without sufficient funds to support the potentially lengthy process of application. Also, in the case of studies involving distributed records, the number of committees to be addressed might be large. Accordingly they advocate guidelines for the use of medical records for research purposes based on the professional status of the researcher, as proposed by the Royal College of Physicians. Specifically: 'Research involving access to medical records... is not considered to require individual patient consent or independent ethical approval provided that... the recipient of the information is a senior professional person... who may be disciplined by his or her professional body' (Working Group to the Royal College of Physicians 1994).

Although such a solution, if adopted, would allow most secondary use of medical records to proceed, it is likely that the majority of potential secondary users would find such a criterion difficult to satisfy.

In addition, it should be noted that NHS patient records are public records under the terms of the 1958 Public Records Act. This has implications for the treatment of medical records which are seldom recognized by medical professionals.

In sum, the issues regarding disclosure of medical records are unresolved both at national and international levels. More comprehensive reviews can be found in Dierks (1993) and Kluge (1993).

Linkage

Record linkage is clearly a major issue for secondary users. From the perspective of the future researcher, the ideal solution would be for all citizens to be assigned a single, fixed, unique, personal identity number, to be used in all documentation pertaining to that individual. It is interesting to note that such a system could sustain record linkage without necessarily compromising confidentiality. Modern encryption algorithms allow the conversion of an identifier to a cipher, such that, first, any given identifier is always converted to the same cipher; secondly, no two different identifies can be converted to the same cipher; and, thirdly, an unknown identifier cannot be recovered from its known cipher, even though the encryption algorithm is also known. Meux (1994) describes the use of encrypted social-security numbers to link medical records, without revelation of the original identifier.

At present in the UK the introduction of general purpose personal identity numbers is unlikely for political reasons, since it would be widely regarded as an infringement of civil liberties. However, NHS identifiers have been in use for many years. In the near future a new, rationalized, ten digit format is to be implemented, incorporating a check-sum digit to facilitate trapping of transcription errors. An alternative identifier pioneered in Scotland is the Community Health Index (Janghorbani, Jones, *et al.* 1993).

In conjunction with the traditional paper case files, the NHS number has proved a disappointing tool for linkage purposes. Maxwell-Stewart, Tough, *et al.* (1994) attribute this to simple failure of patients to provide their number on demand. The fundamental explanation may be that, in current practice, there is no incentive either for the patient to provide their number, or for the recorder to pursue the matter, since neither believes that it would influence the services provided. One might contrast this with the situation regarding National Insurance numbers, equally difficult to memorize, but whose prompt provision might enable the avoidance of tax. There is nothing inherent in the computerization of medical records which resolves this operational problem. In addition, a domain-specific identifier does not satisfy the secondary user who requires linkage between medical and non-medical records.

A different approach to record linkage which has received increasing attention over recent years is the development of probabilistic and heuristic algorithms which make use of multiple record attributes, such as name, sex, date of birth, postcode, various identifiers, and even data items such as height and blood group. This approach has the advantage that useful results can be obtained even if one or more data items are incorrect or absent. Using probabilistic techniques on an array of identifiers, Gill, Goldacre, *et al.* (1993) report much better results than with character comparison. An example of probabilistic resolution of family and household linkage errors is reported by Newcombe (1993). A fuller treatment of linkage theory is given by Jaro (1995).

However, widespread application of these techniques would require the development of standard datatype specifications, and the complexity of this task is surprisingly great. There are at least six different 'standards' for the process of specifying how an individual's name is to be represented as fields in a database (Bidgood and Tracy 1993).

Retrieval

In the above discussion it has been argued that large volumes of data downloaded from EPR DBMSs may be preserved for long periods and thus potentially be available for secondary use. It is, therefore, important to consider the problems in retrieving information from such a collection. Suppose a future secondary user wished to undertake research using data at a particular institution gathered by an EPR of late 1990s vintage. What circumstances and problems might he or she encounter?

Whilst it is quite possible that all the data available to the 1990s primary user might have been preserved, it is highly unlikely that the totality of the primary user's information environment would be available (e.g. application programs). The data would be held off-line in a compressed format on some form of storage device. Clearly the secondary user will need access to facilities for uptake of data from the storage device, a decompression utility, and a relational DBMS into which to load the data. A working knowledge of SQL would also be necessary. A much more serious problem, however, is that the second-ary user must also have detailed knowledge of the data model, i.e. the design of the database, not only covering table and column names and the meaning of the values of data items, but also covering the way in which tables are linked through primary and foreign keys. Data models for an EPR are much more complex than those for financial systems, and the fact that there are many different techniques in use for docu-menting data models is perhaps testimony to the fact that none is outstandingly good. Furthermore, in modern practice it is becoming common to design data models in a rather abstract manner, such that types of information unforeseen at the design stage can be accommod-ated without altering the model. This makes the model even more difficult to interpret. Although there have been attempts to design common, generic models for clinical care (Fowler 1994; Kalra 1994), it is likely that the majority of EPR systems in the near and mid-term future will use proprietary, *ad hoc* models.

A further set of problems for the secondary user lies in the nature of the relational model and of SQL. In a RDBMS all data items must be treated as one of a few simple datatypes—e.g. number, character string, binary large object (BLOB) such as an image or sound file—and there can be no structure within a data item. This means, for example, that a piece of free text has datatype 'character string', and the only means of retrieving this text is by crude string-matching operators. Thus the tyranny of datatypes evident in physical records has not been entirely escaped. Also SQL retrieval is boolean, and, although records which very nearly match a query are more interesting from the point of view of an enquirer than records which match only very distantly, boolean systems are unable to make this distinction—records can only be treated as either matching or not.

In brief, SQL retrieval from a RDBMS is designed for a 'transactional' mode of use rather than an 'exploratory' mode of use. That is to say, it is designed for circumstances where one can specify tightly in advance what information one is interested in (e.g. bank account numbers where the balance is below £0.00), and one is not at all interested in any information which does not exactly match the specification (e.g. bank account numbers where the balance is £0.00 or £0.01). This mode of use is appropriate for primary use, but very limiting for secondary use.

There are developments which may help partially to alleviate these difficulties. There is much research interest in the development of more sophisticated and versatile retrieval techniques, based either on extending SQL, or on probabilistic methods for processing natural language. For instance, Motro (1988) describes an extension to SQL which allows retrieval of information which is similar to the query specification, without necessarily matching exactly, although this requires large amounts of domain-specific information to be added to the database beforehand. Others have extended SQL to handle queries involving temporal reasoning (Das, Tu, *et al.* 1992; Das and Musen 1994). Natural language-processing techniques also generally require large amounts of domain knowledge (Hripcsak, Friedman, *et al.* 1995; Sager, Lyman, *et al.* 1993).

In spite of these and other developments, issues of information retrieval are likely to be one of the major problems facing potential secondary users of EPR data.

Coding and Classification

An issue related to retrieval is that of terminology. The language of clinical medicine is both ambiguous and redundant. Coding systems provide a set of concept identifiers, each of which represents a discrete entity, such as a symptom, disease, or operation. Classification systems provide a mechanism for describing relations between concepts—for example, that angina is a specific type of pain, or that the left ventricle is part of the heart.

There are several medical nomenclatures in use at present, all of which attempt to support both coding and classification, with various degrees of success. Examples are the Unified Medical Language System (UMLS), originating from the domain of bibliography; the Systematic Nomenclature of Medicine (SNOMED), originating from the domain of pathology; the International Classification of Diseases (ICD), originating from the domain of epidemiology; and, in the UK, the Read Clinical Classification, originating from the domain of general practice. Newer representations such as the GALEN Representation and Integration Language (GRAIL) support the construction of compound concepts from combinations of primitive concepts in a controlled manner (Rector, Glowinski, *et al.* 1995). In current practice, assignment of codes to medical records is generally done manually and on a small scale, but work has shown that automated encoding from text can give worthwhile results in restricted clinical contexts (Oliver and Altman 1994).

Using coding and classification systems such as these means that, even though one uses the same retrieval algorithms (e.g. string-matching), the results are likely to be more satisfactory than attempting to match free text.

CONCLUSIONS

For secondary users of medical records, the key issues might be posed as follows:

- What records are subject to long-term preservation?
- Can I gain access to these records?
- Is it possible to link medical records to other medical records and to non-medical records?
- How can useful information be retrieved from medical record collections?

With respect to the now traditional A4-paper unit patient file system, there are major problems with regard to all these issues, as is well rehearsed in previous publications (Maxwell-Stewart, Tough, *et al.* 1994).

More interesting questions concern future secondary use of EPRs based on RDBMSs. Such systems certainly offer the prospect of long-term preservation of complete medical records for entire patient populations. High bandwidth networks would support remote access to such records if available on-line. However, the issues of security, confidentiality, and disclosure are the subject of active debate. As regards linkage, the new NHS number might improve linkage of medical record to medical record, but is unlikely to aid linkage to non-medical records. In any case, there are good prospects of a technical solution to the problems of linkage, in the form of probabilistic and heuristic multi-attribute algorithms. As regards information retrieval from EPR DBMSs, however, current retrieval facilities based on SQL are likely to provide only very limited support for secondary users.

Medical informatics is as yet in its infancy. Major research and development programmes are underway throughout the developed world. In Europe the Advanced Informatics in Medicine (AIM) programme has focused on the specification of international standards and protocols for health data in order to promote integration of care. In the USA a recent authoritative report by the Institute of Medicine has emphasized the need for 'comprehensive, population-based health care databases', and made recommendations for their creation and maintenance (Donaldson and Lohr 1994).

In spite of these initiatives there is a danger of severe frustration among future secondary users, given that there may be a huge information 'meal' on the table, but one which cannot be digested. Accordingly, there is a case for such users to seek to influence the development of EPRs at the earliest possible opportunity.

References

American Medical Associations, (AMA) (1993): 'Users and Uses of Patient Records. Report of the Council on Scientific Affairs. Council on Scientific Affairs, American Medical Association', *Archives of Family Medicine*, 216: 678–81.

Beales, D. (1994), 'Draft Bill Aims at Improving Confidentiality', *British Medical Journal*, 309: 360.

Bidgood, W. D., and Tracy, W. R. (1993), 'In Search of the Name', in *Proceedings—the Seventeenth Annual Symposium on Computer Applications in Medical Care* (1993), 54–8.

Codd, E. F. (1970), 'A Relational Model for Large Shared Data Banks', *Communications of the ACM*, 13/6: 377–87.

Cross, M. (1995), 'Trial by Record', *Health Service Journal* (16 Nov.), 13.

Darling, C. B. (1992), 'Database Technology for Medical Records', *Instructional Course Lectures*, 41: 521–6.

Das, A. K., and Musen, M. A. (1994), 'A Temporal Query System for Protocol-Directed Decision Support', *Methods of Information in Medicine*, 33/4: 358–70.

Das, A. K., Tu, S. W., *et al.* (1992), 'An Extended SQL for Temporal Data Management in Clinical Decision-Support Systems', in *Proceedings—the Sixteenth Annual Symposium on Computer Applications in Medical Care* (1992), 128–32.

Dierks, C. (1993), 'Medical Confidentiality and Data Protection as Influenced by Modern Technology', *Medicine and Law*, 12/6–8: 547–51.

Department of Health, (DoH) (1994): *Consultation Document: Confidentiality, Use and Disclosure of Personal Health Information* (London).

Donaldson, M. S., and Lohr, K. N. (1994), *Health Data in the Information Age: Use Disclosure and Privacy* (New York).

Fowler, M. (1994), 'Application Views—Another Technique in the Analysis and Design Armory', *Journal of Object-Oriented Programming*, 7/1: 59–66.

Gill, L., Goldacre, M., *et al.* (1993), 'Computerised Linking of Medical Records: Methodological Guidelines', *Journal of Epidemiology and Community Health*, 47/4: 316–19.

Hripcsak, G., Friedman, C., *et al.* (1995), 'Unlocking Clinical Data from Narrative Reports: A Study of Natural Language Processing', *Annals of Internal Medicine*, 122/9; 681–8.

Janghorbani, M., Jones, R. B., *et al.* (1993), 'Using the Community Health Index, General Practitioner Records and the National Health Service Central Registry for a 14 year Follow-Up of a Middle-Aged Cohort in the West of Scotland', *Health Bulletin*, 51/1: 28–33.

Jaro, M. A. (1995), 'Probabilistic Linkage of Large Public Health Data Files', *Statistics in Medicine*, 14/5–7: 491–8.

Kalra, D. (1994), 'Electronic Health Records: The European Scene', *British Medical Journal*, 309: 1358–61.

Kluge, E. H. (1993), 'Advanced Patient Records: Some Ethical and Legal Considerations Touching Medical Information Space', *Methods of Information in Medicine*, 32/2: 95–103.

Maxwell-Stewart, H., Sheppard, J., Yeo, G. (1996), *Hospital Patient Case Records: A Guide to their Retention and Disposal* (London).

—— Tough, A., McColl, J. H., and Geyer-Kordesch, J. (1994), *Selecting Clinical Records for Long-Term Preservation: Problems and Procedures* (Glasgow).

Meux, E. (1994), 'Encrypting Personal Identifiers', *Health Services Research*, 29/ 2: 247–56.

Motro, A. (1988), 'VAGUE: A User Interface to Relational Databases that Permits Vague Queries', *ACM Transactions on Office Automation Systems*, 6/ 3: 187–214.

Newcombe, H. B. (1993), 'Distinguishing Individual Linkages of Personal Records from Family Linkages', *Methods of Information in Medicine*, 32/5: 358–64.

Oliver, D. E., and Altman, R. B. (1994), 'Extraction of SNOMED Concepts from Medical Record Texts', in *Proceedings—the Eighteenth Annual Symposium on Computer Applications in Medical Care* (1994), 179–83.

Proceedings—the Sixteenth Annual Symposium on Computer Applications in Medical Care (1992) (Washington).

Proceedings—the Seventeenth Annual Symposium on Computer Applications in Medical Care (1993) (Washington).

Proceedings—the Eighteenth Annual Symposium on Computer Applications in Medical Care (1994) (Washington).

Rector, A. L., Glowinski, A. J., *et al.* (1995), 'Medical-Concept Models and Medical Records: An Approach Based on GALEN and PEN&PAD', *Journal of the American Medical Informatics Association*, 2/1: 19–35.

Sager, N., Lyman, M., *et al.* (1993), 'Natural Language Processing of Asthma Discharge Summaries for the Monitoring of Patient Care', in *Proceedings—the Seventeenth Annual Symposium on Computer Applications in Medical Care* (1993), 265–8.

Smith, M. F. (1995), 'Information Technology into the 21st Century: Impact on Health Care Computing', *Health Informatics*, 1: 85–90.

Spyns, P., Renkens, S., *et al.* (1994), 'Data Compression for Medical Report Archiving', *Methods of Information in Medicine,* 33/2: 164–9.

Van der Leer, O. F. (1994), 'The Use of Personal Data for Medical Research: How to Deal with new European Privacy Standards', *International Journal of Bio-Medical Computing,* 35 (suppl.): 87–95.

Wald, N., Law, M., *et al.* (1994), 'Use of Personal Medical Records for Research Purposes', *British Medical Journal,* 309: 1422–4.

Working Group to the Royal College of Physicians Committee on Ethical Issues in Medicine (1994), 'Independent Ethical Review of Studies Involving Personal Medical Records', *Journal of the Royal College of Physicians,* 28: 439–43.

9

Historians, Archivists, and Electronic Record-Keeping in British Government

EDWARD HIGGS

ABSTRACT

This chapter examines the workings of archival staff within British government based on traditional paper record systems. It concludes that many of the principles upon which these practices are based will be made redundant by the development of new forms of electronic communications. New paradigms for electronic archiving are discussed, and guiding principles for future development suggested.

INTRODUCTION

This chapter examines some of the challenges presented to traditional archival and historical methods by the advent of electronic records. Can existing procedures and structures be adapted to the new digital environment, or do archivists and historians need to rethink their working practices and assumptions from the ground up? The chapter will be in four parts, and will focus mainly on archiving in British central government. First, the working practices of government archivists will be outlined. Secondly, the difficulties inherent in attempting to adapt these procedures to the new electronic records forms will be discussed. The general conclusion drawn here is that new communicative environments require new ways of working. Thirdly, new paradigms for archiving electronic artefacts will be described. The chapter concludes with some suggestions for action.

TRADITIONAL ARCHIVAL PRACTICE IN BRITISH GOVERNMENT

The Public Record Office (PRO), in which the author worked until 1993, has traditionally been dedicated to the preservation of the paper and parchment records reflecting the administrative and legal activities of the central government in Great Britain. It administers the 1958 and 1967 Public Records Acts, which oblige government departments to maintain and select public records for permanent preservation and to transfer them to the PRO when they are thirty years old. There is no freedom-of-information or right-to-know legislation in the UK. The archive has thus always seen its functions in terms of facilitating long-term administrative or historical research rather than as providing access to current records. The Office is now considering the establishment of a computer-readable data archive (CRDA) for electronic data sets, and is beginning to grapple with the issues thrown up by electronic mail (e-mail) and automated office systems. Certain features of the workings of the system should be noted. First, archival appraisal and selection usually take place when records are 'dead'—that is, no longer required for current administration. Typically, records are reviewed by the creating departments when they are five years old to see if they are required for continued use. Those which are rejected at this first review are then destroyed on the grounds that, if they are ephemeral at five years, then they cannot have been important to begin with. The remaining files are then kept until twenty-five years old, when they are subjected to a second review, at which stage departmental and PRO staff apply certain administrative, archival, and historical criteria to determine if records should be selected for permanent preservation (Public Record Office 1993: ch. 3). Although the PRO has always attempted to influence departments to undertake good record-keeping practice, its primary focus has been on the process of appraisal at second review, and the transfer of material to the PRO. This is essentially the approach to records advocated by Sir Hilary Jenkinson, the PRO's deputy keeper from 1947 to 1954, rather than the control of records over their entire life cycles advocated by US archivists (Higgs, forthcoming). The creation of finding aids to these records takes place *post hoc*—that is, manually after records have been selected for preservation. This involves departmental civil servants assigning references to documents and compiling itemized class lists, whilst PRO staff fit accessions into the archives' own guides (Public Record Office 1993: ch. 6).

Turning now to the requirements of historians, it should be noted that they are not interested in the record in its own right but in the manner in which texts reflect processes of communication, and how and why they were used to organize purposeful action, make valid claims, or express feelings. They are interested in texts as purposeful acts of communication which carry meaning and which are related to other texts. The tracking of patterns of communication in modern paper-based bureaucratic systems tended until recently to be fairly straightforward, since the media of communication and storage were the same. A letter carried an address and signature, which defined the parties to, and direction of, a communicative act, and the matter under discussion. Correspondence was placed on registered files which were passed around departments as business was transacted on them. If a text needed to be amended, or comment made on it, this was done on the file itself, either on the relevant paper within the file or on a note attached to it.

The maintenance of such records in departments was traditionally seen as enabling them to see who did what, when, where, and why, and what were the effects of these actions. Records were needed for audit, disciplinary, and precedent purposes, and to enable ministers to take responsibility for the work of their departments before Parliament. In practice, of course, few paper systems delivered all these benefits, but they were the rationale behind their maintenance. Administrative work revolved around files, which were the place where people did their work, transmitted it to others, and, at the same time, stored it. People found their way round such systems by linking issues to file series based on subject, organizational provenance, or function—the Ministry of X's file series about Y, the registered files of the Ministry of X's Y Branch, or the Ministry of X's files on its discharge of Act of Parliament Y. Since paper records were designed to fit into such registry systems, they carried pointers to their position within them; file covers, file numbers, cross references to other files in the same series or related file series, and so on.

Record offices, which classified their holdings according to the principles of archival provenance, maintained this hierarchical arrangement in the manner in which they stored and described their holdings. Thus, in the PRO one finds, in general, the records transferred from a single institution grouped together under a discrete letter code, and the record series, or 'classes', within these clusters described in terms of main institution, branch, and paper series. Departments were expected to ensure that paper series were preserved, that suitable selections were made from them, and that lists itemizing the contents of administrative series were produced. Researchers then use the PRO's guides to the administrative structure of its holdings, original departmental indexes and finding aids, and class lists, to find the information which interests them. Since papers were filed in an order which had meaning within the administrative process, the files and finding aids give researchers a sense of the context within which communicative activity took place. The records were their own 'metadata'. Unfortunately, departmental finding aids, such as docket books, have often not been preserved in central archives. On the other hand, many modern historians do not take the trouble to understand this administrative structure, or the diplomatic of the documents they use, which limits their ability to move between record series and across departments. This is, however, a deficiency in modern academic scholarship rather than in the paper-based systems themselves.

THE IMPLICATIONS OF THE NEW ELECTRONIC ENVIRONMENT

Such traditional systems of documentation began to be undermined in the post-war world by the general spread of the telephone in the office environment and the development of copying. The former removed business from the written sphere altogether, whilst the effects of the latter were more subtle and insidious. It now became easier to send multiple copies of papers to colleagues rather than sending a file on the circuit of an institution. Rather than being the means of communication within business, the file became merely the resting-place for papers circulated separately. As the uniqueness of the written document disappeared, so the status of the file was lowered. Office workers, freed from the veneration of the registry system, increasingly came to keep their own unregistered papers. Whatever the reason for this change, PRO staff working in departments detected a wholesale breakdown in registry systems in the 1970s.

The introduction of automated office systems could carry these processes still further, thus undermining many of the assumptions and procedures which have been conventionally applied to archival work (Gavrel 1990; Hedstrom 1991). The main issues here relate, it could be argued, to the dissociation of communicative activity from record storage, the provision of administrative context for record users, and the timing and nature of archival intervention. In what follows it will be necessary to differentiate between those automated office systems which store unique documents for multiple access, and e-mail, in which multiple copies of documents and messages can be disseminated. The latter is rather more difficult to deal with in an archival setting.

In e-mail systems it is possible to receive a number of related messages from different people on screen, then to go into a statistical package and do some calculations, and, on the basis of this, come to a decision which one communicates to a different set of people. But none of the participants needs to save the particular screen assemblage which was the basis of the final decision. In order to reconstitute purposeful and meaningful administrative acts, one not only needs to save the different communicative acts but also to be able to reconstitute their interrelationships in real time. In automated office systems there may be a unique record but earlier versions of it do not necessarily have to be stored. Communicative acts are multiplied endlessly but could become fleeting and ephemeral. In many ways, information in such systems resembles oral tradition more closely than the object-based holdings of archives and libraries. Will historians be able to reconstruct administrative activity if all that is preserved is the document which initiates that activity and the final formal reply? If intermediate drafts—the electronic versions of pencilled comments, notes, erasures, signatures, and so on, are not preserved—will researchers be able to make sense of bureaucratic processes?

At the same time, the retrieval of information on computer systems is inherently an atomistic rather than a hierarchical phenomenon, horizontal rather than vertical. Instead of files being accessed via clusters of papers in files, the layers related intellectually in a hierarchical manner, computer systems often retrieve individual papers on the same level as discrete entities. In hard-copy systems one finds a paper by applying one's knowledge of how hierarchical systems work. In a computerized system, however, each document could well be accessed at the same level across an entire institution, with access via key-word searching on various fields, or full-text retrieval. In these circumstances the traditional hierarchical arrangement of archives could become redundant, with archivists able to say little more than 'these are the records of Ministry XYZ in the year 2001'. The historian of the future might be able to reconstitute all the documents mentioning a particular subject in an automated PRO, but the manner in which they interrelate might take some time to unravel. I can extract all the files in the Treasury with the term 'finance' in their titles or index fields, but how do I establish the links between them? Directory storage structures might still exist but would not necessarily be used for identifying individual items. In this manner, the structures within which organizational communication went on, at present reflected in the 'metadata' of file structures, could become much more opaque. Will this be a problem, or merely a challenge to discover new historiographical methods? Similarly, how will archivists set about describing and cataloguing such material?

This, of course, might merely reflect the actual flattening effect which information technology (IT) appears to have on organizational structures anyway. As informational flows become less structured, so the watertight internal divisions of institutions break down into a plethora of working parties and task groups with constantly shifting personnel (Handy 1990; Simpson, Chapter 6, this volume). The users of such systems might, of course, create their own directories and computerized registry systems, but these will create even more difficulties for archivists and historians if they go undocumented.

Looking further ahead, one wonders to what extent even the notion of the records of a discrete administrative entity will still be meaningful. In paper-based systems information was 'clumpy', each department holding its own files, and exchanging comparatively little information with other bodies. But, in the age of 'information highways', with government bodies sharing common data banks with other departments and commercial organizations outside Whitehall, to what extent will one be able to identify the records of a government body? Will such organizations own information or merely rent it? Such issues have important implications for traditional archives, where records are organized in discrete institutional blocks, 'groups', or 'fonds', according to the principles of administrative provenance.

To these issues must be added the allied questions of selection and appraisal. Traditionally archives such as the PRO have selected only a small proportion of the records produced in departments for permanent preservation. Historians usually regard this as a scandal and look forward to the day when computerized storage will allow everything to be kept. This is understandable, but reflects, it can be argued, ignorance of the sheer amount of paperwork, often of a trivial or duplicated nature, which departments contain. The Department for National Savings, for example, contains so many papers that, if they were piled one on top of the other, they would reach to the height of nine and a half Mount Everests! It is debatable whether IT managers will wish to migrate such large amounts of dead material across computer systems. Nor will future researchers thank them for leaving a vast amount of dross which makes the location and comprehension of useful material more difficult. There will be those who argue that everything should be kept from automated office systems and that future document search-and-storage facilities will overcome any attendant difficulties. But such systems can only be as good as those who use them in an original research context, and there is a genuine concern that an over-abundance of records will impede search strategies. Archivists are already conscious of the manner in which research students tend to plough the same predictable paths through archival sources. Will records overkill merely accentuate this practice?

But, if selection is to be made, when should it be done, how, and on what principles? One might ask desk officers to make an initial selection of important records as they come off the live system. Experience with paper records shows, however, that this would be poorly done. Should departments dump everything down onto a long-term storage medium and select at the end of a longer period of time with the benefit of historical hindsight—say, after twenty-five years? But how does one ensure that 'long-term' computer storage media are usable after the elapse of such a period of time, and how would the PRO or departments cope with accessing and appraising such a vast amount of material to make a selection?

Also, would the quite lowly administrative civil servants responsible for archival work in departments have the authority or skills to police these issues? When the present archival system was set up in Whitehall in the 1950s, it was envisaged that the person responsible for records work in departments, the departmental records officer (DRO), would be a person of some standing. In practice, registry work and the storage of 'dead' records have been given a low profile and few resources. DROs are not likely to have very great access to the more confidential and high-status activities where many of the most advanced computer systems are being introduced. The PRO itself is hardly over-resourced, with only thirteen inspection and documentation officers to supervise public-records work in all government departments, agencies, and the National Health Service (NHS). The administrative structures for handling archives used in government departments may well need overhauling.

NEW PARADIGMS FOR ARCHIVES

Fortunately, many of these apparent problems may well reflect attempts to apply the principles of traditional paper archiving to the new electronic environment, and it may be necessary to rethink archives to meet the new challenges and opportunities. The new paradigms for archiving electronic records emerging in the USA, Australia, and elsewhere simply make many of these concerns irrelevant, and much of the work of traditional archivists redundant (Bearman 1994; Stuckey 1995).

In the future, archival work will be subsumed within information management, and will precede the creation of records. Computer systems will surround individual records with 'metadata' placing them in their context—including recording the who, what, why, and where of record creation and version control, and will select records based on the administrative needs of organizations. This might take the form of the archiving of certain types of communication between certain types of people, an extension of the retention and disposal schedules beloved of records managers and archivists (Barry 1993: 119).

Archivists would have to broaden their horizons to undertake studies of the flows of information and authority within organizations, and to determine with the departments themselves which are important. Some may baulk at such a suggestion, but it is only making explicit what archivists do implicitly. If one shifts the emphasis of this process from selecting information on certain subjects to capturing certain types of communicative activity between certain people performing certain functions, the dangers of historical relativism are diminished, although not removed. Records might even be maintained and migrated across computer platforms within organizations, rather than being transferred to archives, although this option is plainly problematic (see Higgs, Chapter 12, this volume). The role of the archivist would, therefore, lie in ensuring that suitable archival principles are embedded in computer systems at their design stage, ensuring intellectual control, and providing gateways to electronic information. In addition, archivists might cooperate with historians in designing search engines to locate and contextualize relevant records via networks. The archivist appraising, selecting, and listing documents, and placing them in published guides, would be a thing of the past.

Historians, of course, might feel at this point that they are in some sense losing control over what material is selected for future use (Zweig 1992: 181). But, if selection is to take place, it seems reasonable to attempt to do so on the basis of what an organization saw as important in its own terms at the time, rather than attempting to apply current research criteria to the process. Should one flatter oneself that future researchers will find contemporary concerns of the utmost importance? Historically records have usually been preserved because organizations thought that they were important for their own work, and departing from this principle might well create more problems than it would solve. Also, if technological redundancy implies that electronic records need to be selected for preservation at a very early stage of their existence, it is difficult to see how dispassionate historical criteria could be established for this purpose.

It is also conceivable that some constraints might have to be placed upon communications within computer networks. Automated office systems, which place a premium on the unique record, may have to be given preference over the more ephemeral e-mail. The accessing of such unique documents and the creation of new versions would be logged for future research purposes. Those sending e-mail messages might have to fill in communication protocols which not only identified themselves and the recipients of their message, but required the inclusion of indexing terms and a decision on archiving. To aid this process we might introduce structured directories in which documents could be stored according to a common logic for later retrieval or archiving. These would be the registry systems of the future. Such suggestions might be seen, of course, as an attempt to shoehorn IT into old-fashioned structures, and information scientists may well generate more appropriate solutions to the archival challenge.

These innovations in archival practice will have to be presented to government departments as good business sense—risk management which will enable them to maintain valuable records required for future business, or as an insurance against legal challenge. It is unlikely that the PRO will be able to appeal to the 1958 Public Record Act, or concepts of duty. To those unfamiliar with British public records legislation, especially those from abroad, this proposition might seem rather odd. In many countries the stated role of the state archive is to record the history of the state, and to give members of the public access to information necessary for them to undertake their responsibilities, duties, and rights as citizens. It is a formal requirement that government departments should seek to preserve records to fulfil these functions, to be directed in that task by the state archive, and only to destroy material with the agreement of the national archivist. In some cases, the scheduling of records in departments under the guidance of the national archives is mandatory. Even if this is not quite what happens in practice, it is an ideal to which citizens and archivists can appeal (Frost 1992; Gränström, Chapter 22, this volume).

In Great Britain, however, one is a subject of the Crown rather than a citizen, or a 'customer' for government services at best, and records belong to the Crown (in practice, government departments) rather than to the public. As already noted, there is no UK freedom-of-information or right-to-know legislation. The British state has never had a formal foundation in the aftermath of revolution or war, or as the result of an act of will by an enlightened despot. Legal rights are, therefore, not enshrined in a written constitution or Roman law but are the results of administrative acts by government bodies or courts of law. In this tradition, the role of the PRO is not to direct on behalf of the public good but to guide and coordinate the activities of quasi-sovereign government departments.

The PRO has no direct control over record-keeping in government; rather it gives advice on selection for archival purposes. It does not issue directives on how records should be kept or maintained. Indeed, there is no such overview anywhere within Whitehall. General guidance in computing in government is the responsibility of the Central Computer and Telecommunications Agency (CCTA), but even that can only advise rather than command. The PRO is not, therefore, in a position to issue directives about computer standards, or to advocate the use of model computer systems, as the Canadians have done with the Information Management and Office Systems Advancement (IMOSA) programme (National Archives of Canada 1991). Given that computer procurement is also completely devolved upon departments, and even subsections of departments, the issue of standards becomes a difficult one. The UK is not in the position of North America, where IBM has until recently been a *de facto* standard and a unifying force. Some of these difficulties might be solved with genuine open-systems architecture but not all.

Nor, it should be noted, does the 1958 Public Record Act actually lay down what sorts of records should be preserved and why. It merely indicates that it is the duty of 'every person responsible for public records ... to make arrangements for the selection of those records which ought to be permanently preserved and for their safe-keeping'. But in what subsists the 'ought' of this statement? From the strictly legal point of view, the PRO is not obliged to consider the interests of historians at all. The 1958 Act could be interpreted simply in terms of the needs of departments themselves for information, although in practice civil servants do attempt to apply historical selection criteria. If, however, departments do not feel the need for elaborate electronic archiving systems, structured directories, file use and tracking software, and the rest (however foolish this may be), the PRO might be hard pressed to insist upon them. Many professional archivists and records managers, who see their role as facilitating the work of the organizations which employ them, would probably say that the PRO had no right to do so.

At the same time, the size and nature of the British state is changing in such a way as to reduce the force and scope of the Public Records Acts. The great wave of privatization of the 1980s removed a large number of bodies, mainly nationalized industries, from the schedule of public-record bodies to which the Acts applied. This programme is now moving on to a consideration of the functions of government departments themselves, with proposals to privatize large swathes of government activities, leaving a small, central policy-making core in Whitehall. Proposals are being discussed, for example, in which taxes will be collected by private companies, and social-security benefits distributed directly via bank accounts. As state functions are taken over by private companies, even if made up of ex-civil servants, one will find them dropping out of the public-records net. Ministers of the Crown will no longer be responsible for the internal workings of such organizations, except in so far as they fulfil their contractual obligations. This may affect social-science data users the most, since it might be non-policy areas such as data collection and analysis which are hived off first.

Even within existing state bodies, the workings of legal or administrative imperatives are being complicated by commercial forces, which reflect the revolution in the bureaucratic culture of British institutions since the 1980s. Government has sought to encourage departments to act as if they were commercial organizations, or indeed to become profit-making operations. One no longer administers legislation, one provides products to customers. Even within state bodies, the development of internal markets, as in the NHS, means that their various sections seek to sell services to each other. Getting computer professionals to cooperate with record managers, departmental records staff, and the PRO on imbedding archival requirements in IT systems becomes even more complex. Issues of who pays, when, and why are becoming central to computer archiving. In addition, departments are beginning to see the data they hold as of commercial value, and asking why it should be sent to the PRO for people to view gratis when they can keep it and charge for access.

An additional difficulty for the archivist in British government is the lack of a sense of history. This may seem bizarre, given the manner in which Whitehall and Britain as a whole appear steeped in tradition. In the 1950s there were certainly many state bodies which could trace their history and internal structure back over generations, but much of this has disappeared into the subsequent maelstrom of administrative change. The fluidity of internal administrative structures, the increased turnover of staff, and the break-up of centralized registries have all helped to undermine the role of corporate memory. The recent shift from bureaucratic to contractual imperatives within government has also weakened the importance of precedent. Government is becoming increasingly task- or product-oriented, rather than directed towards carrying out functions over long periods of time in line with established routines. The nature of time in the British Civil Service has changed, cut up into small blocks covered by forward-looking three-year corporate plans, rather than looking backwards to a living corporate tradition. In this fluid, almost postmodern world, the concept of storing records in perpetuity for long-term administrative or research use is almost completely alien, and no more so than in IT units. All these factors point inexorably towards archival, research criteria needing to be smuggled into government record-keeping by the back door.

It should also be noted that many of these issues have not greatly exercised the academic community in this country. Historians are used to asking questions about the closure of paper records, and some are actively interested in the preservation of historical data sets. There has been almost no concern expressed, however, about the implications of automated office systems for future research methodologies. This, of course, may be the proverbial 'chicken-and-the-egg situation', in that historians in this country have not had the opportunity to use such electronic text sources, and have therefore failed to address the issues involved. One might be rather less charitable and argue that the lack of interest reflects a general lack of computer awareness.

THE WAY FORWARD?

The PRO, after a somewhat tardy beginning (Higgs 1995), is moving towards implementing many of the facets of the new archival paradigms noted above, if only in the form of pilot projects. The national archives are taking steps to contract out the preservation of statistical data sets, whilst it concentrates on the challenges of the automated office. Here it is working with other government departments to establish new strategies for capturing and preserving texts of historical, cultural, and administrative importance.

In conclusion, what guiding principles might we draw from the British experience? Amongst the most salient are perhaps the following:

- the need for a clear statement of responsibilities on the part of government departments for the recording of their activities;
- the importance of government organizations accepting that electronic archiving makes good business sense;
- a clear mission and powers for the national archives responsible for maintaining the nation's memory;
- the integration of archive, records, and information-management functions in government; and
- training for the archival community to help reskill it for new ways of working, and a fully informed and supportive user community for the products of all IT systems.

Without these elements, progress can still be made, but the chances of record loss and the expenditure of effort will be that much greater.

References

Bearman, D. (1994), *Electronic Evidence: Strategies for Managing Records in Contemporary Organizations* (Pittsburgh).

Barry, R. E. (1993), 'Managing Organisations with Electronic Records', *Information Management and Technology*, 26/3: 115–21.

Frost, E. (1992), 'A Weak Link in the Chain: Records Scheduling as a Source of Archival Acquisition', *Archivaria*, 33: 78–86.

Gavrel, K. (1990), *Conceptual Problems Posed by Electronic Records: A RAMP Study* (Paris: General Information Programme and UNISIST, Unesco).

Handy, C. (1990), *The Age of Unreason* (London).

Hedstrom, M. (1991), 'Understanding Electronic Incunabula: A Framework for Research on Electronic Records', *American Archivist*, 54: 334–54.

Higgs, E. (1995), 'Information Superhighways or Quiet Country Lanes? Accessing Electronic Archives in the United Kingdom', in Yorke (1995), 52–67.

——(forthcoming), 'From Medieval Erudition to Information Management: The Evolution of the Archival Profession', in International Congress on Archives (forthcoming).

International Congress on Archives (forthcoming), *Proceedings of the XIII International Congress on Archives* (Beijing).

National Archives of Canada (1991), *IMOSA: Information Management and Office Systems Advancement. Overview Document* (Ottawa).

Public Record Office (1993), 'Manual of Record Administration', (unpublished manual).

Stuckey, S. (1995), 'The Australian Archives Policy on Electronic Records—the Technical Issues', in Yorke (1995), 121–32.

Yorke, S., (1995) (ed.), *Playing for Keeps: The Proceedings of an Electronic Records Management Conference Hosted by the Australian Archives, Canberra, Australia, 8–10 November 1994* (Canberra).

Zweig, R. W. (1992), 'Virtual Records and Real History', *History and Computing*, 4/3: 174–82.

PART THREE

The Theory of Preservation and Dissemination

The Implications of Information Technology for the Future Study of History

KEVIN SCHÜRER

ABSTRACT

The focus of this chapter is an examination of the extent to which the developments in the use of computers in history teaching and research in the 1990s have prepared historians for the study of history in the future. In assessing this predicament, a number of issues will be addressed. Principal amongst these are: whether the problems of computing facing historians are different from those in other areas of the humanities and the social sciences; the strengths and weaknesses of the standardization movement; the availability, utilization, and interpretation of source materials; and the position and needs of data-archiving. The chapter will conclude with a plea for the situation to be addressed as a matter of urgency and the case to be presented to appropriate government agencies.

In 1838, having returned from his now famous five-year circumnavigating voyage as naturalist onboard the *Beagle* some two years earlier, Charles Darwin took some paper from the desk in his lodgings in Great Marlborough Street, London, to record his views concerning marriage. This was no general or casual interest; indeed, his thoughts were directed at no other marriage than his own. With Shakespearian echoes Darwin headed the paper thus: *This is the question—Marry— Not Marry.* Below this he set out his arguments for and against matrimony. When viewing the document it is evident that, unlike other aspects of his writing, Darwin's thinking on the subject was not particularly clear. Not only are some of the positive points he makes in favour of marriage repeated in a negative form in the list of arguments against, but also several times the text is annotated and amended. In favour of marriage he noted such things as children, companionship, and home comforts: 'picture to yourself a nice soft wife on a sofa with good fire, and books and music perhaps.' Against marriage Darwin chiefly noted aspects concerned with the lack of one's independence and the financial hardships that a wife and several children might bring: 'forced to visit relatives...the expense and anxiety of children...Loss of time—cannot read in the Evenings...less money for books.' Having contemplated the pros and cons, Darwin came down on the side in favour of marriage. Having made his decision he then took fairly swift action and was married to his cousin Emma Wedgwood on 29 January 1839 (Darwin Papers, Cambridge University Library, DHR.210.10; Macfarlane 1986: 3–5).

An amusing tale maybe, but what does the case of Darwin's marital proposition have to do with the historian's use of primary electronic records? Charles Darwin certainly never used a computer and was not even a member of the 'electronic age'. Although, as a near contemporary and fellow resident of Cambridge, it is possible that Darwin both knew and met Charles Babbage, the so-called father of mechanic computation, the age in which they lived was a far cry from the bits and bytes of present-day society. (Born in 1809, Darwin was eleven years younger than Babbage. Both graduated from Cambridge: Babbage from Peterhouse in 1814, Darwin from Christ's in 1831. Babbage, however, returned to Cambridge to hold the Lucasian chair of Mathematics between 1828 and 1839, while Darwin returned to live in Cambridge in December 1836 before returning again to London in 1837.) But what if Darwin had used a computer? If a present-day Darwin were to agonize over his matrimonial fate, in what ways might it differ from the example above? Changes in contraceptive practices might lessen his fears over large numbers of children, and the string of TV chat shows, radio and press interviews, plus pending film royalties following the voyage of the *Beagle* might well combine to reduce his financial concerns. But what about the physical document itself, how might this be affected? Being a forward-thinking 'man of science', it seems highly probable that our present-day Darwin would be computer literate and, if not an addicted surfer of the Internet, almost certainly he would be a user of word processors. Yet would he use a personal computer (PC) or a Notebook computer for such a document, and if so would he edit it as he reread the text and his thoughts on the subject became more succinct? And, if he should record the note electronically, would he then bother to save it and retain it until the end of his life? It seems unlikely. But even if he did save his electronic jottings, would they be preserved and available for researchers to consult over 100 years after his death, just as his manuscript journals are now? It is doubtful. It seems more likely that, if by chance a computer disk were to be retained beyond his lifetime, that it would be no more than an object of artefactual curiosity, the text and other information once stored upon it having fallen foul to both magnetic deterioration and the combination of hardware and software obsolescence.

So much for speculative games. Historians in the 1990s face a crisis resulting from a marriage of a rather different sort: the practice of history and the use of information technology (IT). Although the battle has been hard and long, and from time to time skirmishes still occur, computers are now widely regarded as a necessary instrument in Clio's weaponry, albeit with reluctance in some quarters. In the 1990s the use of computers in the work of historians has increased dramatically (Igartua 1991; Schürer and Anderson 1992; Greenstein 1994; Harvey and Press 1996). This development is undoubtedly due to the greater accessibility that PCs have brought to computing in terms of cost, ease of use, and reduced dependence on others. Although originally adopted mainly by those sympathetic to quantitative approaches to the study of history, with the increase in computer usage the methodology base has also spread to embrace qualitative analysis and other forms of textual processing (Metz 1987; Teibenbacher 1989; Hall and Colson 1991; British Academy and British Library Research and Development Department 1993). Those that still persist in the belief that within history computers can only be harnessed to quantify statistically orientated source materials are as out of date as the dinosaur-like machines available to the computer-using pioneers of the 1970s. It is true that the acceptance of computing is still greater in research rather than teaching, but it must be said that the latter holds great potential, some of which, hopefully, will be unleashed through the injection of much-needed resources via schemes such as the Computers in Teaching Initiative (CTI) and the Teaching and Learning Training Project (TLTP). Equally, the current trend of research councils to favour formal training, an important component of which for history will be computing and methodology, should bring with it a fuller measure of recognition of the skills acquired by the computer-using historian (Denley 1990; Kruse 1991). In keeping with this life-cycle development, it is also the case that a culture of secondary data use is gradually growing in which there are increasing demands for access to the machine-readable historical data created by others. For some this demand is generated by the increased desire to undertake comparative research, which in part is further fuelled by greater accessibility to information. Computer-aided learning (CAL) also places high demands on access to pre-processed machine-readable source materials. This need both to preserve what is currently being created and to make it available to others has received empathic recognition by the creation of the discipline-wide Arts and Humanities Data Service by the Joint Information Systems Committee (JISC) of the higher education funding councils in the UK (Burnard and Short 1994; Ross 1995). Under the umbrella of this new initiative, the first of the 'service providers' to be appointed has been the History Data Archive at the University of Essex, with a remit to acquire, store, and disseminate machine-readable materials of interest to historians (Anderson 1992).

The mastering of IT and the ability to use today's computers is one thing, but does this necessarily mean that the historians of the future will be able to use the machines of today, in times to come? Although the increased awareness, accessibility, and use of IT by historians has and continues to bring many substantive gains, the impact of technology on contemporary society will undoubtedly also bring a host of problems for the future study of history. Because of the very nature of history with its concern for the reconstruction of the past, these problems lie more so with history than with any other discipline. Not only was the advent of computing perhaps rather longer and more protracted than in some other disciplines, but invariably it is the case that the very nature of computer application in history is rather different, and it is this difference that lies at the root of the oncoming problem. Unlike the vast majority of computer-using social scientists, a basic difference lies in the fact that currently the work of the historian focuses around the computerization of documentary sources originally compiled for manual purposes. This contrasts with non-historians, for whom the data they use are generated from the very start of the research process, either via questionnaire or some other survey method, with computer analyses in view. It is a subtle difference, but one that is fundamental to the problems posed by advances in IT which the historian of the future will at some point, sooner or later, have to face. Because of the historian's reliance on the availability of information compiled by previous generations—back-projected third parties, if you like—rather than the self-compilation of information or the use of that compiled contemporaneously by third parties, the availability of 'documentary' source materials to the historians of the future may prove to be a significant problem hindering the study of history.

Awareness of this problem is by no means new (Hedstrom 1984; Schürer 1985; Mallinson 1986). Yet familiarity with the problem has not, as yet, generated any adopted solutions and much still needs to be done to overcome it. In brief, developments in technology have resulted in a situation in which increasing amounts of information are stored and communicated electronically. In the USA it has been estimated that, by the year 2000, three-quarters of all government transactions will be undertaken electronically (United States Congress, House Committee on Government Operations, 1990: 2). It is doubtful if the corridors of Whitehall and the British Civil Service will quite match this record, but the simple point is that a host of records of potential interest to the historian that would have manifested themselves on paper will no longer do so. And the same is true of non-governmental records. Businesses large and small are increasingly using 'office automation systems' to communicate internally and externally, to maintain staff records, and to monitor financial transactions in the form of sales, costs, and budget forecasting. Nor should we forget our latter-day Darwin— the diarist, novelist, or would-be intellectual sitting at home with his word processor. Clearly paper will not be abandoned altogether and it is likely that trivial notes of the type cited at the beginning of this article will invariably be recorded as manuscripts. Yet much, even if publication or long-term preservation is not intended, will be recorded and stored electronically. To return to Darwin, leaving aside curious insights to his personal life, it is clear that the examination of his manuscript notebooks and papers preserved in the Cambridge University Library alongside the publication for which he is most well known adds a richer and more penetrating interpretation of the man and his ideas. But how would these be preserved if he were writing them now, and what would the historian of the future make of the sanitized, word-processed, spell-checked notes that might be left behind, with every trace of the intellectual evolution of his argument having been edited and re-edited from the text? My point here is simply this: assuming that electronic records do survive and are readable, which itself is questionable, the interpretation of such source materials will require substantial revision in the light of current-day practice, since the very nature of the source materials themselves will have changed. In other words, the practice of history itself will be subject to change.

Having said this, the historian can, of course, analyse and interpret only the sources that survive the destructive tendencies of previous generations and societies. With this in mind, it is perhaps rather ironic that, despite all of the advantages of information capture and storage offered and promised to us by developments in computer technology, owing to the inherent instability of magnetic media and the hardware and software environments through which access is gained, it is still in many respects easier and safer to preserve information over a longer term on paper rather than on disk or tape. If this sorry state of affairs is to be reversed and the historian of the future is to be presented with the tools to do his job, it is clear that the archival preservation and main-tenance of machine-readable files must take a high priority. The archiv-ist must become the keeper of disks as well as of the printed and handwritten word. It is, after all, a relatively straightforward logical development of the archivist's role as custodian of records detailing information transactions of one kind or another: at a national level, between states, between government departments, and between govern-ment and subjects of the Crown; at a local level, between private individuals, within and between local administrative bodies, and between such administrative bodies and the individuals they serve. Traditionally the records of these transactions have tended to be recorded for the purpose of storage on parchment, vellum, or paper. Consequently, archives have developed expertise in the preservation and conservation of such materials. The fact that the storage media are changing rapidly and increasing amounts of transactions are now being stored digitally on magnetic media rather than on a physical 'page' does not change the logic of the archival process. Archivists need to raise their heads above the paper mountains that surround them in order to develop a realistic strategy for the preservation of the new generation of records. And not a moment must be lost. The pace of technological change has already rendered obsolete many items that few would argue against the worth of preserving. Since 1980 researchers wishing to have special tabulations compiled from the 1961 census of England and Wales have been refused owing to 'technical difficulties', and it has been discovered that the machine-readable 10 per cent sample of the 1971 census for Scotland is no longer accessible (Marsh 1980; Schürer 1985). This is not to imply that archives and archivists are standing idle, Nero-like, with Rome burning around them. A lead of sorts has been given by the national archives of North America, with the Center for Electronic Records of the National Archives of the United

States having already archived in excess of 10,000 records of varying size and complexity, and with the Canadians also pursuing an active policy of storing governmental records in machine-readable form (National Historical Publications and Records Commission 1991; NARA 1991). As for the UK, the Public Record Office (PRO) is implementing a two-pronged strategy to handle electronic records—outhousing so-called 'structured sequential data sets' while at the same time developing recommendations for governmental departments for the preservation of the products from office automation systems.

The preservation of information captured in machine-readable form undoubtedly presents a host of problems to traditional archives. First, the magnetic storage formats which are fundamental to computing have been demonstrated to be inherently unstable. Anyone with a home cassette player can testify to the questionable long-term durability of tape recordings. The same is known to be true of the reel-to-reel tapes favoured by the older mainframe computers. The lifetimes of digital audio tapes (DAT) and Exabyte tapes (similar to home video cassettes) are claimed to be longer, but how will they perform over ten, twenty or fifty years? Without fairly constant monitoring it will be hard to tell. Equally, the same story holds true for optical laser and compact discs (CDs), although hopefully to a lesser degree. Hi-fi buffs are already advising people not to be too hasty in relinquishing their black vinyl record collections for fear that the CDs that they are replacing them with will fade in sound quality after ten years of use. The same fears must apply to non-audio recordings.

A second problem is caused by the ever-changing nature of computing hardware and software. Machines that were seen to be at the forefront of technology just a few years ago are now readily replaced and cast off with little or no second-hand value. It is true that the market-leading software packages have perhaps displayed greater longevity, but, whilst the base product apparently remains the same, version numbers change rapidly, with incompatibilities being introduced with each new version. Although in the PC world the pre-eminence of Bill Gates's Microsoft Corporation products has produced a *de facto* standard of sorts, how much longer is this situation likely to remain? And what of those that have already fallen by the wayside? It is a rather risky business building preservation and interchange standards upon the shifting sands of commercially based proprietary software. In search of a solution to the seemingly constant change, some have advocated an approach which broadly demands the long-term maintenance of the hardware and software environments required to interpret the machine-readable files to be preserved (Swade 1990; Chapter 13, this volume). Although such an approach may appeal to those interested in the operation of machines as historical artefacts and is vital, in some cases, to the ability to 'read' those files which technology has already passed by (a classic example being the maintenance of punched-card readers to process the already long-forgotten decks of eighty-column cards currently being rediscovered in the corners of filing cabinets, broom cupboards, and the like), a more efficient strategy is to be found in the transfer of machine-readable files to a hardware and software independent format. Yet, despite the soundness of this principle, the practice may prove to be far from straightforward. It will require constant monitoring of the technological situation and may in the longer term necessitate several changes of format to keep pace with changes in storage devices and storage techniques. And, of course, as more complex relational-based software products are developed—multimedia packages, hypermedia, and hypertext—the task of rendering the information stored within them truly software independent without significantly reducing their contextual framework becomes more challenging (Zweig 1992; Gardner, Chapter 8, this volume).

A particular problem is posed by the rapidly developing world of super highways and the Internet. For the clientele of the fashionable cyber cafés, it is invariably of little interest or relevance to know how, or from where, and even from whom their daily dose of information is being served. The whole point of Internet resources such as Mosaic or NetScape is that they make the interface between information consumer and information provider invisible. This will become even more so with software developments like the so-called Hot Java. Developments in IT may serve to bring people closer together in the sense that academics, for example, can communicate globally and search remote library catalogues without leaving the comfort of their own studies, but equally the technology on which this communication is based also serves to distance the information producers and the end-users. If the interface is lost, taken away, or superseded, will the historians of the future be able to 'read' let alone interpret this vast mountain of information? However, all this said and done, just as historians and archaeologists are today able to reconstruct the meaning of obsolescent forms of recording such as hieroglyphics or the structure and form of ancient buildings through the analysis of postholes, one must not underestimate the ability of future generations to decode the electronic records that are being created by today's society. Future 'magnetic archaeology' may solve some problems, but we should not rely on it totally.

Lastly, a further problem, and in practical terms possibly the most daunting, is the general lack of technical skills and awareness displayed by the traditional archivist. Without wishing to be demeaning, computer literacy and competence are not particularly high on the list of archival training. Gaining the human skills and physical infrastructure necessary to meet the challenge that the large-scale preservation of machine-readable records demands presents enormous resource implications to an already under-resourced archival service (Cox 1987). Quite rightly, strategies to cope with the problems of electronic records are being implemented from the top down, with the various national archives taken a leading role (Higgs 1992). But, if the problems of training staff and investing in the necessary hardware and software systems are proving burdensome to national institutions, they will surely place an intolerable strain on the budgets of local archival services, many of whom are already faced with reduced hours of opening and the like simply in order to survive. However, it must be remembered that technological innovation has a positive as well as a negative side. An obvious advantage can be seen in the reduction of the physical storage space required to keep machine-readable records, and in this regard optical scanning may also prove beneficial in alleviating current storage problems (van Horik 1992; Robinson 1993; van Horik and Doorn 1994). Equally, the fact that in the case of machine-readable files technological advances reduce the need for archival records and their users to be located in physical proximity to one another, the possibility to link and integrate electronic cold stores removed from the archive *per se* may result in significant economies of scale (Morris 1992).

Unfortunately the mere preservation of machine-readable documents is not the only problem confronting the archivist. As archivists are acutely aware, even if electronic records are made 'readable', to be of use to the historian of the future the context in which the document was created also needs to be retained (Higgs 1992; Zweig 1992). This is true of paper records, just as it is so for those stored in any other form. Indeed, traditional archivists devote much time and resources to providing users with a description of the administrative framework that gave rise to the generation of a particular record or class of records. The many detailed catalogues and calendars stand as testimony to the archivists' skill in providing this information. But the skills required to produce the necessary documentation giving details of the provenance of electronic records, enabling the future researcher to determine how the information was collected and stored, why it was collected, and the responsibility for the collection, are markedly different from those displayed in conventional archival practice. Guidelines for the documentation of machine-readable files have already been suggested for historians currently generating computerized transcripts of historical source materials, and the adaptation of these may prove to be very beneficial. But the process differs significantly from the source criticism which forms the mark of good historiography (Reinke, Schürer, and Marker 1987; van Hall 1989). In addition to the administrative setting of the record, a detailed account of the technical environment in which the record was created is also required—for example, did encoding of information take place, and if so how was this performed? Again, this requirement not only stresses the need for the traditional archivist to acquire new skills, but also has important implications in regard to the collection of this information. Currently, much of the archival work reconstructing the administrative framework of the deposited documents is carried out retrospective to their creation. Yet in the case of electronic records the details of provenance are all too quickly lost following the process of generation. The result is that to be effective the documentation of machine-readable files has to be compiled in parallel with their creation rather than in serial. This simple requirement would demand a radical change in the relationship between the eventual custodians of machine-readable records and the depositors—those generating such records. Again, the resource implications are potentially enormous. For national institutions such as the PRO with their government departmental record officers, a practical solution may be found, but for provincial archives this demand may prove impossible without the introduction of wide-reaching enforceable legislation.

The problem of documentation is further confounded when one considers the nature and range of electronic documents currently being produced. Detailing the provenance of files such as letters, departmental policy documents, and surveys may not prove too problematic, but what of internal electronic mail (e-mail) and memoranda? How does one ensure that the history of their generation—who received them and when, and how they relate to other items of information—is fully documented (Zweig 1992; Samuel, Chapter 7, this volume)? And what should happen when living or organic forms of data, such as continuous updated accounts, or records of employment or social benefit, are preserved? Not only does their documentation create a problem, but the intellectual definition of what constitutes a record is clearly troublesome. Should one take sample cross-sections of the material on an *ad hoc* or regular time basis, or should one attempt to capture the 'record' in its entirety? For information created and disseminated via the ever-growing Internet or trapped in the World Wide Web, the recording of provenance in line with current archival convention may prove an impossible task. Yet is this taking things just a little bit too far? To the medieval historian who is invariably left with just the concluding record of administration procedures, this discussion on documenting the provenance of data generation may smack a little of over spoon-feeding the historian of the future. The interpretation of what remains as historical evidence is after all fundamental to the historian's craft, but the deliberate preservation of historical source materials in the absence of context (or worse still the failure to preserve them at all) surely does little justice to the society in which we live.

Irrespective of the immense problems posed by the preservation of electronic record that the traditional archives are now having to face, it would be wrong to claim that many of these problems are entirely new or unchallenged. In the social sciences and humanities, specially designated data archives already have a benefit of some twenty-five years of experience in storing and disseminating machine-readable files for secondary use (Anderson 1992; Lievesley, Chapter 17; Marker, Chapter 20; Doorn, Chapter 21, this volume). Indeed, they already store numerous records generated by government agencies and have developed strong links with the producers of machine-readable data. Moreover, they have developed internationally agreed models of study description and are particularly active in the production of guidelines for the documentation of electronically produced data, and standards for the storage and archiving of machine-readable holdings (Nielson 1974; Rasmussen 1981; Dodd 1982). It is true that in an environment which is independent of computer hardware and software the materials they hold do not embrace the full range of information that future historians would wish to have at their disposal, but the expertise and experience that they have established should not be underestimated. Given the resource implications facing traditional archives in their attempt to provide archival coverage for the electronically produced records outlined above, there is a real danger in reinventing the wheel, or worse still, several wheels. The UK faces a particular problem in that the peculiarities of the Public Record Acts empowers the PRO to act only as custodians of the records generated by government. The 'ownership' of records, whether in machine-readable form or not, is still vested in the departments that generated them. The social-science Data Archive at the University of Essex has even less muscle, relying entirely on the goodwill of governmental departments to deposit their material. Acknowledging the problems of information confidentiality and the need to retain machine-readable records for up to 100 years before they can be publically released, it still seems feasible for the various interested parties to forge links in order to share expertise and avoid the needless duplication of effort. Local archives also need the support of larger institutions if they are to provide the necessary technical facilities demanded by the storage of electronic records. Surely, all of this points to the urgent need to define a common strategy and a corporate working agenda. Above all, if the machine-readable records of today's society and those of future societies are to be preserved for future use, both resources and direction in terms of policy have to be provided centrally.

References

Anderson, S. (1992), 'The Future of the Present—The ESRC Data Archive as a Resource Centre of the Future', *History and Computing*, 4/3: 191–6.

British Academy and British Library Research and Development Department (1993), *Information Technology in Humanities Scholarship: British Achievements, Prospects, and Barriers* (London).

Burnard, L., and Short, H. (1994), 'An Arts and Humanities Data Service', Report of a Feasibility Study Commissioned by the Information Sub-Committee of the Joint Information Systems Committee of the Higher Education Funding Councils.

Cox, N. (1987), 'Computer-Readable Records from a Government Archivist's Point of View', in M. Cook, (ed.), *Approaches to Problems in Record Management: Computer-Generated Records* (Winchester).

Denley, P. (1990), 'Computing and Postgraduate Training in Britain: A Discussion Paper', *History and Computing*, 2/2: 135–8.

—— and Hopkin, D. (1987) (eds.), *History and Computing*, (Manchester).

—— Fogelvik, S. and Harvey, C. (1989), *History and Computing II* (Manchester).

Dodd, S. (1982) *Cataloguing Machine-Readable Files, an Interpretative Manual*, (Chicago).

Greenstein, D. I. (1994), *A Historian's Guide to Computing* (Oxford).

Hall, W., and Colson, F. (1991), 'Multimedia Teaching and Microcosm-HiDES: Viceroy Mountbatten and the Partition of India', *History and Computing*, 3/2: 89–98.

Harvey, C., and Press, P. (1996), *Databases in Historical Research: Theory, Method and Applications* (London).

Hedstrom, M. L. (1984), *Archives and Manuscripts: Machine-Readable Records* (Chicago).

Higgs, E. (1992), 'Machine-Readable Records, Archives and Historical Memory', *History and Computing*, 4/3: 183–90.

Igartua, J. (1991), 'The Computer and the Historian's Work', *History and Computing*, 3/2: 73–83.

Kruse, S. E. (1991), 'Computing and History Courses for Undergraduates: Issues of Course Design', *History and Computing*, 3/2: 104–12.

Macfarlane, A. (1986), *Marriage and Love in England 1300–1840* (Oxford).

Mallinson, J. C. (1986), 'Preserving Machine Readable Records of the Millenia', *Archivaria*, 22.

Marsh, C. (1980), 'Computers and Historical Research', unpublished paper presented to the Department of Social and Political Science, University of Cambridge.

Metz, R. (1987), 'TUSTEP: A Software Package for Source Oriented Data Processing in History', in Denley and Hopkin (1987), 241–50.

Morris, R. J. (1992), 'The Historian at Belshazzar's Feast: A Data Archive for the Year 2001', *Cahier VGI*, 5: 42–51.

NARA (1992): National Archives and Records Administration, 'Information about Electronic Records in the National Archives for Prospective Researchers', General Information Leaflet 37 (Washington).

National Historical Publications and Records Commission (1991), *Research Issues in Electronic Records*, (St Paul).

Nielson, P. (1974), *Study Description Guide and Scheme* (Copenhagen: Danish Data Archive).

Rasmussen, K. B. (1981), *Proposal Standard Study Description* (Odense: Danish Data Archive).

Reinke, H., Schürer, K., and Marker, H.-J. (1987), 'Information Requirements and Data Description in Historical Social Research', *Historical Social Research*, 42/43: 191–200.

Robinson, P. (1994), *The Digitization of Primary Textual Sources* (Oxford: CTI Centre for Textual Studies).

Ross, S. (1995), 'Preserving and Maintaining Electronic Resources in the Visual Arts for the Next Century', *Information Services and Use*, 15: 373–84.

Schürer, K. (1985), 'Historical Research in the Age of the Computer: An Assessment of the Present Situation', *Historical Social Research*, 36: 43–54.

—— and Anderson, S. J. (1992), *A Guide to Historical Datafiles Held in Machine-Readable Form* (London: Association for History and Computing).

Swade, D. (1990), 'Computers and Antiquity', *Interdisciplinary Science Review*, 15/3: 203–6.

Teibenbacher, P. (1989), 'The Computer, Oral History and Regional Studies', in Denley *et al.* (1989), 286–90.

168 KEVIN SCHÜRER

United States Congress, House Committee on Government Operations (1990), *Taking a Byte out of History: The Archival Presentation of Federal Computer Records, House Report no. 101–987* (Washington).

Van Hall, H. (1989), 'Towards a Standard for the Description for Historical Datasets', *Historical Social Research*, 14/1: 89–117.

Van Horik, R. (1992), 'Optical Character Recognition and Historical Documents: Some Programs Reviewed', *History and Computing*, 14/1: 211–20.

—— and Doorn, P. K. (1994), 'Scanning and Optical Character Recognition of Historical Sources', in H. J. Marker and K. Pagh (eds.), *Yesterday: Proceedings of the 6th Annual Conference of the Association of History and Computing, Odense 1991* (Odense: Danish Data Archive).

Zweig, R. W., (1992), 'Virtual Records and Real History', *History and Computing*, 4/3: 174–82.

Defining Electronic Records: Problems of Terminology

JEFFREY D. MORELLI

ABSTRACT

This chapter examines the qualities of 'recordness' in the electronic environment and describes the relationship between a record and computing system. It describes the problems associated with the preservation of the qualities of an electronic record through changes in the system environment.

INTRODUCTION

In our technological society we recognize that specialists may need to employ terminology different from everyday language because they require more precision or, alternatively, they need to refer to new or otherwise unfamiliar concepts. This is particularly noticeable with respect to information technology (IT), where new words appear with alarming rapidity, and terminology may get borrowed from other disciplines and applied to similar (but not identical) concepts.

This chapter examines some of the similarities and the differences between traditional hard-copy (paper) records and the 'electronic records' created and held by computers. It looks at how and why using similar terminology may be concealing some fundamental differences which should not be ignored.

'RECORDNESS' AS AN EMERGENT PROPERTY

Records are typically comprised of symbols, usually represented by words. We prepare and preserve records and often spend time and effort indexing them on the assumption that they will be useful—in the ways in which we expect—to those who come after us. In the process of labelling things as records we automatically attribute properties to them which may not be appropriate—particularly in respect to electronic records. Until the age of microfilm, written records were confined to formats which could be read without the imposition of any specialized device for interpretation between the reader and the object being read. Even microfilm, it could be argued, falls into the first category, because it required only magnification using an optical device, a lens. One of the corollaries of these formats is that they are fairly static and inaccessible to manipulation and editing. Today, we can sort, search, merge, separate, and manipulate records in computers in a host of ways. In fact, computer records are potentially so plastic that one is tempted to question the very concept of a 'record' itself. Do records, as such, exist in computers or are we dealing only at the level of *information* or even just *data*?

These are interesting questions and I propose to begin by discussing what a 'record' might be. My dictionary states that a record is 'an account in written or other permanent form serving as evidence of a fact or event' and also 'something on which such an account is made e.g. a document or monument' and even 'information on facts or events which are handed down . . . '. It seems that a record can be *information* (possibly an account of a fact or event) which is recorded. It can also be the *paper* (or other medium) on which this information is preserved. Thus within the very word 'record' we perceive a confusion as to whether or not it involves information and whether it is the *container* or the *content* which is the record. This is a source of ambiguity inherent in the term *record* from which it is impossible to free ourselves and which echoes through all discussions about records—including this one.

In the heady world of records management, the problem of defining exactly what constitutes a record (even in hard copy) continues to be a subject of intense discussion and debate. We have seen many attempts at a definition, but they all suffer from being either very specific and limited to a particular context, or else so general and bland as to be of little practical use. This lack of clarity with hard-copy records is only multiplied when we try to examine the matter of *electronic records*. Yet, it is worthwhile exploring the characteristics and properties of hard-copy records, if this will help clear up some of the added confusion which emerges when we begin talking about electronic records.

A record is proof of an act of communication. Records are preserved over time, they are *recorded*. This may seem painfully obvious—even a tautology. But if we think of our experience with records, the length of this 'span of time' seems to have an effect on the 'recordness' of the record. That is to say, items which have only a short life span (e.g. a Post It note), although technically *recorded*, are usually excluded from being classed as a *record*, at least in normal conversation. I add this qualification because, as we will discuss later, almost anything can become a record if it is left long enough. Meanwhile, one can think of other examples of information presented for short duration (e.g. data displayed on a VDU screen) which are not normally considered to be records because of their transient nature (but see Gränström, Chapter 22, this volume). In this respect, the act of recording anything (e.g. writing it down) does not necessarily result in the creation of a record. I often have occasion to ask individuals what records they keep and a surprising number insist that they keep *no* records even though their office is full of paper and they periodically send boxes for filing and storage. Either these people are wrong, or they are unwittingly creating records by failing to throw away transient information which has been recorded for short-term purposes only.

Carrying this line of thought a little further, we normally think of records being created and preserved *intentionally* for some purpose relevant to the information which they contain. However, we cannot ignore the fact that many records in business (and elsewhere) are preserved more by accident than by design. An extreme example of this is a fossil record, but every filing system (and ultimately every archive) contains items which have long ceased to be of use for their original purpose and which are preserved only because their creator neglected to destroy them. As most historians will agree, these unintentional records are often an extremely valuable source of information later, and it is probably true to say that much of the recorded material available to historians has traditionally originated partly or wholly in this way. Do we deny that these are records?

So the process of recording or preserving is essential. The questions raised earlier about whether or not computers contain information or data can be put aside—it is the process of recording or preserving which is important. However, the process of recording and preserving may be only the first step. What about items which have been recorded and preserved but are never retrieved? Can we say that information *whose very existence is unknown* constitutes a record? Clearly, we can refer to such objects in the abstract as falling into the *class* of recorded or preserved entities. However, it would be impossible to refer to a specific case without it becoming known. This suggests that there is a further step in becoming a record which involves a process of *instantiation*, i.e. the recognition that 'Here is a record'. This must necessarily happen after a suitable period of time has elapsed during which the record has been preserved. Instantiation occurs most obviously when we retrieve a record (as with a fossil or something which was accidentally preserved), but it is possible to conceive of instantiation without necessarily leading to retrieval. In fact, instantiation must logically precede retrieval, since without it we could not recognize the existence of the record.

I suggest that the acts of preservation and instantiation are prerequisites, but by themselves they are not enough to make a record. During my days at university we buried a student time capsule in the foundations of the new library building. I sometimes wonder what the fate of that time capsule will be. Will anyone ever discover it in the dim and distant future? What if it is never discovered by anyone, Will it ever serve as a record of how we lived and what we thought? Indeed, the *use* of a record begins with its retrieval and examination. That is to say, it *functions* as a record only at this stage. The importance of this functional quality is apparent if you consider that there is a vast amount of recorded material in the world which will never be retrieved and will therefore never exercise this function as a record even though we know it is there. Yet, for practical purposes, it might as well not exist at all. If no one ever retrieves the student time capsule, it will never be a record.

So far, we have explored the process of becoming a record which appears to have three stages:

- preservation (whether accidental or intentional);
- recognition and instantiation that 'Here is a record'; and
- retrieval and examination, i.e. the functioning as a record.

I have used the term recordness to describe a property which arises as a result of these three events occurring over time. Recordness is, therefore, an emergent property which becomes a potential in objects when they are preserved but which cannot be realized until they are identified as a record and then retrieved for examination. It seems to me, therefore, that recordness is dependent upon *preservation, identification*, and *use*.

THE MEANING AND PROPERTIES OF RECORDS

When we begin to use a record, we are faced with the problem of its meaning. What information can we glean from it? The student time capsule will mean something completely different in the twenty-third century from what it did to the students who buried it in 1968. It is probably true to say that all records mean something different to each individual who uses them. This depends partly on the natural ambiguity inherent in language, but there are other dimensions as well. Sometimes the nature of the record may change dramatically—i.e. the object which is instantiated as the record may have different boundaries from what the originator intended. Those people in the twenty-third century may well think that the galvanized dustbin and the plastic carrier bags have real historical significance. This plasticity is particularly important with electronic records, which may be created with new boundaries at *run time*. Different users will have different interpretations and each instance in itself may define the boundaries of a different record. How long do these instantiations last? If they are merely screen images, are they records? I think not.

This is perhaps one reason why it is valuable to create indices of records for future use. Creating metadata about the data involves a process of structuring which presumes certain meanings in the records. Although these meanings may not be relevant to future users at all, indexing is a process of instantiation which makes the records easier to work with and retrieve than unstructured data. Thus, indexing enhances recordness.

There are some properties of records which seem to persist in all occurences. For example:

- any entity which is preserved over a period of time has the potential to become a record;
- as the length of the preservation period increases, the potential for recordness also increases;
- in order to achieve its potential recordness, an entity must be instantiated as a record by recognizing that it exists through indexing or some equivalent process;
- the ultimate criterion is retrieval, because using it as a record provides realization of the potential recordness of the object; and
- the meaning of a record will change according to the point of view of the user and the circumstances of its use. In this respect a record has no objective meaning, only its meaning in a particular context.

PROTO-RECORDS AND ELECTRONIC RECORDS

In 1993 I introduced the concept of a *proto-record* to describe computer data which required the employment of a computer system for access and retrieval (Morelli 1993). Proto-records were seen to be incomplete records because, although recorded, they were not directly accessible to human beings—only potentially so. Today I would suggest that the term *proto-record* can be applied to *any* entity which has been preserved and instantiated but which has yet to achieve recordness through exercising its record function during retrieval and use. A proto-record is a potential record awaiting the chance to divulge meaning to a human witness—e.g. the student time capsule waiting to be discovered. Until then it is just a time capsule—a proto-record. Thus, fossils, relics, and other unintentionally preserved materials which persist over time have some potential as records but they are not at the same state of potential as stored documents which may have already been instantiated as records by various means such as creating an index of them. Once records have been instantiated, they are proto-records waiting to become records.

Electronic records are generally considered to be records which are generated and/or held within a computer. In a computer, the confusion between the container and the content (noted earlier) is compounded. If a record can be the information *or* the material on which it is written, how does one instantiate an electronic record? When we try to answer this question, we are faced with a bewildering array of options. For example, a word-processor operator may think of an electronic record as a word-processor file on a computer disk. A person with an imaging system may think of a scanned image as a record. These are actually both stored within a computer system as computer files. Therefore, we might be tempted to instantiate all electronic records as computer files. This is a common view and gives rise to the notion that backing up, archiving, purging, and other computer file-management activities are the electronic equivalent of records management—which is only partially true.

However, there are many entities other than computer files which can be (and are) considered to be records under different circumstances. For example, a database designer will think in terms of a database record as being a logical grouping of data items (i.e. the fields within a data table). This type of record (which we will term a 'database entry') may have nothing directly to do with the file structure in the computer system. We have also heard the term *record* used to describe items of media on which information has been recorded—e.g. floppy disks.

Listed below are some of the computer-related entities which people sometimes refer to as 'electronic records':

a database entry;
a computer file;
the data written to the file;
a database table;
a raster image;
a floppy disk;
a hard disk;
an optical disc;
a CD-ROM disk;
a computer tape;
an entire database;
a VDU screen displaying data;
a computer-tape library;
a box of floppy disks.

The list goes on to include almost any logical and/or physical entity, associated with a computer system, in/on which data may reside, or, alternatively, the data which reside there. In addition to this, we can divide up the data at run time in an infinite variety of ways thus presenting a different set of data each time. In short, we can instantiate an electronic record in a huge variety of ways. Because the process of instantiating an electronic record is so plastic, the next stage—retrieval and use—must be the determining factor in defining electronic records.

RECORDS MANAGEMENT

So far we have included in our thinking the vast numbers of unintentional or accidental records which are created and preserved and which are often of great use to historians. However, in the world of records management, such records are an anathema. Records managers go to great lengths to ensure that records are *only retained intentionally* and that these are the specific records which have been designated for retention for a specific reason or purpose. All other material should be destroyed, not retained. If records managers have their way, there will be a lot less historical material preserved for use by historians in future generations!

The recognized method of achieving this type of control is via a records-retention schedule which lists the categories of records produced, received, and filed by an organization. Such a schedule defines the policy with respect to the retention (or destruction) of different categories of records. However, very few records retention schedules reflect the actual filing practices of 'live' records within the organization. The result is that retention schedules usually give a rather simplistic view of the reality of the organization's records (although the records managers responsible would not admit to this). When this happens, it is not unusual for a large number of 'accidental' records to be preserved along with those which are designated for retention. Maybe historians do not have much to worry about after all.

In the 1990s, records managers in business have been invited to provide similar classification schemes for electronic records as they have in the past for hard-copy records. The objectives are the same as for hard copy—to preserve or delete records (in this case computer data) in line with their function within the organization. This is a logical step today, because many hard-copy records start their life as computer data and the question arises why we should keep the hard copy at all when the computer version is (apparently) much more compact to store and easier to manage? Ultimately, the problem of destruction is much less of an issue with electronic records, because the storage media do not take up much space and the records are destroyed automatically by becoming unreadable through degradation over time (more about this later). In any case, systems administrators often clear away unused and unwanted data as part of their house-keeping activities. Therefore, most organizations do not worry too much about records-management issues with respect to off-line data unless the information stored could be an embarrassment to the organization in the future.

Looking at the list given earlier of all the entities which could be considered electronic records, it is clear that some of the items of storage media can be physically detached from the rest of the computer system. When detached from their system (i.e. off-line), computer tapes, floppy disks, optical discs, and other such media cannot possibly divulge their content and fulfil their function as records by means of retrieval. Therefore, the further 'off-line' they get, the more they lose their potential recordness. Their status even as proto-records may be lost under certain circumstances. Once these entities become unreadable, it is probably fair to say that they are no longer records.

Virtually all off-line storage media ultimately become unreadable either due to degradation and data corruption or because the devices to mount and read them are no longer operational—unless special measures are taken to refresh and/or convert them to new media (van Bogart 1995). This same process of obsolescence occurs with all 'electronic records' on our list—e.g. a database entry, a computer file, and so on. All of these ultimately depend upon some form of physical media and an operational computer system platform which can read the media and display the data to a user. If the media become degraded or the delivery mechanism is decommissioned, the data become completely inaccessible. Conversion and migration must be undertaken to maintain such data in a readable condition by a currently available system platform.

This is an additional barrier to the retrieval of electronic records which is not present with hard-copy records because hard-copy records include within them their own information delivery mechanism—i.e. the printed page.

THE COMPUTER SYSTEM AS RECORD

With electronic records, the computer system itself is an integral part of the record. That is to say, it is the system as a whole which constitutes the record, because it is required for the functions of access and retrieval. No isolated part of the system (e.g. file, disk, or tape spool) can fulfil this role alone. With the aid of the system, we may output information in various forms. For example, we may wish to view a database entry on a VDU screen. In order to do this we must have the appropriate software program, as well as hardware which is capable of reading the storage media. The form which our record takes is dependent upon the context—the needs of the moment. Only if we choose to print the selected information onto paper do we obtain a record which can be both preserved and used without the aid of a computer system. This process of retrieval demonstrates one of the great powers of the computer system—the ability to manipulate data and to deliver it in different forms according to our needs. Here, more than in hard copy, we can see how the meaning and identity of a record changes according to the user's needs and capabilities. By reformulating our query we can make the recorded data available in new and previously unexpected ways, thus compounding its usefulness and enhancing its recordness.

Thus, electronic records are potentially much more useful than hard-copy records because of the enhanced accessibility of the data in different combinations for different purposes. However, we are faced with a fundamentally volatile delivery mechanism: the data and the system are subject to change, both intentional and due to gradual degradation. Computer systems are also subject to sudden failure. Doron Swade describes the predisposition to sudden catastrophic failure as 'inherent brittleness' (Swade, Chapter 13, this volume).

The simple conclusion from all of this is that it is much more difficult to preserve electronic records over an extended span of time than hard-copy records. Computer systems are 'brittle' because the whole system depends upon a large number of individual components, any one of which can bring the system down when it fails. This has significant implications for archivists and historians. Often, if one of the hundreds of components that comprise a computer system are missing, the system cannot function and the information held within the system cannot be used as a record.

Computers have not been around long enough for any organization actually to try to maintain a reliable stock of hardware components, correctly assembled in working order, over periods of time of historical relevance (say 50–100 years or more). However, the problems of doing so are formidable, especially when we know of organizations forced to dispose of systems which are only five years old because they can no longer obtain spare parts to keep them running. This problem is actually much worse than maintaining other types of machinery, because many of the components of computer systems are proprietary and could not be remanufactured in the future because the technology is secret or else too expensive to make a 'one-off' repair. While maintaining hardware over long-time periods presents almost insurmountable difficulties, the problem is perhaps more insidious and more catastrophic with respect to software.

Computer manufacturers continue to improve their products and this evolution effectively precludes users keeping out-of-date hardware and software. Thus, continuous upgrade is the norm and at any moment in time we would expect the current information held by the system to be upgraded or converted along with the system platform. However, a tape made last week or last year for back-up or archive purposes may not get the same treatment. Today, many organizations have data tapes and disks in their 'archive' which are less than ten years old (and which are regularly copied and 'refreshed') but which they cannot actually read with their current system, even though it is *nominally the same system* that created the tapes several years ago. For example, satellite observations form a valuable record in establishing evidence for environmental change. Those taken in the 1970s of the Amazon basin could provide evidence for change over time, but these records are now inaccessible because the obsolete tapes to which they were written cannot be read (Eisenbeis 1995: 173–4).

In theory, it might be possible to put an entire computer system 'in mothballs' at some point in its life. This is termed 'heroic measures' in certain government-regulated industries. However, the ravages of time and the environment take their toll and a mothballed system would be very unlikely to start up and run without expert attention, spare parts, and so on—even after a few months, let alone years. In short, the economics of 'heroic measures' together with the poor chances of success make such an exercise of academic interest only. Doron Swade concludes that a lifetime extension of about ten years beyond the manufacturer's support period is a realistic maximum for a modern computer system (Swade, Chapter 13, this volume).

For all these reasons, archived tapes, disks, and other media are unlikely to be of any long-term use. Claims made by optical-disc manufacturers of a thirty-year read life for their WORM (write once read many) discs have little relevance if the rest of the system to read them will not be there as well.

DATA CONVERSION

Maintaining a computer system in an operational condition is a major and continuous undertaking, but it is possible, theoretically at least. It might well be possible to preserve computer data intentionally in on-line or 'near-line' conditions for a considerable period by maintaining them on such a system and converting them as necessary when the system is upgraded. In business, computer systems are migrated over time and the current data migrate with the rest of the system—although not over the extremely long periods which are relevant to archivists or historians. However, it is expensive to convert retrospectively old data to be compatible with each new system upgrade. This expense usually means that continuous data conversion is undertaken only with data of extremely high commercial value, where the value would be lost if the data were not available on-line.

From a historian's or archivist's point of view, care would need to be taken during the migration process with the data themselves to ensure that the information is *preserved* and not altered during conversion. This could be something of a problem, since computer data are inherently easily altered. Computers are much better at holding and manipulating *current* information rather than preserving *static* records. Thus, preservation requires special security and validation measures as well as great care and attention every time there is an upgrade and conversion.

An interesting adaptation of this strategy is to convert computer data into a form which is less likely to become obsolete. A format which is more 'platform independent'. This process is actually being attempted at selected locations throughout the world and may well be valuable to future historians. The process usually involves identifying potentially valuable data and copying them onto a standard medium (e.g. 1600 bpi magnetic tape) in some standard format (e.g. ASCII (American Standard Code for Information Interchange) or SGML (Standard Generalized Markup Language). SGML is favoured in some applications, because the files incorporate metadata about their format and content. Some of those preserving ASCII data are attempting to provide this metadata in the form of a separate index to the information which will (notionally) assist in its future retrieval and use. In other cases work is being carried out developing standards to encapsulate data in information about their structure, context, and use history.

In some respects, attempts at conversion for preservation are like King Canute trying to hold back the tide. Apart from the ever-present threats of data degradation and catastrophic failure, the range of ongoing maintenance and upgrade required is considerable. Standards themselves evolve, and file formats such as SGML, TIFF (Tagged Image File Format), and others will inevitably be superseded and require conversion to new formats. Ultimately, media such as 1600 bpi tape, magnetic and optical discs will also become obsolete and will need to be replaced. This evolutionary process means ongoing retrospective conversion of file formats, media, operating systems, and hardware will never end—whether the data is held on-line or off-line.

The reality is that preservation of computer data is therefore not a single act but a continuous process requiring continuous investment. Without this investment, electronic records soon lose their potential to be records or even proto-records—they become meaningless magnetic, optical, or other signals—like a time capsule which can never be found and opened. In business, it has not normally been possible to guarantee that funds for ongoing retrospective conversion will always be available throughout the required retention life of the records. When this happens, records managers must take the decision to print valuable computer data or else make computer output microfilm (COM) for retention purposes. While this may satisfy statutory or regulatory requirements to keep records, it does not address the real issue of preserving electronic records *per se.*

Maintaining data by means of retrospective conversion means that only data which are specially selected for long-term retention will remain viable: all other data will be lost. In recognition of this awful fact, it has been suggested that the solution to obsolete hardware is to write a software program which emulates the original system platform and which can be run on modern machinery (see Swade, Chapter 13, this volume). Thus we do not have to convert data, we simply run the emulation program in order to have access to them. We might be able to emulate a Superbrain DQD using a program running on some other machine. In this way we could mount a database created some time ago on a Superbrain DQD, together with the application software to interrogate it and have on-line access.

Unfortunately, there are a number of problems with this approach and, in fact, this is just a concealed form of heroic measures. The first problem is with media. We must be able to mount the media and read the data, and this is the first hurdle. Although our Superbrain DQD data may be recorded on a conventional floppy disk, the track formats, signal density, and other parameters are proprietary. Thus, it is not just a question of emulating a Superbrain DQD operating system (a proprietary version of PC DOS), we must also be able to configure a disk drive to recognize the Superbrain DQD formats. Anyone who has tried to make his personal computer (PC) read a foreign format disk will understand the difficulties, because it requires tinkering with the operating system software of the host computer as well as some of the mechanical elements in the disk-head management mechanisms. The next problem we face is actually emulating the Superbrain operating system and the application software which wrote the data (in this case, by the way, a program called 'Muse'). Not even the original authors of

PC DOS and Muse (the application program) fully understood the whole of their software code (there were undocumented bugs in both program suites), so how do we propose to emulate them?

The question as to whether or not it is possible fully to emulate any hardware and application environment in this manner is largely academic, because there is a more fundamental problem to face. In the long term, this apparently seductive approach only compounds the problems of perpetual conversion and upgrade by adding yet another layer of computer-readable records (i.e. the hardware emulation software) to contend with. This software will need to be converted and upgraded onto new media, hardware, operating systems, etc., as time passes. So, we are back at the beginning again, except that we have dug a hole for ourselves which is a little deeper and a little more complex than before.

Thus, it is probably better to ignore hardware emulation and to concentrate on converting and maintaining the target data in a viable environment. This means that most data captured on Superbrain DQDs in the past will inevitably become unreadable and that only data which have been targeted for continuous preservation can be kept in readable format.

CONCLUSIONS

Although the problems of defining and maintaining electronic records seem insoluble, there are a few conclusions we can reach which may be of value:

- Electronic records offer much greater potential for information value for future users if they are available on-line: their *recordness* is enhanced beyond that of ordinary hard-copy records because of the flexibility with which they can be accessed and retrieved.
- Without a computer system available to read them, electronic records cannot achieve this potential—they are not even proto-records but just useless media or meaningless signals.
- The technology incorporated in computer systems is evolutionary and therefore inherently volatile. Maintaining a working system takes expertise, support from the manufacturer, and *money*.
- It is neither economically nor technically feasible to preserve computer systems much more than ten years beyond the point after which the system is no longer supported by the manufacturer.

- Longer-term preservation of electronic records requires ongoing retrospective conversion of the records onto each new technology platform. Using 'industry-standard' file formats does not alleviate the burden of preservation, which must be an *ongoing process.* Hardware emulation only compounds the difficulty and the cost.
- If archivists and historians wish to ensure that information held within a computer system is preserved for extended time periods, they should direct their attention to securing sufficient funds for the ongoing (perpetual) preservation of the electronic records throughout their retention life.
- The only certain alternative method for preserving computerized records is to make a human-readable copy by printing onto paper or computer output to microfilm. However, these are no longer electronic records.

References

Eisenbeis, K. M. (1995), *Privatizing Government Information: The Effects of Policy on Access to Landsat Satellite Data* (Metuchen, NJ).

Morelli, J. D. (1993), 'Defining Electronic Records: A Terminology Problem ... Or Something More', in Ross and Higgs (1993), 83–92.

Ross, S., and Higgs, E. (1993) (eds.), *Electronic Information Resources and Historians: European Perspectives* (St Katharinen).

Van Bogart, J. W. (1995), *Magnetic Tape Storage and Handling: A Guide for Libraries and Archives* (Washington: Commission on Preservation and Access).

The Role of Tomorrow's Electronic Archives

EDWARD HIGGS

ABSTRACT

This chapter examines the differing functions of traditional archives—as a resource for record-creating organizations, the source of historical artefacts for historical research, and the place of record for the maintenance of the rights of citizens. The needs of historians may be overlooked if the emphasis currently being placed on information management in electronic archiving comes to dominate future implementation.

INTRODUCTION

Historians need records, but it seldom crosses their minds to ask why archives hold them. Many historians assume that archives are run for their benefit, and find the intrusion of other researchers, such as genealogists, an inexplicable nuisance. The fact that the use made of historical records by family historians is what keeps most local and national archives open is usually overlooked. In reality, the origins of archives predate their use by the historical profession. They were the offspring of organizational need and, at least in some countries, of the desire to safeguard the rights of citizens. Archivists, on the other hand, are very conscious of this plurality of archival roles, and have struggled to balance the competing demands of organizations for a safe place for their non-current records, of citizens for records of proof of valid legal claims, and of historians for historical evidence.

This balancing act is largely an internal matter of resources as long as records are stable artefacts, and archives are places set aside for the safekeeping of 'dead' records. Records find their way into the specialized vaults of archival institutions once they have ceased to be of interest to their creating bodies, and can then be accessed by the differing interested parties on an equal footing. Thus, in the Public Record Office (PRO) in London, government paper records usually find their way into the archive when they are thirty years old (see Higgs, Chapter 9, this volume). Archives are public places, neutral spaces. Archiving is seen by organizations as an external cost which will be borne by others. In addition, the technologies of information management and access for paper records are so cumbersome and expensive that few organizations know exactly what information they hold.

The advent of electronic archives threatens to turn an internal problem of housekeeping into a public clash of principles. This reflects the fragility of electronic artefacts, the need for powerful hardware and software intermediaries to interpret the records, and the modern revolution in the manipulation of information. With electronic records it is not possible to wait for them to become 'dead' after a period of decades. If they are to be saved, they need to be earmarked for preservation at an early date, preferably at the point of creation. Archival considerations need to intrude into the life cycle of records at their birth. Similarly, the complexities of maintaining electronic records in a usable condition, including their migration across hardware and software platforms, may simply be beyond the capacities of archival institutions. David Bearman (1991) has argued that organizations may thus have to be charged with maintaining their own records for posterity. At the same time, the advent of new technologies to manage electronic artefacts makes them both a valuable corporate resource, and a target for rivals and external parties with a grievance (Bearman 1993). Suddenly records have become an internal asset, cost, and threat to organizations, and need to be managed. This may well have important implications for access to historical records in electronic form.

The purpose of this chapter is to sketch out the development of the differing roles of traditional administrative archives, and then to analyse in more detail how and why the stakeholders which correspond to these roles might come into conflict in the new world of virtual electronic archives.

THE TRADITIONAL FUNCTIONS OF ARCHIVES

In the original Greek the *archeion*, the Latin *archivium*, was a magisterial residence and public office. The early history of record-keeping in medieval Europe is similarly associated with institutions founded on the Church and State. The position of the Catholic Church as the single stable and literate European organization with a long-term frame of action gave it pre-eminence in the field in the first millennia AD, as witnessed by the splendours of the Vatican archives. But, as monarchical rule began to stabilize across Europe at the dawn of the present Christian millennium, so the administrative functions of the State expanded and differentiated. In Italy, of course, the urban communes performed similar functions. These developments led to the creation and expansion of repositories for the preservation of administrative, legal, and financial artefacts, and the creation of a cadre of officials to maintain them. As early as the reign of Henry III of England (1216–72), one of the king's clerks was known as 'Keeper of the Rolls of Chancery' (Maxwell-Lyte 1926: 5). Such developments were mirrored across the European subcontinent, as existing archive collections were arranged and listed (Posner 1967: 24).

Such administrative archives under the *Ancien Régime* were maintained essentially for administrative purposes. They were utilized, in the main, by state functionaries going about their business. This business was that of the Crown, rather than that of the subject. During the eighteenth century, countries such as Sweden passed laws to give citizens the right to see official documents for the purpose of facilitating public debate (see Gränström, Chapter 22, this volume). During the French Revolution, however, the concept of public access to such records was given a radical form. Thus, under a decree of 24 June 1794, a central archives institution for the revolutionary French state was established, and existing repositories in the provinces were subordinated to it. The principle of the accessibility of archives to the public was proclaimed by Article 37 of the Messidor decree, 'Every citizen is entitled to ask in every depository...for the production of the documents it contains', ushering in what Ernst Posner has described as 'the beginning of a new era in archives administration' (Posner 1967: 24–5). The archivist now served, not discrete institutions but the citizen body at large.

This opening-up of the archives was part of a much wider movement to enable the new revolutionary citizen to play his or her proper role in a property-owning democracy based on markets and the unhindered ability to alienate one's property. Nor were such developments confined to France. In anti-revolutionary England similar principles were given institutional form in the course of the nineteenth century. Thus, the

PRO in London, established under the 1838 Public Records Act, was originally conceived as a repository for the safekeeping and public use of the legal records of the state. The 'public records' were to be a repository of material in which the citizen could establish his legal right to property (PRO 1963: 2).

The staffing of these new public archives, which sprang up all over Europe in the course of the century, was soon dominated, however, by the nascent breed of records-based historians. This professional cadre saw itself as part of the contemporary project of nation-building in post-Revolutionary Europe. According to Posner:

As a struggle against the levelling tendencies of the Revolution and against the foreign domination of Napoleon, the beginnings of nationalism developed. The peoples of Europe gradually became conscious of their national individuality and began to use national history as a source of encouragement in the time of national disaster. Romanticism began to glorify its past, its works of art, and its literary and documentary monuments. Publishing the documentary sources, making them available for the history of the country, and writing its history out of the newly discovered materials became the aim of a vigorous and enthusiastic movement in historiography.   (Posner 1967: 30)

The qualifications for entry into the early public archives were predominantly scholarly, and when archive schools were established they were often created as graduate schools for instruction in historical research methodologies. Indeed, as late as the 1970s formal training for newly appointed archivists in the PRO revolved around the translation and editing of medieval legal documents.

The narrow scholarly aspect of many of these traditional national archives was to make it difficult for them to adjust to the informational revolution unleashed by modern administrative and managerial practices. Across Europe and North America in the late nineteenth century, spurred by increasing state intervention in society, central administrations were growing in relative terms, and creating increasing masses of paper. In the private sector similar developments were under way which led, especially in the USA, to the emergence of new forms of records management. In the UK, for example, the size of the central Civil Service grew from 39,147 in 1841 to 280,000 in 1914 (Cook and Keith 1975: 150). Over roughly the same period, the public, professional and clerical workforce grew from 6.7 per cent of the occupied population to 18.1 per cent (Deane and Cole 1969: 142). In the period from 1850 to 1920, with the increasing size of capitalist enterprises (Hannah 1976), a new philosophy of management based on system and efficiency arose in which internal communications came to serve as a mechanism for managerial coordination and control. JoAnne Yates has summed up this revolution as follows:

Procedures, rules, and financial and operational information were documented at all levels, making organizational rather than individual memory the repository of knowledge. Impersonal management systems—embodied in forms, circular letters, and manuals—replaced the idiosyncratic, word-of-mouth management of the foremen and owners of earlier periods. Information and analysis, increasingly in statistical form, were drawn up by the lengthening hierarchies to enable upper management to monitor and evaluate processes and individuals at lower levels. (Yates 1989: 271)

This movement of 'systematic management' was the informational equivalent of the contemporary movement for 'scientific management' on the work floor associated with Frederick W. Taylor and his followers. With 'systematic management' went the systematic control of records and information. In 1914 Irene Warren, librarian at the University of Chicago, brought together a group of people interested in records-handling and began the Warren Filing Association. This was associated with the Warren School of Filing, which she had also founded for the training of filing clerks and supervisors. By 1954 these bodies had developed into the American Records Management Association, which began to issue professional qualifications, the Certificate of Records Management, in 1974 (Gill 1988). In this manner a new profession of record managers was created within the commercial sector, unconnected with developments within traditional national archives. As Evans, Himly, and Walne have noted, this new grouping carved out a new role within organizations, responsible for that 'area of general administrative management concerned with achieving economy and efficiency in the creation, maintenance and disposal of records, i.e. during their entire life cycle' (1984: 139).

Although many traditional European national archives worked fruitfully with government registries to ensure that the latter adopted methods of retrieving and holding records which facilitated their transfer to the archives, they seldom intervened actively in departmental records management. Thus, according to Sir Hilary Jenkinson's *Manual of Archive Administration* of 1937:

The Controller of Registry is not an Archivist and is not even tied by the Archivist's Rules. Though it is part of his work to preserve, he is really creating;

while the Archivist preserves only and is not in the least concerned with what Archives are made.... The Archivist, of course, may lighten his future labours by persuading Registry to adopt certain systems of numeration and physical arrangement in the documents which will presently come to him as Archives, but this will be the limit of his personal concern in them until they are finally handed over to his charge.   (Jenkinson 1937: 189–90)

The third edition of his manual, published in 1965, still retains this passage. Jenkinson was, of course, the administrative head of the PRO from 1947 to 1954.

It was in the USA that the national federal archives developed the modern theory of the integrated management of records over their entire life cycle now current in the developed West. This may reflect the comparatively late creation of the National Archives and Records Administration (NARA) in 1934. The professional formation of the newly appointed federal archivists took place, therefore, at a date when the vast bulk of modern administrative files was already apparent. Also, many of the skills traditionally associated with archives work in European institutions—palaeography, languages, diplomatic, dating, and so on—were unnecessary, given the recent foundation of the USA. This 'reinvention of the records manager' in the USA was intimately bound up with the urgent necessity of controlling paper, especially during the Second World War. American federal archivists thus developed the concept of the 'life cycle of records', and argued that archivists had a legitimate interest in the creation and management of documents. This role was formalized by the 1950 Federal Records Act, which mandated a government-wide records-management programme (Dollar n.d.: 9–14).

ARCHIVES IN THE NEW ELECTRONIC ENVIRONMENT

The three professional roles of records manager, guardian of public accountability, and keeper of the historical memory of nations dominate the work of the modern archivist. In a paper world they could be integrated to great effect, since records could be managed over their life cycle with the aim of creating well-documented records which could be transferred to an archive once they had reached the end of their business life. Information management may, however, be about to become the *raison d'être* of the archival profession.

If one follows some recent trends in archival research, in the Brave New World of electronic preservation, archivists will not administer dead records in archives but will work in record-creating organizations imbedding archival considerations into software systems. Computer software itself will document records as they are created, surrounding them with metadata indicating who created them, when, for what purposes, who they were sent to, and so on. Such software might also make its own decisions about which records should be preserved, based on the operational or legal risks to the organization of losing certain predetermined forms of information. Electronic records will be preserved to meet the requirements of accountability laid on organizations by law. Electronic records will not be held in central archives but retained and migrated across software environments in the bodies which created them, based on the long-term needs of those bodies. This scenario is a composite of the work of a number of archival theorists, not all of whom would agree on every detail ('2020 Vision' 1994; Bearman 1994b; Hedstrom 1995; McDonald 1995), but there are signs that some archives are moving in this general direction. The Australian National Archives (ANA), for example, have already told their government departments that this is the archival strategy which they will now be pursuing. Archivists will provide signposts and gateways to these organizational resources over the Internet, rather than maintain the central vaults of traditional paper-based national archives (Stuckey 1995: 121–32).

Although there is much in this vision of the archival future which should commend itself to historians, there is no guarantee that organizations will wish to keep records for long-term research or cultural purposes when they cease to have an organizational use. Given statutes of limitation, and the death of interested parties, there must come a time when the risks to businesses of destroying records become minimal. As Stephen Ellis, the Director of the Systems Integration and Redevelopment Project at the ANA, argued at a conference in 1994:

the preservation of accessibility to records for the protection of current rights and entitlements of living and future people is of a higher value than the mere preservation of the historical record of the activities of dead people for cultural purposes. . . . In relation to every record in every format, society will eventually come to the decision that the game is not worth the candle and that the cost of preserving access is too great to be justified by the expected benefits. (Ellis 1995: 119)

Increasingly businesses are becoming interested in 'archiving' valuable records, but their time horizons are usually extremely short. For example, Ulrich Kampffmeyer (1995: 56), an expert in business re-engineering, has stressed the need for the proper archiving of information. But he advises only that manufacturers of hardware and software should be required to supply products which can provide readability of media over at least two drive generations—i.e. seven years. 'Archiving' in this sense is what archivists used to conceive as the function of 'intermediate repositories', where semi-live records were stored prior to selection for more permanent preservation and transfer to archives proper.

One needs to enquire if the public interest is exhausted in organizations doing their work efficiently and being formally accountable before the courts? Would one want to keep the records of the Stalinist era in Russia only for the purposes of 'continued administrative need'? What happens when the organization ceases to exist, or abandons a particular business function? This issue is taken to its extreme when whole states disappear, as described by Michael Wettengel (Chapter 18, this volume). The argument, emanating from the USA, that organizations can be expected to take on board long-term cultural functions appears to reflect the relative stability of the institutional structures of the Union. In an interesting historical reversal, one could argue that it is now Europe that is the new political entity with all the difficulties associated with documenting emerging and collapsing organizational frameworks.

Similarly, will the concept of the citizen's right as citizen to access records in a neutral environment, free of the constraints imposed by the functionaries of organizations, whether state or commercial, be protected? Will access to electronic files in organizational computer systems be unconstrained, as in modern archives, or will organizations take it upon themselves to vet material, as under US freedom of information legislation. Organizations will always be interested parties to their own information, unlike the neutral archives of the past. This comes down essentially to the interest which the archivist/information manager serves. If the professional is employed by an organization and works within it, he or she is likely to identify with its interests. As one information manager recently noted: 'Put very simply, information resource management is the totality of planned and directed activities within an organization which result in usable, accessible, timely, secure, integral, economical, and accurate information for that organization' (Campbell 1989: 146). Similarly, are organizations impartial, or do they systematically distort the historical record in their own interests? It might be argued that records have always been preserved because of administrative requirements, but this has not always been with the express understanding that they would be made available to the public. It could be argued, moreover, that in the past much has survived because organizations had no control over information. Information is no longer a buried treasure lost in attics and basements but capital to be made to sweat, and to be consciously managed. Some of the new archival theorists appear to assume that organizations exist in a world of perfect information, where they need to be able to document all administrative processes. All that may survive in practice, however, are the sanitized, formal processes of decision-making. An information specialist has, for example, recently advocated the destruction of all company e-mail and voice mail after fifteen to thirty days on the grounds that,

Electronic mail rarely represents the 'offiical' position of the organization. These communications reflect preliminary thoughts or ideas, have not been reviewed by the organisation and typically only reflect the personal opinion of the parties involved. Yet, since employees of the organisation created these communications, courts and regulatory agencies can construe these records to reflect the organisational view.   (Skupsky 1993: 42)

Much depends here on the culture of organizations, and one might (possibly) expect public bodies used to democratic accountability to take more kindly to transparent decision-making than commerce. The concept of the transparent organization will also have more purchase in a society such as Sweden, which passed its first Freedom of Information Act in 1766, than in the UK, where legal rights to access to information are absent (Gränström, Chapter 22, this volume). It is also a moot point as to whether or not the nation state, or larger entities such as the European Union, are willing, or able, to impose a regulatory regime on the private sector.

CONCLUSION

It is not inevitable that the role of information management should absorb the archival profession. The Canadian national archives, the US National Archives and Records Administration, and many European archives, are currently exploring the possibility of integrating the information management and traditional archival approaches. There is no reason why archivists should not involve themselves in the life cycle of administrative records, with the end view of transferring records worthy of permanent preservation to a specialist archive, where they can be consulted in a neutral environment. There are plainly technical problems with respect to accessibility, but, as long as minimum standards and rules for documentation have been adhered to, these should not be insurmountable.

Before technological convenience is allowed to dictate how society uses new technologies, some basic questions about what archives are for need to be asked. If archivists are to make the transition to the electronic world successfully, they need to think fundamentally about the ends, as well as the means, that they are pursuing. Technology is only determinant if one allows it to be so.

References

'2020 Vision' edition (1994), *American Archivist*, 57.

Bearman, D. (1991*a*), 'An Indefensible Bastion: Archives as a Repository in the Electronic Age', in Bearman (1991*b*), 14–24.

—— (1991*b*) (ed.), *Archival Management of Electronic Records* (Pittsburgh).

—— (1993), 'The Implications of *Armstrong* v. *Executive Office of the President* for the Archival Management of Electronic Records', *American Archivist*, 56: 674–89.

—— (1994), *Electronic Evidence: Strategies for Managing Records in Contemporary Organizations* (Pittsburgh).

Campbell, T. M. (1989), 'Archives and Information Management', *Archivaria*, 28: 140–50.

Cook, C., and Keith, B. (1975), *British Historical Facts 1830–1900* (New York).

Deane, P., and Cole, W. A. (1969), *British Economic Growth 1688–1959* (Cambridge).

Dollar, C. M. (n.d.), 'Archivists and Record Managers in the Information Age', unpublished paper.

Ellis, S. (1995), 'The Background to the Development of the Archives' Policy', in Yorke (1995), 114–20.

Evans, F. B., Himly, F., and Walne, P. (1984), *Dictionary of Archival Terminology* (London).

Gill, S. L. (1988), *File Management and Information Retrieval Systems*, (New York).

Hannah, L. (1976), *The Rise of the Corporate Economy*, (London).

Hedstrom, M. (1995), 'Finders Keepers, Losers Weepers: Alternative Program Models for Identifying and Keeping Electronic Records', in Yorke (1995), 21–33.

Jenkinson, H. (1937), *A Manual of Archive Administration* (London).

Kampffmeyer, U. (1995), 'Is Time on your Side?' *Document Manager*, 3/2, 50–6.

McDonald, J. (1995), 'Managing Records in the Modern Office: The Experience of the National Archives of Canada', in Yorke (1995), 84–92.

Maxwell-Lyte, H. C. (1926), *The Great Seal* (London).

Posner, E. (1967), *Archives and the Public Interest* (Washington).

Public Record Office (1963), *Guide to the Contents of the Public Record Office*, i (London).

Skupsky, D. S. (1993), 'Establishing Retention Periods for Electronic Records', *Records Management Quarterly* (Apr.), 40–9.

Stuckey, S. (1995), 'The Australian Archives Policy on Electronic Records—the Technical Issues', in Yorke (1995), 121–32.

Yates, J. (1989), *Control through Communication: The Rise of System in American Management* (Baltimore).

Yorke, S. (1995) (ed.), *Playing for Keeps: The Proceedings of an Electronic Records Management Conference Hosted by the Australian Archives, Canberra, Australia, 8–10 November 1994* (Canberra).

Preserving Software in an Object-Centred Culture

DORON SWADE

ABSTRACT

Computer software is not yet an explicit part of the custodial mandate of the museum establishment and there is a growing alarm at the historical implications of this exclusion. The nature of software is philosophically problematic. In practical terms, a programme of acquisition and conservation is technically forbidding as well as resource intensive. This article attempts to locate software as an artefact in the material culture of museums and explores some of our preconceptions and expectations for a software preservation programme. It examines some respects in which software is both like and unlike traditional museum objects. It briefly considers the prospects for extending the operational life of obsolete systems through physical restoration as well as logical simulation.

Museums are part of an object-centred culture. Their essential justification is the acquisition, preservation, and study of physical artefacts. Physical objects, their meaning, significance, and care, dominate a curator's professional psyche. One of the first tasks, then, is to locate computer software in the artefactual landscape. Computer hardware, as a category of object, is seemingly unproblematic. It is the physical stuff of computer systems and falls painlessly into the custodial universe of conventional object-centred curatorship. Software, a term in general use by the early 1960s, is usually defined negatively—that is to say, a component of computer systems distinct from hardware. *The Oxford Dictionary of Computing* (1986: 352) defines software as 'a generic term for those components of a computer system that are intangible rather than physical'. *Prentice Hall's Illustrated Dictionary of Computing* (Nader 1992: 412) irreversibly severs the material link by noting that 'software is independent of the carrier used for transport'. The non-material features of software have ominous implications. The Science Museum's Corporate Plan for 1992–7 states that one of its core objectives is to 'acquire the most significant objects as physical evidence of science worldwide' (National Museum of Science and Industry 1992: p. vii). Physical objects are explicitly identified as the evidentiary medium. We have a prima-facie conflict. If what distinguishes software is something non-physical, and software is in some sense irreducibly abstract, then it falls outside the mandate of material culture, and a conscientious museum curator might have qualms about mobilizing resources to acquire and preserve it. The dilemma may seem pedantic. But there is a real issue: in whose custodial territory does software fall? Is it the responsibility of the archivist, librarian, or museum curator? Some software is already bespoke: archivists and librarians have 'owned' certain categories of electronic 'document'—digitized source material, catalogues, indexes, and dictionaries, for example. But what are the responsibilities of a museum curator? Unless existing custodial protection can be extended to include software, the first step towards systematic acquisition will have faltered, and a justification for special provision will need to be articulated *ab initio*, in much the same way as film and sound archives emerged as distinct organizational entities outside the object-centred museum establishment. The National Sound Archive (NSA), which became part of the British Library in 1983, opened in 1955 as the British Institute of Recorded Sound (Day 1981). The National Film Archive was founded in 1935 (Butler 1971).

One way of bypassing philosophical misgivings about the materiality of software is to appeal to the broader mandate of science museums to maintain a material record of technological change. Software represents a substantial human endeavour, and the intellectual, economic, and material resources involved in its production and distribution represent a major technological movement. Its importance is not in dispute. So perhaps we can bluff it out and collect software by day, leaving philosophical disquiet to the troubled night. In practical curatorial terms, the abstraction of software is, in any event, something of a pseudo-problem. We do not collect prime numbers or polynomials. We collect instead mathematical instruments, physical models, and the written deliberations of mathematicians. In much the same way, our curatorial concern for software centres on the external physical record—coding sheets, punched-paper tape, punched cards, flowcharts, manuals, magnetic disks, publicity literature, i.e. the distinct physical media of creation, representation, distribution, and storage. Floppy disks are often loosely referred to as 'software'. If the term 'software' is reserved for the abstract relational element of programs, then the floppy disk is strictly speaking not the software *per se* but the physical medium of record. Solid-state read-only memory chips (ROMs) containing programs and data are often referred to as 'firmware', which at first sight seems to occupy some middle ground between hardware and software. However, the ROMs are still strictly speaking no more than a more permanent physical medium of record for software, and, like floppy disks, should be kept distinct from the relational element of the information they contain. So we could perhaps make a case for offering curatorial protection to artefactual software by regarding it as part of the contextual and functional extension of hardware without which technical history would be incomplete.

But the lump under the carpet is still visible. Once we grant ourselves the licence to collect the physical artefacts of software, there remain, at least at first sight, respects in which artefactual software is both like, and unlike, the archetypal museum object. There is the issue of permanence, and the related issue of artefactual identity. Objects decay, despite our best efforts to conserve them. In the conventional acquisition model, physical deterioration does not apparently affect the identity of the object. The brass telescope remains a brass telescope notwithstanding inevitable degeneration. We refer to a rusted telescope as a 'rusted telescope' or, more impressively, 'telescope, condition poor'. The time scale of its degeneration does not seem to threaten its identity as a telescope—that is to say, its physical deterioration is sufficiently slow to support the illusion of permanence. That it is a telescope seems not to be at risk. Ultimately when time reduces our prized telescope to some orphaned lenses adrift in a little heap of metallic oxide we sadly shake our heads over the debris and say 'this was a telescope', or, in Python-esque terms, 'this is an ex-telescope'.

Magnetic media, the most common means of information storage for machine-readable software and data, are notoriously impermanent. Banks, required to retain computer records for audit purposes, were advised in the USA in the early 1980s that no archived magnetic medium over three years old should be regarded as reliable. Posterity stretches ahead without limit. In contrast, disk and tape manufacturers, when they are prepared to commit at all, are reluctant to do so for more than a few years. There is a fundamental incompatibility between the life expectancy of magnetic media and the long-term custodial needs of museums. Jeff Rothenberg (1995) cites two separate life-expectancy figures for various storage media (magnetic audio tape, video tape, magnetic disk, and optical disc). The two figures cited for each medium are 'physical lifetime' and 'time until obsolete'. In the case of optical disk, 'physical lifetime' is estimated at ten years and 'time until obsolete' at thirty years. So even the most durable of our current 'permanent' media offer storage durations that qualify as ephemeral when measured against the archaeological time scales of our custodial ambitions.

What are a curator's responsibilities? At the centre of curatorial practice is an inventory procedure. This procedure formally transfers the 'title' of the object from the donor/lender/vendor to the museum. Each inventoried object is the direct responsibility of a named curator, the collecting officer, who signs a formal declaration of responsibility for each object when it is acquired. 'I hereby take responsibility for the objects described overleaf', is the forbidding form. An object once inventoried is subject to formidable safeguards against disposal and unqualified alteration. In museum culture, the physical integrity of an inventoried object is sacrosanct, and the act of inventorying marks its transition into protective custody. In what sense can a curator, the official custodian of the object's integrity, responsibly sign the acquisition declaration knowing full well that there is no guarantee that a floppy disk or tape will be readable in a few years, even if pampered with executive-class conservation treatment—acid-free packing, humidity- and temperature-controlled environment, and low ambient light levels? While magnetic media are, in general, demonstrably more robust than worst-case fears indicate, it is only worst-case life-expectancy figures that can responsibly be adopted in the context of systematized software archiving. Thirty-year-old magnetic tapes have been successfully read at the Science Museum, London. The 35 mm tapes were created on an Elliott 803 discrete component germanium transistor computer dating from 1963. This computer was restored to working order and original tape stock read on the original hardware. The tapes, stored in metal canisters, were stowed in an unregulated garage environment for many years without any special conservation measures taken. In the personal-computer (PC) context, material written to floppy disks over ten years ago is commonly still usable. It is worth bearing in mind that storage conditions (for example, temperature or humidity) have a significant effect on the physical lifetime of media (van Bogart 1995).

The acknowledged impermanence of the medium leads to the question of artefactual identity. Is a set of floppy disks for Windows 1.0, say, like the telescope with an identity that transcends its state of repair? If the information content, represented by the magnetic configuration of the disk coating, is what makes a set of disks Windows, then does 'Windows 1.0, condition poor' mean anything? If the magnetic configuration of a disk is the determinant of the object's identity, then this identity is no less ephemeral than the magnetic information, itself impermanently stored. In more practical terms, does meaningful collection of software imply a functionally intact copy with the promise or potential of running it? If so, then we have at least one clear respect in which artefactual software, acquired in accordance with the canons of conventional museum practice, differs from software acquired for archival purposes (Bearman 1987). We do not ask 'functional intactness' of the telescope. 'Telescope, broken' does the job.

We can perhaps draw a useful analogy with pharmaceutical products. I learn from my medical sciences colleagues that the Science Museum has recently placed some proprietary drugs on inventory. Panadol, say, is now an inventoried object. There is valuable cultural information in the physical artefact: tablet form, blister-pack press-through dispenser, advertising imagery used in the logo and packaging, and information to decode about consumer appeal. But we can be reasonably sure that the drug company will not guarantee the potency of the sample beyond its sell-by date. We are clearly acquiring Panadol at least partly as a cultural artefact on the understanding that its chemical infrastructure and therefore its potency are ephemeral. In museological terms, Panadol does not cease to be Panadol when it is no longer chemically potent. Similarly, the centuries-old 'poison-tipped arrow' remains so-called, though the likelihood of any residual toxin is remote. Is the Windows disk like Panadol? Apart from the facetious difference that the one gives headaches which the other alleviates, there are strong similarities. 'Potency' in both cases is not visually meaningful. Function is not manifest in external form. Further, the Windows disks are no less a vehicle for contextual and technical messages than the Panadol pack: symbolism and imagery in brand logos and packaging, quality of label print, physical size, soft or hard sectored, whether or not factory write-protected, presence of reinforcing ring, and so on. The disks are informative as generic objects (media) as well as conveying product-specific information about Windows. However, the richness as a cultural object of a deteriorated Windows 1.0 disk pack is cold comfort to an archivist or historian preoccupied with preserving or regenerating the operational environment of the product. So we return to the question of functional intactness.

Software we know is 'brittle'. It degrades ungracefully. We are all familiar with the awful consequences of what in information terms may be a trivially small corruption. One bit wrong and the system crashes. There are, however, situations in which the value of magnetically stored information is not bit-critical. Disks used as storage media for textual data, as distinct from programs, provide one example. Parchment deteriorates, leaving us with partial or fragmentary records. Like the parchment example, a progressively corrupt magnetic record is simply a partial record but a usable record none the less. The residual data are not deprived of meaning or access by partial corruption. The 'all-or-nothing' fears do not in this case apply, and we may be encouraged to re-examine whether there is some give in the apparently uncompromising need for bit-perfect records of program software.

If we look at the effects of corruption on program performance, we can identify three broad categories. Non-critical corruption covers situations in which unused portions of the program are compromised—unused print drivers, irrelevant utilities or subroutines, for example. If we use a steam engine, say, as an example of a conventional museum object, 'non-critical corruption' would correspond to the damage to an unused or non-critical part—a nut dropping off, a dented panel. Damage in this case does not compromise the primary function, that of producing traction. Critical corruption leading to evident malfunction is a second category—the system hangs, the cursor freezes, the operating system fails to boot, or the program produces obvious gibberish. In our steam-locomotive comparison, the engine loses traction, or makes an explosive noise and stops. So far the comparison with physical machines works. The third and most worrying category is critical corruption that produces non-evident errors—a maths program that produces an incorrect numerical result, a database manager that cross-labels data records, for example. Comparison with the stalled steam engine is not obvious. Perhaps a closer analogy would be with a telescope that misrepresented what we were looking at. The distant unsighted object is a church steeple. But, observed through our telescope (condition, good), it produces the image of a mosque. There is a representational dimension to a great deal of software which renders correspondences between reference and referent vulnerable to a different class of derangement—misrepresentation. It is the possibility of non-evident critical corruption that makes it prudent to conclude that, if archived program software is to be run, the need for bit-perfect records is uncompromising.

If the medium of issue is magnetic, then the indefinite maintenance of bit-perfect records commits us to an active program of periodic renewal and integrity checking, or a one-off transfer to a more permanent medium (Thorvaldsen 1992). Thorvaldsen, formerly of the Norwegian National Archives, reports on integrity checks on archived tapes being carried out every two years and routine transfer to new tape stock every five years. Engineering instinct favours retaining the medium and format of issue to ensure compatibility with the original hardware. Transferring software to a more permanent storage medium—optical disc, for example—offers a tempting liberation from the fate of perpetual periodic renewal. However, the interdependence of hardware and software poses formidable technical difficulties to running programs so transferred. Machine-independent software is frequently anything but. Correct operation of applications software relies more often than not on particular revisions of system software, program patches, hardware upgrades, firmware revisions, and machine-dependent interfacing to peripherals. Transferring to an alternative medium requires new data formats yet to be standardized, and dependence on a new generation of hardware to read or download stored information. Interfacing to these devices and executing code so stored is not straightforward. Transfer to a more permanent medium is not without penalty, despite its promise of releasing Sisyphus from his fate in the copying room.

The requirement for functional intactness of software not only entails the maintenance of bit-perfect records but also implies the provision at some time of operational contemporary hardware or a functional equivalent. Neither the provision of contemporary hardware nor a functional equivalent is trivial. In 1989 the Science Museum, with the British Computer Society, founded the Computer Conservation Society, which is dedicated to the restoration and preservation of historic computers, and to the capture of the operational know-how of computing machines. The Society has had signal success in restoring to working order a Ferranti Pegasus, a large vacuum-tube machine dating from 1958 (Fig. 13.1), and an Elliott 803, a discrete component germanium transistor machine dating from 1963. At best such ventures can extend the operational life of obsolete systems. The life expectancy of the Pegasus, for example, has been extended by an estimated five to ten years. But, however successful these endeavours, we have to accept the eventual demise of such systems. The intractable fact of the matter is that, in terms of archaeological time scales, the operational continuity of contemporary hardware cannot be assured, even when suitable specimens

Fig. 13.1 Ferranti Pegasus vacuum tube computer (1958) restored to working
order at the Science Museum, London

are available to begin with. What meaning, then, does an archive of
bit-perfect program software have if the material cannot be run?

One way forward presently being explored by the Computer Conservation Society is to simulate early hardware on present-generation
computers using the restored original as a benchmark. Two simulations
are well advanced, one for the Pegasus, the other for a German Enigma
cypher machine. In the case of the Pegasus, console switches, console
oscilloscope traces, input/output peripherals (paper tape, teletype-style
printers) are visually simulated in facsimile and animated on-screen
(compare Fig. 13.2 with Fig. 13.3). The operator can write, run, and
debug programs by 'driving' the simulated controls, and the simulator
responds appropriately, even to the extent of execution times. The
original storage medium for Pegasus software is paper tape, and surviving software libraries have been captured and preserved on modern
hardware by interfacing to contemporary optical tape readers, and
storing the programs in a form that can be executed by the simulator.

The museological implications of such simulations are intriguing. An
implicit tenet of museum life is that the original object is the ultimate
historical source. In museum culture the original physical artefact is

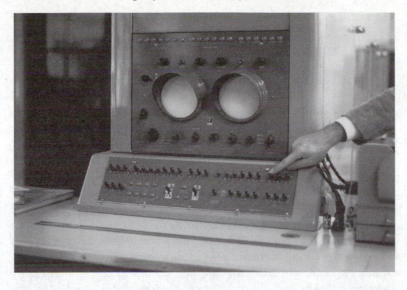

Fig. 13.2 Engineer's console of the Ferranti Pegasus

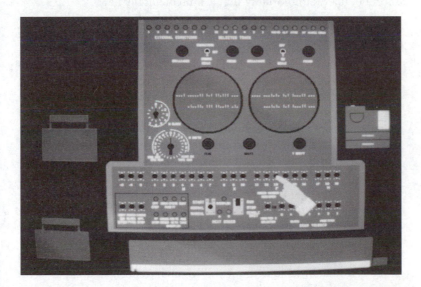

Fig. 13.3 Simulation of the Ferranti Pegasus

venerated at the expense of a replica, duplicate, reconstruction, or hologram. If we wished to test a new theory about Napoleon's allergy to snuff, say, it would not make sense to examine replicas of Napoleon's clothing, even contemporary lookalikes. Prior to the snuff-allergy hypothesis, snuff content would not be a consideration in the making of a garment replica. Only the original artefact with authenticated provenance would suffice for this forensic purpose. Physical replicas can incorporate only features and characteristics perceived to be significant at the time of replication, and part of the justification for preserving original objects in preference to a copy is that the original can be interrogated in an open-ended way in the light of unforeseen enquiry (Swade 1991). Physical replicas are inherently limited as historical sources for practical as well as for psychological reasons. However, logical replication seems to offer more. Capturing the operational persona of an early machine on a later machine promises possibilities for open-ended analysis of the kind formerly offered only by a working original. As computer languages used for the simulations become increasingly machine-independent, the simulation program, which embodies the logical and functional identity of the original machine, can be migrated from one generational platform to the next. The technique seems to offer a form of logical immortality that is museologically new.

The resource implications of a meaningful software acquisition programme are formidable. However persuasively we argue to include software in the existing fold of custodial protection, the need for the special provision of resources cannot be evaded. The maintenance of bit-perfect records requires an open-ended commitment to periodic copying and checking. This requires staff and equipment. The transfer of program software to optical media invokes a raft of technical issues of operational compatibility that would require a prohibitively large (for a museum with a conventional mandate) engineering and hardware design investment to solve. The restoration and maintenance of contemporary hardware on an indefinite basis demand vast financial resources, and the opportunity cost is likely to be politically indefensible. The development of simulations and emulations is technically promising, but the necessary skills levels are high, and the financial implications of programming, development, and verification are substantial. The progress made in this field at the Science Museum would have been unaffordable without the voluntary efforts and expertise of the Computer Conservation Society's members. In custodial terms, even a successful simulation exercise does no more than transfer the operational persona of a historic early machine to a currently support-able platform which will itself be duly subject to generational obsoles-cence. The potential of the technique lies not in the immortality of current hardware but in the prospect of machine-independent software. But the Utopia of machine independence may not ultimately appear on the custodial atlas of the future. In the meanwhile, simulation buys time and allows us to pass the baton to the next generation, which may well have to face similar problems.

Despite the formidable obstacles that face a fully-fledged software preservation programme, there is at least one modest but significant programme of software acquisition that is technically achievable and that has affordable resource implications—namely, software for PCs—'shrink-wrapped' consumer software, as well as custom-written special applications software. Acquiring working specimens of significant volume-production PCs since 1977, and their variant upgrades, is still a realistic acquisition objective. The technical skills required to recom-mission, repair, and maintain such machines are still available, and there is still time to reach back into the past and trawl relevant examples into the present. The complementary task is to identify and acquire significant examples of contemporary consumer software, from Visi-Calc (an early spreadsheet package for the Apple II, available in 1979) and Electric Pencil (a word-processing package for the Tandy Model I, 1978), through to the latest release of DOS (Disk Operating System) and Windows for present-day PCs. The acquisition of these products can be accomplished with existing resources. Recommissioning the hardware, copying onto fresh stock, and documenting the operational quirks of the systems would require additional but affordable technical support. Once established, the 'archive' will be relatively easy to keep updated—by purchasing off-the-shelf current software products and contemporary hardware. In the absence of an independently resourced organization with a specific brief to preserve systems and applications software, this acquisition programme represents one practical step we can take. In overall archival terms, the venture is no more than a holding operation. Perhaps the cavalry will still arrive in time.

References

Bearman, D. (1987), 'Collecting Software: A New Challenge for Archives and Museums', *Archival Informatics Newsletter and Technical Report*, 1/2 (Pitts-burgh, Pa.), 1–15, 36–42.

Butler, I. (1971), *'To Encourage the Art of the Film': The Story of the British Film Institute* (London).

Day, T. (1981), 'Sound Archives and the Development of the BIRS, Recorded Sound', *The Journal of the BIRS*, 80: 121.

Nader, J. C. (1992), *Prentice Hall's Illustrated Dictionary of Computing* (London).

National Museum of Science and Industry (1992), *Corporate Plan 1992–1997: The Next Five Years* (London).

Oxford Dictionary of Computing (Oxford, 1986).

Rothenberg, J. (1995), 'Ensuring the Longevity of Digital Documents', *Scientific American* (Jan.): 26.

Spiegel, J. van der (1996), 'ENIAC-on-a-Chip', *Penn Printout*, 12/4: 7.

Swade, D. D. (1991), 'Napoleon's Waistcoat Button: Modern Artifacts and Museum Culture', *Museum Collecting Policies in Modern Science and Technology* (London).

Thorvaldsen, G. (1992), 'The Preservation of Computer Readable Records in Nordic Countries', *History and Computing*, 4/3: 211–27.

van Bogart, J. W. (1995), *Magnetic Tape Storage and Handling: A Guide for Libraries and Archives* (Washington: Commission on Preservation and Access).

Electronic Information and the Functional Integration of Libraries, Museums, and Archives

W. BOYD RAYWARD

ABSTRACT

The increasing availability in electronic form of information generally and of new kinds of information more particularly will lead to a redefinition and integration of the different categories of 'information' organizations. Traditionally these have been created to manage different formats and media such as print and its surrogates (libraries), objects (museums), and the paper records of organizational activity (archives and records repositories). Differences in organizational philosophy, function, and technique have arisen from the exigencies presented by these different formats and media. These exigencies no longer apply in the same way when there is a common electronic format. It is clear that, if electronic sources of information are to be effectively managed for future access by historians and others, differences between libraries, archives, and museums will largely have to disappear and their different philosophies, functions, and techniques integrated in ways that are as yet unclear.

INTRODUCTION

The thesis of this chapter is that the advent of electronic sources of information and their ever-increasing volume and variety will require a major redefinition and integration of the role of archives, museums, and research libraries. It is my view that the distinctions between all of these apparently different types of institutions will eventually make little sense, though we can anticipate continuing turf battles between the professional groups that manage them as we get to this point. Moreover,

some of the functions typical of these institutions will be performed—
are already being performed—by other players in the information
generation and dissemination game, especially publishers, networks,
data archives, and various kinds of information brokers.

New kinds of functional realignments between the agencies involved
with electronic information sources, and a new approach to understanding the kind of market in which they operate, are needed. Until
the fact of these realignments is accepted and understood, until the
integration of the roles and functions of libraries and archives especially
is accepted, we will not be able properly to come to grips with the
information needs of historians. These and other scholars need access to
more information in electronic form than is currently available through
commercial and non-commercial services of various kinds. Problems
created by new kinds of information and the possibilities of new kinds
of information access and manipulation for scholarly purposes will not
be solved. The key issues are the impact of new electronic technologies
on the custodial, keeping, archival role of 'collecting' institutions such
as museums, libraries, and archives and the increasing availability of
information sources in electronic form.

THE TRADITIONAL COLLECTING INSTITUTIONS

In the past the distinctions between libraries, museums, and archives
rested on the formats of the typical artefacts that were in their care.
Specialized techniques were required to manage these different formats.
Libraries and librarianship have been centred on the acquisition of
printed books and journals, or surrogates of them such as microfilm.
To manage the collections that they created, librarians have developed
special techniques for cataloguing, classification, and physical arrangement of these materials. In addition, extensive and often complicated
systems of bibliographic control, backed up by interlibrary lending
procedures, have been devised to provide 'intellectual' and physical
access to what has not been acquired.

Modern librarianship has tended to stress the importance of the
library as an access mechanism because of the volume, complexity, and
cost of the information sources which fall within the purview of libraries
but which no one library, no matter how great a research collection it
aspires to acquire, can hope to obtain. Though librarians talk of information storage and retrieval as their *raison d'être*, they usually do not tell

an enquirer what he or she might want to know: they provide texts or locations for texts that might be useful in a particular case. They perform their professional functions by identifying and retrieving whole or parts of recorded texts that are held in their own collections or in the collections of other libraries to which they have access. The texts are printed and written collections of books, manuscripts and personal papers, for example. They may also be images derived from collections of documentary photographs, maps, prints, or pictures.

The research library in particular has a clear archival function. It preserves texts over time against possible future uses. The size and comprehensiveness of its collections set it apart from other kinds of libraries and provide the basic criteria for its usefulness to many kinds of scholars. Such libraries are literally documentary archives.

In another sense they are also museums of printed or written artefacts, though this notion seems more appropriate to the rare and other special materials that they contain in an original format. The parts of their collections in print-surrogate form, such as microfilm, would not normally be seen to have the kind of artifactual value that typically attaches to museum objects. Nevertheless, most research libraries functioning to this extent as museums, segregate certain items in their collections for special treatment, including exhibition or display. These items are usually books and manuscripts whose texts, illustrations, and binding are important examples of the book arts. They may also be considered rare, valuable, or 'curious' for other reasons, as might be the case of books with foredge paintings or a collection of miniature books. The texts of these items are of secondary—or of no—interest. It is their artefactual importance as 'codicological' printed or manuscript objects that counts. Another major category of these special materials comprises items whose physical characteristics provide important evidence for the scholarship centred on the texts—the province of analytical bibliographers and others concerned with establishing the authenticity of texts and patterns of textual transmission, for example. While these texts, like any texts, are readily reproducible in microfilm or electronically, for example, there are scholarly needs for access to the physical documents as such.

In general, however, the major functionality required of the library is to retrieve the texts in its own or other collections so that the texts can be read or consulted. Except in the instances outlined above, the form in which the text is made available, apart from convenience of consultation, is not an issue. Original book or journal or microfilm or electronic versions are equally acceptable. In libraries, collections of images, such as photographs or print and picture collections, are usually not permanently exhibited but form part of the stored collections of the library and are retrieved and consulted in the same way as other texts.

The objects collected by museums theoretically have no limit. There are natural history, science and technology, and ethnographic museums; there are museums of musical instruments, costumes, furniture, and household equipment, maritime and railway museums. Aquaria and botanical gardens are 'living' museums; national and regional art galleries are museums.

Museums are identified by their commitment to the collection, storage, and educative display of physical, three-dimensional, objects which are in some way representative of the classes of objects, the genera and species, to which they belong. The major use to which the museum puts the objects in its collection is exhibition. They are typically 'viewed'. Nowadays, touring 'blockbuster' exhibitions or special temporary exhibitions for which items are borrowed are important aspects of the work of many museums, especially art galleries.

Most museums have an important research function. This typically involves identifying, acquiring, and processing the objects that fall within a particular museum's ambit. It also underpins the museum's display activities and informs the labelling of items and the special guides to collections or catalogues produced for exhibitions. Depending on the nature of the material, this research function is usually carried out by a permanent staff of specialist personnel such as ethnographers, palaeontologists, archaeologists, art historians, and so on. In terms of their permanent collections, whether in storage or on permanent display, museums may be considered in a general way to be archives or libraries of objects or specimens. They preserve objects as evidence of the past.

Traditionally, archives collect the records that government and other organizations create as part of their day-to-day operation. Special techniques have been required to appraise what is often the vast bulk of these records in which individual items are of relatively little predeterminable value—although, subsequently, identification of such items may well be crucial for the research of a particular investigator—to determine what will be retained and for how long. However, as Bearman observes, unlike the case of bibliographic material in libraries, 'when we accession, transfer, arrange, weed, document and inventory archival material we change their character as well as enhance their evidential and informational value. The fact of processing, exhibiting, citing, publishing and otherwise managing records becomes a significant fact in their meaning as records, which is not true of library materials' (Bearman 1992: 10)—but may well be true of museum objects.

The anchor of modern archival science is the principle of provenance or *respect des fonds*, the identification of the agency creating the records essentially in terms of its institutional relationships and the maintenance of the integrity of the body of records as originally created (Gavrel 1990). This is not dissimilar to the extension that librarians have had to make to what once seemed the relatively simple idea of the author of a book or article which has now become 'primary responsibility' for a 'work'. Because of the nature of the activities of government and other organizations, traditionally archives have contained much library-like material as well as many museum-like objects—maps, printed documents, photographs, motion pictures, sound recordings, architectural models, and so on. Unlike libraries and museums, these items are acquired as part of the records that document a particular activity, function, or responsibility of the creating body.

AN UNDIFFERENTIATED PAST

It is clear that modern libraries, museums, and archives are different mainly because of the nature of the materials for which they have primary responsibility and because of the ways in which they provide for the educative and research uses of these materials. The emergence of their specialized functions can be traced in modern times from the previously undifferentiated collections of books and objects of seventeenth- and eighteenth-century rulers, aristocrats, and scholars. In England at the time of the great intellectual movement that began with Bacon and was fuelled by the Puritan rebellion, many scholars and divines speculated about how knowledge of God's creation might be more effectively advanced and disseminated than in the past. For the circle of reformers that surrounded Samuel Hartlib, for example, the advancement of learning required the creation of a centrally located complex of new kinds of institutions. These would undertake, when appropriate, the systematic collection of antiquities, items of natural history and books and manuscripts. In this complex of institutions would be found scientific colleges and societies, herbaria, laboratories, workshops, and specialized information bureaux called Offices of Publick Addresse which would function in association with new kinds of professionalized library services (Webster 1975; Rayward 1994*a*).

The cabinets of curiosities, so much a feature of the households of gentlemen of the period, reflected not only an interest in what was rare, valuable, and out of the ordinary but, as Hudson (1988: 21) has pointed out, also an acute, eager interest in the natural world. There was little of the division between the sciences and humanistic disciplines so widespread today. All learning was seen as having a fundamental unity, ultimately deriving from religion. 'Curiosity' and 'antiquarian' were terms widely in use then with strongly positive connotations. They have acquired in recent times a more restricted, in the latter case indeed a pejorative meaning, that they did not have in this earlier period. What was important was the acquisition of whatever artefacts—books or objects—were appropriate to the social status, world view, and broad, multi-disciplinary intellectual interests of these individuals. No real distinction of library and museum, nor, at another level, of personal from government papers, was contemplated.

Thus, towards the end of the seventeenth century, the Ashmolean Museum at Oxford, reflecting John Tradescant's Closet of Curiosities in which it had originated, consisted among other things of collections related to natural history and antiquities, a library, and a chemical laboratory (Hudson 1988: 21). Some seventy years later, Sir Hans Sloane's great collection, the basis of the British Museum, 'contained specimens of plants, animals, birds, fossils, minerals, as well as antiquities, works of art, coins, books and ethnographical materials' (Hudson 1975: 18). It is only today that the final separation of the library from other parts of the British Museum, set up by Act of Parliament in 1753, is occurring, though the natural history collections were removed to South Kensington in 1857. It should also be noted that the other foundation collections for the Museum were the extensive manuscript collections of Sir Robert Cotton and the earl of Oxford, Robert Harley, which contained large and important collections of state papers and other archives, along with the library of George III which came to the Museum in 1827 (Miller 1974).

An interesting expression of the early complementary relationship of library and museum was the Charleston Library Society. Created in South Carolina in 1748, its collections contained scientific instruments as well as books, and it lent both to its members. In 1773 it initiated an appeal for natural-history specimens and in a few years it had amassed 'an extensive collection of Beasts, Birds, Reptiles, Fishes, Warlike Arms, Dresses and other Curiosities'. This became the nucleus of the collections of what was described in the mid-nineteenth century as 'one of the best museums in the United States' (Hudson 1975: 32–3).

The point being made here is simple and perhaps obvious. It is that the functional differentiation of libraries, museums, and archives as reflected in different institutional practices, physical locations, and the specialist work of professional cadres of personnel is a relatively recent phenomenon. This functional differentiation was a response to the exigencies of managing different kinds of collections as these have grown in size and have had to respond to the needs and interests of an ever-enlarging body of actual and prospective users. It does not reflect the needs of the individual scholar or even the member of the educated public interested in some aspect of learning or life. For the individual, the ideal is still the personal cabinet of curiosities that contains whatever is needed for a particular purpose or to respond to a particular interest, irrespective of the nature of the artefacts involved—books, objects, data, personal papers, government files.

How to regain this functional integrity has been an implicit theme in speculations over the recent centuries about how to mobilize the growing knowledge that is potentially available in the service of society, if only a firm enough grip could be taken on it. Hartlib's Office of Publick Addresse, Leibniz's Encyclopedia, Otlet's Office of Documentation and Palais Mondial, Wells's World Brain all imply distress at, or explicitly lament, the problems of complexity and dispersion created by the ever-escalating growth of knowledge. Each represents a special suggestion for a single institutional framework within which the world of learning might be encompassed and better managed (Rayward 1994*a*).

'INFORMATION-AS-THING' AND ITS ELECTRONIC REPRESENTATION

The distinction between 'information-as-thing' and its electronic representation is found in an important paper by Michael Buckland. Buckland suggests that the institutional arrangements of libraries, museums, archives, and the like are concerned with 'information-as-thing', things which are informative, which constitute evidence which 'could change one's knowledge, one's beliefs, concerning some matter' (Buckland 1991: 353). He seeks to reintroduce into the analysis of information and information systems the extended notion of 'document' formulated by Paul Otlet at the turn of the century in Europe and accepted by the English and European 'documentalists' (Buckland 1991*b*; Otlet 1991), a notion that reaches across institutional distinctions.

Buckland observes that:

information storage and retrieval systems can only deal directly with 'information-as-thing', but the things that can be stored for retrieval in actual or virtual collections vary in significant ways. Historic buildings, films, printed books, and coded data impose different constraints on the tasks associated with information retrieval systems: selection, collection, storage, representation, identification, location, and physical access. Put simply, a museum, an archive, [a] library of printed books, an online bibliographic database, and a corporate management information system of numeric data can all be regarded as species of information retrieval system. But differences in their physical attributes affect how the stored items can be handled.   (Buckland 1991*a*: 359)

Increasingly, 'information-as-thing', as text, image, object, datum, specimen, record group, or file, is represented or representable electronically or indeed may be available only in that form. In so far as these electronic representations are adequate for a particular purpose, the physical distinctions between the different formats or media of record disappear. That is to say, digitization eliminates physical distinctions between types of records and thus, presumably, the need for institutional distinctions in the management of the systems within which these records are handled.

Modern telecommunications systems now make it of little concern to the individual researcher where the record he or she wishes to access is held—library, archive, museum, commercial database vendor, or any personal or institutional location on the Internet—provided only that what is wanted is available electronically. In effect he or she can at will create ever-changing virtual 'cabinets of curiosities' in which any kind of digitized document—text, image, or object—can be introduced and used. The kind of almost science fiction-like speculations of Paul Otlet, are now realizable practically (Rayward 1994*b*). Nevertheless, the information retrieval functions outlined by Buckland remain of the greatest importance, though they may be distributed institutionally in new and different ways that require urgent attention.

The fundamental question is: *what is to be collected, by whom, and under what circumstances of preservation, availability, and access.* This is not a new question. Modern libraries, archives, and museums represent historically determined, institutionalized answers to it. Now, however, answers to such a question are no longer certain. In so far as the media of the past continue to be centrally involved, there is little problem—books for libraries, objects for museums, and government and organizational records for archives. But the electronic versions of these media create problems as to who has responsibility for identifying and collecting them, preserving them physically, and maintaining systems of access to them. The new kinds of electronic information sources in their turn present even more pressing problems of this kind, because there is no real precedent for dealing with them.

PROBLEMS OF 'ELECTRONIFICATION'

Traditionally the library has served as a major intermediary between the publisher of bibliographic and substantive information and the scholar. An important function of the library has been to provide access to bibliographic services and to the journal and other literature represented in these services. As the publication of what were formerly printed materials—books and journals particularly—increasingly takes an electronic dimension, publishers and the brokers of on-line database services are exploring new ways of packaging and marketing this material. It is now possible for individuals quite independently of libraries to search bibliographic databases and to acquire copies of articles and reports and so on from databases held by commercial organizations. These organizations have entered the document-supply business, and their new services are intended to circumvent what they would consider to be the slowness cumbersomeness and inefficiency of traditional libraries. These bibliographic and document-supply services, however configured and labelled, are performing important 'library' functions, clearly recognizable though not usually acknowledged as such.

To what extent are these services based essentially on what is currently available and commercially practicable to supply at the moment? The complement to this question is the extent to which older, out-of-date, less-used parts of these electronic files will be effectively and permanently 'archived'. These issues have hardly become a problem yet, because most of the files now being dealt with cover a relatively short period of time. But in two or five or ten or fifty years, one may assume that the commercial organizations responsible at the moment for these services, given the rapidly increasing size of most of the files and assuming that the pace of technological change will continue unabated, are unlikely to want to preserve the files permanently in an always currently accessible database. Presumably the responsibility for the preservation and the provision of access to these files after their current commercial exploitability has passed will at some point be given over to what have hitherto been called libraries or data archives.

It may well be that libraries will enter the life cycle of formally published material of this kind, the knowledge food chain, if you will, at a later point than in the past. Less concerned with current availability than now because of the way in which commercial organizations have taken over this aspect of their work, they will become essentially archives of databases that no longer have current commercial viability. Critical in this electronic archival process will be the extent to which the files will have to be 'remastered' or converted for preservation and access, as system software and hardware change.

Museum collections have been undergoing similar processes of digital representation and transformation. In some cases, the traditional 'viewing' function that they have performed has been amplified by new kinds of information systems. In these systems, electronic representation of objects allows for manipulation, a more intimate, detailed, multidimensional inspection than is possible conventionally. It can also provide a variety of explanatory and/or analytic contexts for them. Museum information systems involve the enormously complex business of contextualizing and indexing and retrieving images. The systems use a variety of library-related or language-based techniques and graphical expert-system techniques. In 1988 it was suggested that there were 'almost 250 automated projects of various types . . . including databases for institutional collections, typological corpora and inventories of monuments' (Cawkwell 1992: 308). Multimedia or hypermedia applications—from museum tours to recreations of eighteenth-century Montreal to the exploration of Piero della Francesca's fresco *Legend of the True Cross* (Bearman 1991; Trant 1993)—pose special problems of storage and access beyond the occasion of their initial development and use as working databases. They are important electronic information sources about which typical 'library' decisions about collection, physical preservation, and the maintenance of access systems have to be made.

Similar decisions have to be made for the various manifestations of expert systems used in architecture, engineering, city planning, astronomy, and medicine, for example. They represent the status of specialist knowledge at a given time.

Apart from current use, they too have important archival value in documenting the development and history of the aspects of science and scholarship to which they relate. If they are routinely updated as new information comes to hand or if they go through various stages of development, unless 'copies' of earlier versions—'editions?'—are kept and 'archived', there will be an incomplete record of these developments, and potentially valuable historical information will be lost.

A similar 'edition' problem is presented by various reference databases that are constantly updated without new versions of the database being created. The information handled in this way knows theoretically no limit. It can be cartographic, economic, social and demographic, meteorological, and company and business related, for example. These databases are electronic versions of directories, handbooks, and other reference sources. They are regularly updated in traditional libraries by new editions and supplements, one coincidental function of which allows changes in the information presented over time to be tracked. Knowledge of such changes may be critically important for particular purposes. Of course, loose-leaf services present this same problem in the paper environment. Unless libraries implement some sampling procedure for these databases, important historical, developmental, time-series information will be lost.

Certain new forms of electronic 'information-as-thing' that have now to be brought within the set of functions that libraries, archives, and museums entail, present these problems in a particularly striking way. Like the databases mentioned above, electronic journals and hypertext systems contain text that may be regarded as unstable, as shifting in meaning as it accumulates commentaries, revisions, and interpolations. The hypertext document, it has been observed somewhat hyperbolically, 'functions as an elastic palimpsest allowing access to and reworking of layered texts'. For Davenport and Cronin, 'Hypertext may transform the practice and culture of science by opening up texts for comment and verification in ways which previously have been impossible' (Davenport and Cronin 1990). As texts shift and change and merge, not only are general questions raised about the responsibility of the author and the integrity and authority of the document, but practical issues of what parts or states of the text will be kept and how changes in it will be monitored and recorded become pressing. Perhaps this is an area to which archival appraisal techniques, which focus centrally on the evidential value and uses of records and are concerned as much with disposal as retention, may well be brought to bear.

The electronic office which utilizes an enormous range of software and hardware has dramatically affected the work of archivists. It epitomizes some of the major problems that are created by electronic information sources that originate in new processes of communication based on telecommunications and electronic networks. As Gavrel points out,

sophisticated systems provide access to a variety of software and hardware, as well as gateways to exterior information systems. In most cases, these systems do not have record management capabilities and documents can be destroyed voluntarily or involuntarily by the creators at any point in time. Naming conventions for documents are not standardised within organisations and the choice of document names is left to the creators of the documents.... The knowledge of file classification systems within a particular organisation is limited and documents are often given acronyms which may have meaning at the time of the creation of the document but usually not several weeks later and certainly have no meaning to others in the organisation. Most creators manage their documents within their own personal filing systems without reference to any corporate system or link to existing hard copy records within the organisation.   (Gavrel 1990, 18)

Gavrel notes that, while hitherto few documents related to policy development, programme management, and other organizational activities have been maintained in electronic form, with the development and use of more and more local area networks this can be expected to change. She also points out that many of the sources of information 'do not reside inside the organisation but are accessed by communication links or gateways outside the organisation' (ibid. 19). Not only, then, do the records have to be appraised and account taken of the particular problems of inter-organizational databases, but

it may also be necessary, to ensure that the archival record is complete, to preserve certain software and access records of the system. If certain records only existed for seconds on the screen, it may be important for the archivist to select, along with the records, the access logs for the system which identify by whom and when the system was accessed. The value of these logs will not be in the records themselves but in providing proof that certain systems were accessed at a particular time and by whom. In a similar vein, it will become important to retain certain software, particularly if decision-making processes are a fundamental part of the software.   (ibid. 22)

THE ARCHIVAL FUNCTION

It can be expected that archival records in electronic form make possible the use of indexing techniques that have been developed for more general applications. The principle of provenance or *respect des fonds* is essentially inadequate for all but the few users of archives who are interested in the nature of the organization that the record arrangements reflect. Most users are interested in general problems or topics on which they are seeking information. With records in electronic form, it should be possible instantly to recreate or change information about provenance to reflect shifting organizational alignments of functions and offices if this is required. The records themselves can be copied and manipulated in any way that available software allows; their original order should be capable of being regenerated automatically. It should be possible to search them for personal, corporate, or geographic names and by subjects either in full text mode or on text surrogates to the degree that such surrogates have been provided. Effectively the archive and the library become identical as bodies of text, though record volume in the archive, its 'legal, fiscal and operational need for evidence' (Bearman 1992), and the complexity and variability of record structures may remain a problem for the design of the data content of archival documentation and for information-retrieval techniques.

Equally appropriate for the application of archival techniques is the ever-changing list servers and electronic noticeboards available through the Internet (Samuel, Chapter 7, this volume). Who is to assume responsibility for the appraisal of these 'record groups' and the development of a permanent archive from them? This is an important conundrum, given the near universality and the informality of access that is possible to them. Are there to be special libraries or computer-based archives into which these 'records' will go. Certainly contemporary data archives pay no attention to them. How are the bulletin boards and list servers to be monitored, weeded, sampled, acquired, processed, and stored? Is it sufficient to leave this to chance, in the same way that in the past libraries have left to chance the collection of ephemeral materials that document social movements or other phenomena, relying not on their own collecting activities to ensure continuous contemporary coverage but on later bequests and donations? Is someone cumulating a special-interest file related to an issue or subject now being explored nationally or internationally through these Internet functions? In what form might this file come to a library?

This raises the more general problem of casually created files that might be of later value—what might be called a personal archive. In the past this took the form of drafts, sketches, notebooks, files of correspondence, all involving the creation of paper records whose preservation was often purely accidental. Libraries and archives have collected these 'personal papers' as an important part of their archival function. These personal records are now increasingly kept electronically on hard disks or downloaded onto floppy disks.

Managing access to the contents of these electronic files constitutes a far greater problem for libraries and archives than managing access to the contents of paper documents. The disks that contain the electronic files, like their paper counterparts, will be found in drawers and boxes and attics, either separately or as parts of machines (e.g. hard disks), at long periods after their creation, perhaps at long periods after the death of their authors and the obsolescence of the machines. In principle of the greatest value for biographers, historians, literary critics, and others, just as their paper counterparts were, they cannot be appraised visually as paper records can. They require software and hardware that so far has quickly been superseded and become obsolete. Thus with the passage of time these electronic records may not easily be converted from one format to another, if at all. All of the problems mentioned above in relation to the electronic office characterize such files. As industry standards become more widespread and inter-convertibility easier, some of these technical difficulties will lessen. Nevertheless, how to acquire these files and from whom, and how to manage them—above all how to read them—will constitute, are currently constituting, important challenges for the librarian and archivist. They will need access to museums of computer hardware and software that are supported by historical research collections of system documentation. These will be the tools with which technical specialists, who will function in effect as system archaeologists and cryptographers, will in the future decode the mysteries of 'found' electronic files.

It is becoming possible to replace paper materials with electronic versions which can be manipulated in various ways not possible in the original versions. As new kinds of high-volume scanning techniques and new kinds of cheap, high-density storage media emerge, it will be possible to capture electronically the text, the information content, of printed materials ever more quickly and cost effectively. Preservation and space problems that bedevil libraries attempting to manage huge paper collections might well then be obviated by electronic storage. The 'electronic' archive, representing runs of journals or large bodies of special materials—texts in the Short Title Catalogues, for example, or the correspondence and other papers of important historical or literary figures—may replace microfilm as the way to build up research collections. Such archives will become increasingly easy to create; they are readily duplicated and are certainly saleable.

It may be that for libraries, for example, the increasing volume of information available in electronic form may not only require them to redefine their archival function as discussed in this chapter it may also change their relationship to their traditional materials. If paper is largely replaceable for everyday library use by text in electronic form, then libraries will begin to view paper sources differently. Perhaps some of the paper-based sources will be for current casual use, to be replaced by electronic forms for preservation and storage. The analogy here is the cumulation on microfilm of the issues of newspapers and journals, the paper copies of which are then discarded when the microfilm copy becomes available. Other sources, as mentioned earlier, may have artistic, evidential, rarity, or exemplary value that electronic versions of text cannot replicate. These will tend to be relatively few in number, if past experience is anything to go by. What is fundamentally important about them is their physicality as books and manuscripts, and they become functionally little different from traditional museum objects. Thus libraries, because of the emphasis they place on the artifactual value of materials that are retained in that format, will begin to resemble museums. The question may well become: why would one wish to retain materials in printed form except for what they represent as artefacts if their texts can be cost-effectively transferred to electronic systems which provide better storage and access capabilities?

PRESERVING ACCESS TO DIGITAL INFORMATION IN LIBRARIES, MUSEUMS, AND ARCHIVES IN AUSTRALIA

In Australia there have been sustained attempts to find practical and policy-based answers to the questions raised in the preceding sections. In 1985 the Australian Council of Libraries and Information Services (ACLIS) created a Task Force on the Preservation of Australian Electronic Information, observing that 'the preservation of Australian information in electronic format will be the responsibility of Australian libraries, archives and possibly museums' (ACLIS 1992: 4). The work

of the ACLIS task force, with its limited approach and slow development, was eventually subsumed by a much more comprehensive and
far-reaching initiative. In March 1992, sponsored by the National
Library of Australia, a national conference, 'Towards Federation 2001:
Linking Australians with their Heritage' was held in Canberra. Its
purpose was to explore how to provide cooperatively across the range
of national heritage and other interested organizations improved access
to the Australian documentary heritage. One of its resolutions was 'that
the Australian Archives, the Australian Council of Library and Information Services (ACLIS), the National Preservation Office and the
National Film and Sound Archive establish a working party to develop
guidelines for the management of material in electronic format' (URL
http://www.nla.gov.au/dnc/tf2001/pr9496.B.html). The involvement of
the archive sector in this venture 'was identified as critical since the
issues were seen to be basically the same regardless of the nature of the
organization' (URL: http://www.nla.gov.au/dnc/tf2001/auccrep2.html).
The working party, known simply as PADI (Preserving Access to Digital
Information), now comprises as well as the organizations listed above
representatives of the Mathematical and Information Sciences Division
of the Commonwealth Scientific Industrial and Research Organization
(CSIRO), the Commonwealth Government's Department of Communications and the Arts, and the National Museum of Australia.

PADI's 'major goal' is 'providing mechanisms that will help ensure
that digital information is managed with appropriate consideration of
preservation and future access'. The Medium Term Plan, available only
in digital form through the World Wide Web, lists six objectives for the
working party:

- to facilitate the development of national strategies;
- to develop and maintain a Web site for information and promotion purposes;
- to establish a forum to exchange views;
- to develop preservation and access guidelines and strategies;
- to impact on preservation aspects of national digital information
  initiatives;
- actively to identify and promote relevant activities (URL: http://
  www.nla.gov.au/dnc/tf2001/medplan.html).

The Working Party has developed a range of strategies by which it hopes
to meet its objectives and each strategy is targeted at major players in

the game. 'While collecting institution, governments and the records management industry will remain the key players in PADI's activities, attempts will be made to involve universities, the information technology industry, publishers and creators of digital information, and commercial business sectors' (URL:http://www.nla.gov.au/dnc/tf2001/med plan.html). With funding from the Australian Vice Chancellor's Committee, in 1996 PADI commissioned a survey of 242 cultural bodies grouped as archives, galleries, libraries, museums and others 'to determine policies and procedures associated with the acquisition, production and preservation of Australian digital information. A Web site has also been established.'

PADI represents a coordinated, sophisticated policy initiative as well as a practical attack on the problems thrown up for the historian and other scholars by 'electronification' of information. Implicit in its work is a recognition that the boundaries between collecting organizations such as libraries, archives, and museums are now necessarily blurred, as has been argued in this chapter. It is clear that the active involvement of representatives of all of these kinds of organizations is necessary in the search for solutions that will allow appropriately managed preservation of electronic information for the future.

CONCLUSION

It is clear that the availability of increasing volumes of information in electronic form and the emergence of new kinds of electronic information sources are presenting critical professional challenges for librarians and other 'information professionals'. How they meet these challenges will determine how the institutions under their care respond to the needs of historians and other scholars for the sources they need to fulfil their scholarly roles and responsibilities. Being able to respond to these challenges effectively will largely depend on how well these 'information professionals' are able to transcend the limitations that their highly developed professional cultures impose upon them. These professional cultures have defined themselves to some extent in opposition to each other, and personnel influenced by them necessarily tend to see the world differently. Libraries, archives, and museums are agencies that represent institutionalized organizational practices that the different professional cultures have evolved and sanctioned. The key element around which the cultural differences have crystallized has been the different kinds of artefacts for which historically the different professional groups have assumed responsibility.

At least for the foreseeable future each of the professional groups will still have to continue to deal—perhaps preponderantly—with its 'traditional' materials. Thus there is no reason to suggest that differences between them will cease to exist and that we must envisage their complete amalgamation in the near future. Nevertheless, the argument of this chapter is that 'electronification' can be dealt with adequately only by questioning and rising above traditional modes of territorial demarcation between these groups, and this is beginning to happen. To the extent that they are having to deal with the same kinds of 'thing'—electronic records—we must begin to explore the idea of functional integration between the agencies—libraries, archives, and museums—that are responsible for collecting and managing the public's access to them. In this way we will be able to secure a future for historians and others in an increasingly electronic past.

References

ACLIS (1992): Australian Council of Libraries and Information Services, Task Force on the Preservation of Australian Electronic Information, 'The Need for the Preservation of Australian-Created Electronic Information: A Position Paper' (unpublished draft circulated for information; Canberra: ACLIS).

Bearman, D. (1991) (ed.), *Hypermedia and Interactivitvy in Museums: Proceedings of an International Conference* (Pittsburgh).

—— (1992), 'Documenting Documentation', *Archivaria*, 34 (Summer).

Buckland, M. (1991*a*), 'Information as Thing', *Journal of the American Society of Information Science*, 42: 351–60.

—— (1991*b*), *Information and Information Systems.* (New York).

—— (1992), *Redesigning Library Services: A Manifesto* (Chicago).

Cawkwell, A. E. (1992), 'Imaging Systems and Picture Collection Management: A Review', *Information Services and Use*, 12: 301–25.

Davenport, E., and Cronin, B. (1990), 'Hypertext and the Conduct of Science', *Journal of Documentation*, 46: 175–92.

Gavrel, K. (1990), *Conceptual Problems Posed by Electronic Records: A RAMP Study.* (Paris: General Information Programme and UNISIST, Unesco).

Hudson, K. (1975), *A Social History of Museum* (London).

—— (1988), *Museums of Influence* (Cambridge).

Miller, E. (1974), *That Noble Cabinet: A History of the British Museum* (Athens, Oh.).

Otlet, P. (1991), *The International Organisation and Dissemination of Knowledge: Selected Papers of Paul Otlet*, ed. and trans. W. Boyd Rayward (Amsterdam).

Rayward, W. Boyd (1994*a*), 'Some Schemes for Restructuring and Mobilising Information in Documents: A Historical Perspective', *Information Processing and Management*, 30: 163–75.

——(1994*b*), 'Visions of Xanadu: Paul Otlet (1868–1944) and the History of Hypertext', *Journal of the American Society for Information Science*, 45: 235–50.

Trant, J. (1993), 'On Speaking Terms: Towards Virtual Integration of Art Information', *Knowledge Organisation*, 20: 8–11.

Webster, C. (1975), *The Great Instauration: Science, Medicine and Reform, 1626–1660* (London).

PART FOUR

The Practice of Preservation from the European Perspective

Research-Library Directions in the 1990s

LYNNE BRINDLEY

ABSTRACT

This chapter will consider the impact of the increasing availability of electronic information on major research libraries. It will raise issues such as the organization, integration, and management of research materials in a variety of formats—print, images, multimedia, and digital texts; the increasingly complex task of providing access to such information; and the requirements for training and support of readers. The need to rethink our concept of the research library in this wider information environment will be discussed. Relevant national developments from the UK higher education funding councils' Libraries Review and of the Joint Information Systems Committee will be assessed.

INTRODUCTION

'Humanists depend to a very considerable extent upon libraries, both in their own and other institutions, and upon a network of museums, galleries, and archives' (British Academy and British Library Research and Development Department 1993: 30). Indeed, the pattern of research work in the humanities and social sciences is such that perhaps the only generalization which can be made is that no article or book is written using only the resources of one library, still less the home library of a researcher's institution.

A not atypical list for anyone working in a history-related discipline has been outlined by Dr W. Ryan, Librarian of the Warburg Institute. As an active researcher, he uses, as well as his own research library, the libraries of the Institute of Historical Research, School of Slavonic and East European Studies, School of Oriental and African Studies,

University of London Library, British Library, Public Record Office, National Maritime Museum library, Society of Antiquaries library, British Library of Political and Economic Science, Bodleian Library, Taylorian Library, John Rylands Library, as well as libraries in Moscow, St Petersburg, and Helsinki. Obversely he comments that, whilst the History Department at Birkbeck College in London got a well-deserved five in the latest research-assessment exercise, neither the quality of the research nor its subject area could possibly be seen as being solely dependent on the strengths of the library of that college. On the other hand, Oxford received a three for Russian, despite having one of the best collections of Slavica in Western Europe (Ryan, pers. com.).

The British Academy and British Library report cited above also concerns itself with the growth in projects creating electronic resources in the humanities, and the increase in those wanting access to information electronically held. It mentions as well the growth of new ways of accessing information, from on-line public access catalogues (OPACs), through CD-ROMs and on-line searching, to the more recent network navigation tools.

Taken together, these observations highlight what is in my view perhaps the major challenge facing research libraries in the 1990s—namely, to develop a model whereby consultation of our cultural inheritance manifest in print and manuscript form can be beneficially combined, and handled conjunctly with, access to electronic information in a wide variety of forms. Getting the balance between these activities right and appropriate to changing academic needs, particularly in an era of severely constrained resources, will require skill, continuing dialogue between the library and its users, and imaginative collaborations.

TRENDS AFFECTING THE RESEARCH-LIBRARY ENVIRONMENT IN THE 1990S

It follows from the introduction that one can conceive of a university scholarly information resource infrastructure of the 1990s comprising several overlapping areas:

- the 'library' taken narrowly as the traditional collection of books, journals, and a wide range of other media, with its existing set of facilities, operations, and services;
- the 'library of the future' or the 'virtual library', taken broadly as the entire set of information resources and facilities, bringing in

other stakeholders, such as computing centres, media centres, film and data archives, museums, electronic information providers, and telecommunication networks; and

- the research library network, consisting of the entire set of national and research libraries and other kinds of information resources acting as a cooperative and integrated whole in support of scholarship.

A very major concern for the 1990s is the economics of research libraries, narrowly interpreted. Indeed it would not be an exaggeration to say that the pressures on the acquisition budget are almost certainly the most pernicious economic problem faced by academic research libraries today. Rates of inflation in journal prices threaten every other commitment of the acquisitions budget.

Another major economic concern is with the collections themselves—their storage, preservation, and the tools for physical access. Major research collections are still growing in the 1990s, even though probably at a slower rate than in the 1980s, so they require housing, and the collections of every major research library are in states of disintegration and embrittlement. Capital provision to support these two areas is scarce, and the 1990s have tested even the most supportive administrations to meet urgent demands for library extensions and preservation/substitution programmes, neither of which has been an established part of institutional budget-planning, nor likely to receive much more than sympathy from the funding councils, except perhaps in cases where enormous growth in student numbers have caused such pressures on space.

Libraries are also having to deal with costs incurred in new means of data access—indeed most libraries welcome the opportunities offered by the new media to extend access to information sources. However, lack of funding, which will force more hard choices between competing 'good causes', has been a major preoccupation of the 1990s, pitting disciplines against each other, libraries against other information providers, clashes with senior administrators, and so on.

As yet, the costs of electronic information sources represent a relatively minor part of a research library's budget. However, the funds require to be met from a virtually static budget. *University Statistical Record* figures indicate a decline in the financial priority of the library from 1980/1, when the library accounted for some 4 per cent of institutional expenditure, to 1989/90, when the expenditure was 2.89

per cent. Only to a limited extent are these new electronic services yet replacing specific print products. Indeed, the commercial aspirations of publishers are precisely to ensure additionality, not direct substitution for print in their pricing and packaging structures.

Moving to the 'library of the future', many libraries have long given up their comprehensive collecting aspirations: they purchase selectively and rely on access, for example, through interlending and document supply, and also on access to bibliographic and other electronic information sources. Just-in-time management philosophy has moved from manufacturing to the university-library sector. This approach requires very different kinds of investment, unlikely to save institutional funds overall, although it will shift funds towards areas such as networking infrastructure. Wide access to electronic information resources requires an investment and continuing reinvestment in information technology (IT), particularly in networking bandwidth, gateways to international networks, workstations at the desk, and public clusters in the library and elsewhere.

A US study (Hayes: n.d.) has indicated that on average a university spends 4 per cent of its budget on the library. A further 6 per cent is spent on computers, telecommunications, and other IT hardware and software. Hayes forecasts that up until the year 2000 the library proportion will remain stable at 4 per cent, but growth will occur in the IT proportion, rising to 11 per cent of the institutional budget. This implies an increasing shift to access services, based on experience of networked information delivery, with continued severe budget constraint on traditional material acquisition.

Most UK universities publicly aspire to such intensive provision—e.g. 1:1 ratio of workstations : academics, 1:4 for research students, and 1:10 and then 5 for undergraduates—but are finding the level of resources required to achieve and sustain such provision very difficult to engineer in an environment of devolved budgets and uneven 'soft-money' distribution. Research libraries and humanities departments should be natural allies in promoting equity of provision across disciplines and user groups.

The development of the 'virtual library' is causing some universities to re-examine their organizational structures to bring the range of stakeholders into a closer relationship. Whilst there is unlikely to be any prescriptive model of such a structure, organizational change will be a feature of the 1990s. An increasing number of universities are bringing the library and the computing service together, under one operation, or linked through a senior academic administrator post. Whatever the structure, it will be increasingly important for the institution to take a strategic view of its information requirements and the supporting technological structure, as well as for the library to ensure that it plays a leading role in any new arrangement.

The third strand of the university scholarly information-resource infrastructure for the 1990s was identified as the national and international research-library network, and this will be discussed later in the chapter in the context of national initiatives.

THE IMPORTANCE OF ELECTRONIC ACCESS TO CATALOGUES AND RETROSPECTIVE CONVERSION OF CATALOGUE DATA

The topic of cataloguing and catalogues may not be an exciting one, yet, in the context of research-library provision for the 1990s, there is some special pleading to do on its behalf. In particular, I wish to address the development of the OPAC and the associated issue of retrospective conversion of catalogues of 'important' collections and networked access to them. Access to the OPAC is cited by humanities departments as one of the key benefits that campus local area networking can bring, both to identify appropriate material and its location and potentially for document supply (electronic or otherwise).

However, with notable exceptions, the major OPACs of UK universities contain mostly recent material, for monographs and serial titles. A coherent strategy for retrospective conversion has not been attempted for the UK (although it is known that there are stirrings of such an initiative in a European context, involving the British Library), and lack of institutional funding for such unglamorous activities has ensured at best a piecemeal approach. If one relates this position to citation studies in the humanities which show that well over 50 per cent of books cited have imprint dates up to thirty-five years ago and earlier, the increasing tendency to search only the OPAC, and ignore the card catalogue, is doing a major disservice to scholars and their potential exploitation of the resources of research libraries. It is for the humanities to speak up for the value of retrospective conversion, and for some national planning to be undertaken to achieve this, as they, and to some extent the social sciences, have most to gain from such an investment.

Where systematic retrospective conversion has been undertaken, resulting in a fully converted catalogue, there are still significant problems of interpretation and retrieval. Just as manual catalogues are not harmonized retrospectively, so electronic versions are unlikely ever to be. What is required is the education and assistance of users if their research depends on access to a multiplicity of databases and catalogues to understand the construction of electronic catalogues, and their associated approaches to subject indexing and cataloguing. I am much indebted to Professor Robin Alston for stimulating these comments, based on his extensive work with individual researchers as they approach the resources of the British Library (BL), both through the converted catalogue and through mediated access to Internet and other database resources (Alston: n.d.).

Many researchers come to the electronic version of the BL catalogue with experience of its printed version, and so are arguably more fitted by experience to know its idiosyncrasies and quirks. What, asks Alston, will happen when remote users have access to these electronic versions only, and to readers who have no understanding of the way in which the catalogue has developed? Limitations in subject access in on-line databases are also a serious concern, not by any means eliminated by the increasingly ubiquitous full-text searching capabilities offered by database hosts.

An issue for research libraries over the next few years is to seize the opportunity offered by technology for enrichment of OPACs as electronic access tools. Possible enrichment includes adding images of contents pages, indexes, thesaural-searching and electronic-browsing capabilities, the development of intelligent access tools, and so on. Such developments would seem to offer an opportunity for libraries, archives, and museums to work together, drawing on their range of experience to ensure that new designs and software development meet the needs of humanities scholars. Significant further research and investigation of the possibilities and benefits to be derived from such an approach are recommended.

NEW SKILLS REQUIREMENTS

Alston argues strongly for a new breed of reference librarian who can understand the nature of the collections in his or her care, their description, and the range of access tools. Such an individual should embody knowledge of cataloguing and indexing rules, at least in the context of a particular research library's collection, its process of catalogue conversion; knowledge of data structures, telecommunications, and network gateways; search protocols; and relevant electronic sources.

Librarians are increasingly defining the requirements for a new type of employee within 'converging' information services who possesses the best qualities of current professionals in both organizations. Stronger subject and technical background and training are important for these new information staff, as well as the ability to work effectively in a more fluid organizational environment.

Assuming that research is likely to depend on access to a multiplicity of sources and databases, users will need such expert advice. This is an interesting perspective and reinforces the key challenge referred to earlier for the research library—namely, the simultaneous access to and consultation of material in all forms to support research, particularly in the humanities, and the need for both 'ancient and modern' skills.

Argument for such mediation and user support is not uncontested: indeed much library policy and practical imperatives tend towards the encouragement and support of the 'self-service virtual library', where academics at their desks can roam information resources without any intermediary intervention. Practically, the two extremes may be reconciled through more initial effort in training to ensure user understanding of the range of information sources, combined with more in-depth support from 'database or information surfers' (navigators), targeting particular subject groups to optimize their exploitation of this increasingly complex information environment.

NATIONAL DEVELOPMENTS

Key national activities in the UK have been led by the JISC, which was set up in 1993 by the Department of Education Northern Ireland, the Higher Education Funding Council for England (HEFCE), the Higher Education Funding Council for Wales, and the Scottish Higher Education Funding Council as a successor body to the Computer Board and the Information Systems Committee (ISC). It is responsible for the national infrastructure and standards for networking and the encouragement of the effective use of information technology in information systems. It has a core programme comprising two elements—the provision of a national networking infrastructure for the academic community and specialist information services and data sets, complemented by a range of programme initiatives.

The national networking infrastructure (SuperJANET) is now a world leading network. Very few countries have 34 million bits per second (mbps) network links (the UK higher education and research community has some sixty such connections) and only the USA can match the 140 mbps PDS network (SuperJANET has fourteen connections). Higher bandwidth and the flexibility of the multimedia ATM protocol ensure that there will be an advanced underlying networking capability for the community to exploit by 2005.

Progress has been made not only with bandwidth, but also on the 'reach' of the network. There are over thirty additional higher speed connections currently being installed: metropolitan area networks (MANs) are also being promoted as a cost-effective way of extending connections—for example, to small colleges—and the HEFCE has announced a £22 million programme over two years for MAN development. What is equally important in this context is the complementary investment at campus level to ensure the creation of appropriate local area network (LAN) and workstation infrastructures, to ensure that the potential multimedia highway does not grind to a halt at the campus gateway.

The second core programme of the JISC is for the acquisition and provision of data-set services (embracing all categories of bibliographic, text, and research data and information) to the higher education community. Initial mounting of such bibliographic files such as the Institute of Scientific Information citation indices and the Excerpta Media Database (EMBASE) at Bath, and the continuing support for data centres at Manchester, are manifestations of this programme. The policy is to seek a wide range of complementary databases, and it is important for the humanities community to make its requirements known, directly or through the Datasets Inter-Agency Group (DIAG), an advisory body bringing together data-set providers and funders.

Early in their existence the higher education funding councils set up a Review of Higher Education Library Provision, under the chairmanship of Sir Brian Follett, Vice-Chancellor of Warwick University. They were led to do this after major expressions of concern about the difficulties institutions were facing in their libraries in coping with the massive expansion in student numbers. The brief was early on extended to consider resource-sharing across libraries, particularly research resources, which, in the context of a new (at the time) unified university sector, are very unevenly distributed. The Review reported in December 1993 (Joint Funding Council's Libraries Review Group 1993), and ideas for development have since significantly advanced through a range of initiatives under the umbrella of the Electronic Libraries (e-Lib) programme. Below I wish to consider in some more detail the major thrusts of the e-Lib programme and a major initiative for the non-formula funding of specialized research collections in the humanities. Let me take the non-formula funding initiative first.

£10 million was set aside over four years for competitive bids in the humanities (scope fairly widely drawn) in the areas of conservation, cataloguing of collections, in a format suitable for networking or to be made available on-line, and preservation. In addition, recurrent bids were also invited for activities intended to enhance access to collections through publicity for, or development of, the collections, or support for user-related services. The announcement of the awards for these specialized research collections was made in HEFCE circulars issued in 1995 (HEFCE 1995*a*, *b*)—Scotland had a separate competition. A condition of funding is that institutions will provide free access to the collection to bone fide researchers funded by the funding councils and the Department of Education Northern Ireland.

The circulars make interesting reading for the richness of activity in these areas which will benefit humanities researchers in very important and practical ways. First, there is included a significant amount of retrospective conversion of catalogue records, so knowledge of, and access to, this material should be made significantly easier. Secondly, it is evident that archives collections feature very strongly in the awards, again a welcome outcome, which will bring a much wider knowledge of and accessibility to these outstanding primary sources. Preservation activity at this stage is via microfilming, but again a substantial corpus of material will then be available for digitization and improved remote access. Supporting activity is also bringing together the archives community for discussion of standards and the need for improved 'resource discovery tools'.

As a direct response to the Follett report, the JISC established the e-Lib programme. The programme has a budget of some £15 million over three years, and its objectives include the use of IT to improve delivery of information through increased use of electronic library services, to allow academic libraries to cope better with growth in demands, to explore different models of intellectual property management, and to encourage new methods of scholarly publishing.

The Follett Implementation Group for Information Technology (FIGIT) was set up to oversee this programme. FIGIT called for expressions of interest in seven major areas in 1994. They were electronic document and article delivery, electronic journals, digitization, on-demand publishing, training, and awareness, access to network resources, and supporting studies. Over 350 expressions of interest were received, and panels were set up to evaluate proposals, interact with proposers where appropriate, and recommend funding. Numerous major projects have been funded and are under way. Details of the projects are available both in print through a programme pack and via the World Wide Web (URL: http://ukoln.bath.ac.uk/elib/intro.html).

The interests of the humanities are well represented within the projects. *Internet Archaeology* (URL: http://intarch.ac.uk), an international electronic journal of archaeology, offers exciting multimedia possibilities for the dissemination of archaeological research findings. On-demand Publishing in the Humanities is a project exploring the issues involved to deliver supporting readings to students in the humanities. The Institute of Historical Research has two projects using their IHR server to conduct electronic seminars in history and to develop the electronic journal *Reviews in History*. Many of the more general projects will, of course, also be significant for the future nature of library and information services to support the humanities.

Discussions with the Consortium of Research Libraries (CURL) on the development of their database as a national resource have proceeded very positively since the Follett report recommended this approach. The CURL libraries represent major research-library collections, around 22 million volumes from 500 years of collecting and maintenance, comprising some 56 per cent of the total stock of pre-1922 universities. Some seven million catalogue records of their stock are available, as a potential national database and on-line catalogue. A contract was awarded to Manchester University to host this service. There are also discussions commencing on the potential augmentation of this catalogue through the material retrospectively converted through the non-formula funding initiative. By a roundabout route, the UK higher-education community will thus create a national database of its holdings, complemented by the major on-line catalogue of the BL, for the significant benefit of UK researchers, especially in the humanities.

In 1993 there was an 'idea' for an arts and humanities data centre under discussion. Since then, after a substantial report of a feasibility study commissioned by the Information Services Sub-Committee (ISSC) of JISC (Burnard and Short 1994), followed by a full consultation exercise, funding has been made available, some £500,000 per annum for three years. The contract for an Arts and Humanities Executive function for the Arts and Humanities Data Service (AHDS), with the emphasis on service, has been awarded to Kings College London. This development is both exciting and of major significance for the humanities community, in that it offers a coherent, distributed approach to making available a range of electronic sources and services to support humanities research into the twenty-first century (Ross 1995).

Under the e-Lib programme two studies of significance for humanities have been conducted. A study was undertaken into the requirements for retrospective conversion of library catalogues in UK higher education (Bryant *et al.* 1995). A national programme is recommended with a price tag of some £25 million. The report is under consideration and any funding and prioritization is likely to be developed in the light of the non-formula funding initiative mentioned earlier. The second study focused on the area of images, and a feasibility study has been completed which outlines the needs of the higher-education community, potential materials, and possible organizational structures for a national service, bearing in mind the AHDS model already established.

Perhaps one of the most difficult and yet important issues to be tackled is that of long-term digital preservation. The e-Lib programme is responsible for the development of a range of digital library resources, and there is now an urgent need to address the long-term implications of these developments. Under the e-Lib programme a joint BL/JISC seminar late in 1995 set this task in motion, drawing on the excellent work already undertaken in the USA by the Research Libraries Group (RLG) and the Commission on Preservation and Access (CPA) (RLG/CPA 1996). Obvious questions relate to the potential role of the research library to undertake the long-term preservation of electronic materials.

Outside the JISC e-Lib programme there is of course significant additional activity. The problems faced are international in scale and applicability, and digital library programmes of the EU and in the USA are all relevant and of serious interest for the humanities. It would be impossible in this short chapter to do justice to these programmes, but some pointers should be suggested.

INTERNATIONAL DEVELOPMENTS

The European Libraries Programme is well documented. The third framework programme (3FP) had three calls, and details on individual projects can be found at the following URL (http://www.echo.lu). The libraries budget under 4FP (1994–8) is about 30 million ECU. A first call has been completed and further calls for projects are likely. The main action lines are broadly: network-oriented internal library systems; interconnection of library systems; and library-mediated access to network resources, providing a focus respectively on the library service itself, access to a distributed library resource, and access to the world of (non-library) networked information.

A different approach has been taken in the USA National Science Foundation (NSF) digital library programme, which has made about $24 million available over four years to fund only six, very large projects. These are based at Carnegie Mellon University, Illinois, Michigan, Stanford, Berkeley, and University of California Santa Barbara, are primarily research projects rather than service developments (unlike the e-Lib programme), and take a holistic view, tackling all or a large part of each project's view of what is a digital library. None is specifically humanities focused. Each project has a World Wide Web address for further information, and the following URL provides a useful overview of USA digital library developments (http://www.cnri.reston.va.us).

CONCLUSIONS

John Laver, Chairman of the Humanities Research Board of the British Academy, has recently said: 'the library is the laboratory of the humanities: the unification of the world's libraries into a single virtual collection, at least at the level of their catalogues, with a swiftly growing proportion of digitized textual and other material made widely available over the network, will transform the laboratory of the humanities into one of global scale' (Laver 1995).

The future reshaping and conception of the role of the research library, indeed its very survival, in the context of international developments outlined in this chapter, are daunting tasks. They depend on evolving a flexible model, balancing access and holdings, new and traditional skills, and integrating access to electronic, networked and print sources available worldwide. This in turn requires a technological appreciation of the possible, far beyond that presently attained in most libraries. This challenge comes on top of the enduring and more traditional challenges of space, finance, and preservation. In summary:

- Research libraries face severe economic, space, and preservation problems through the 1990s, which are likely to have a particularly adverse effect on the libraries' ability to acquire traditional research materials, and may inhibit their participation in new developments.
- Campus technology infrastructure developments are required as an essential support to the emerging 'virtual library'.
- Research is required into how the working patterns of scholars are likely to change to cope with the complexity and variety of information sources available to them, and what support they will require in this information-seeking process.
- Cooperation between research libraries, museums, and archives should be encouraged to define and develop the design requirements for enriched access tools for humanists.
- Research libraries require a new breed of professionals with both subject and technical background to support new access routes to information.
- It is important for the humanities community to make its requirements known for the national acquisition and provision of data-set services.
- It is recommended that there should be a national strategy for the digitization of materials in research libraries, closely related to user requirements and priorities.
- At the national level, there is significant activity relating to electronic library developments that is important for the humanities community and major humanities research libraries.
- The challenges of the electronic library are global not national, and there needs to be wide awareness of relevant developments wherever they are taking place.

References

Alston, R. C. (n.d.), *Charting the Bibliographic Seas: Research and the Art of Navigation* (n.p.).

British Academy and British Library Research and Development Department (1993), *Information Technology in Humanities Scholarship: British Achievements, Prospects, and Barriers* (London).

Bryant, P. *et al.* (1995), *Retrospective Conversion of Library Catalogues in Institutions of Higher Education in the United Kingdom: A Study of the Justification for a National Programme* (University of Bath).

Burnard, L., and Short, H. (1994), '*An Arts and Humanities Data Service*': *Report of a Feasibility Study Commissioned by the ISSC of the Joint Information Systems Committee of the Higher Education Funding Councils* (Oxford).

Hayes, R. M. (n.d.), *Libraries and Information Resources in Research Universities in the United States: A Contribution to Information UK 2000* (n.p.).

HEFCE (1995*a*), 'Libraries Review: Non-Formula Funding of Specialised Research Collections in the Humanities: 1994–95 Non-Recurring Allocations' (Circular 5/95; Feb.).

—— (1995*b*), 'Libraries Review: Non-Formula Funding of Specialised Research Collections in the Humanities: 1995–96 Recurring Allocations' (Circular 14/95; July).

Joint Funding Councils' Libraries Review Group (1993), *Report* [Chairman: Sir Brian Follett] (Bristol: HEFCE).

Laver, J. (1995), 'Light Shed by Lone Scholars', *Times Higher Education Supplement* (8 Sept.).

RLG/CPA (1996): Research Libraries Group and Commission on Preservation and Access, *Preserving Digital Information: Report of the Task Force on Archiving of Digital Information* (Washington: RLA/CPA).

Ross, S. (1995), 'Preserving and Maintaining Electronic Resources in the Visual Arts for the Next Century', *Information Services and Use*, 15: 373–84.

Special Collections in the British Library and Electronic Media

ALICE PROCHASKA

ABSTRACT

This chapter discusses the work being undertaken by the British Library (BL) to provide services in an electronic form. This includes electronic publications and access to unpublished research materials in a digitized format. The status of digitized data under the 1911 Copyright Act will also be considered, with special reference to the deposit of mapping data by the Ordnance Survey. The chapter will conclude with a section on the physical and intellectual problems of preserving electronic records from the point of view of BL Special Collections.

INTRODUCTION

The British Library (BL) is devoting a very considerable proportion of its resources during the 1990s to the automated provision of information. The challenge of the electronic media informs much of its *Strategic Objectives for the Year 2000* (British Library 1993). From the enhanced provision of electronic delivery by the Document Supply Centre to a huge programme for retrospectively converting music, map, and manuscript catalogues which have been created over a period of more than 150 years, to the question of how to extend the provisions of the Copyright Act 1911 to include legal deposit of digital publications, the Library faces a formidable set of tasks arising from the electronic revolution. Much investment has borne fruit already: in the publication of the BL *Catalogue of Printed Books to 1975* on CD-ROM (British Library 1992), in the electronic output (including CD-ROM publications) of the National Bibliographic Service, in the publication by Bowker-Saur of the retroconverted *Catalogue of Printed Music* (British Library 1997), a joint venture with Research Publications International to publish the retroconverted map catalogues, and so on. The Library's on-line public access catalogue (OPAC) has been networked and its World Wide Web site (URL: http://portico.bl.uk), developed from the Portico information server, contains a rapidly increasing range of current information about BL collections and services. The ambitious aim of BL Network Services 'to be able to supply to the remote user text, sound or visual images from all parts of the collection', while curtailed by the deep cuts in the Library's overall funding which were announced following the November 1995 Budget, remains a central plank of BL policy. The commitment of the Library's Research and Development Department to information technology (IT) is illustrated both by the seminars and research projects it has sponsored and by the publication of its R&D Report no. 6097, *Information Technology in Humanities Scholarship*, which was a cooperative venture with the British Academy (British Academy and British Library Research and Development Department 1993). In all of this, the Library recognizes that it can only advance with the closest possible cooperation and consultation with those organizations, most notably university departments and university libraries, which have already set in place the academic and technological infrastructure to which we hope to make an increasingly useful contribution.

An overwhelmingly important consequence of the electronic revolution for the BL is the question of how to acquire, preserve, and make available unpublished research materials which happen to have been produced in electronic form. A working group on the legal deposit of non-print publications, chaired by the then Chairman of the BL Board Sir Anthony Kenny, including representatives of other interested organizations and working in close consultation with publishers, put together in 1996 a proposal for the consideration of government. The issues include the fundamental question of how to define a publication, and, amongst many others, how to arrange for selection and preservation from the great spectrum of electronic published output including sound and film, and how and at what stage of a publication's life to ensure access for readers, while preserving the commercial rights of the publishers. From the historian's and archivist's point of view, there are question marks over the distinction between unpublished databases of organizations including government, and information formerly made available in published form.

My own area of responsibility as Director of Special Collections covers the Manuscript Collections, Map and Music Libraries, the Oriental and India Office Collections, and the Philatelic Collections. All of these are treasure houses for the historian. Together they form the main, though not the only area within the Library where the selection and purchase of material tend to be governed by considerations of 'national heritage'. (And here, I hasten to add, we are of course one part of a nationwide network of collectors of 'heritage' material.) Large-scale purchases by the British Library as well as others are often supported by grants from the National Heritage Memorial Fund or other bodies, and can involve protracted discussion of their research and monetary value, before they can be acquired. Similarly, when individuals or organizations offer us extensive personal collections or archives, some thought must be given to their research potential and their contribution to the national-heritage profile of the collections, in relation to the Library's capacity to store, preserve, catalogue, and make available the material in question. It is to the connected questions of developing and making available our unpublished collections, and dealing with the problem of what constitutes a published source, that I propose to devote most of this chapter.

With the exception of some early state papers in private collections and, most notably, the very extensive India Office records, which effectively ceased to be produced in 1948, the Special Collections of the BL are for the most part private in their origin and unpredictable in the manner and timing of their acquisition. We are not, therefore, in the position of being able to foresee or systematically to plan for large accessions of unpublished, electronically generated material. Nor do we face, in the way that government repositories do, the problems of how and whether to cope with vast bodies of statistical material. (Published statistical material, incidentally, is made available through the Science Policy Information Service, newly established to bring together social science data from the science and humanities collections to provide a focused service for applied social science in particular.) We do not have to decide whether to keep in bulk, or alternatively to sample, particular instance papers which electronic data-handling techniques now make potentially useful to the historian in ways that they simply were not before. The issues raised by handling census and other survey data are not so central to the management of our collections.

A fundamental question in this area which does concern curators and readers at the BL involves the nature of the text itself. Digital technology has introduced (or perhaps I should say that it has reintroduced, for the first time since the establishment and dominance of printing) the unstable, or infinitely variable, text. I will offer you a few examples of what this means for the British Library, in particular in its role as the provider of sources for historical research.

DIGITIZED PUBLICATION AS A REPLACEMENT FOR PRINT: THE CASE OF THE ORDNANCE SURVEY

One issue slowly being resolved is that of the provision of large-scale Ordnance Survey mapping. In 1997 the Ordnance Survey will cease to produce its large-scale mapping in analogue form, and will move to wholly digitized output. Having become an Executive Agency of the government, it is under an obligation to cover most of its costs through sales of data and services. Most of its cost recovery will be achieved by providing to customers such as surveyors, planners, property developers, and the like a vastly enhanced and continuously updated digital database. This huge and exciting advance in the degree of up-to-date detail which Ordnance Survey can provide to its main customers presents difficulties for the copyright libraries. At present, our Map Library receives microfiche sets of Ordnance Survey mapping covering the whole of the UK, under the provisions of the Copyright Act 1911. Until a few years ago, we received it absolutely free of charge. We still receive it free of charge, but we now pay a substantial sum for jacketing the fiche. From 1997 onwards, we could have had to pay well over ten times that cost in order to receive the equivalent digitized output. We also have to take account of capital investment in the necessary equipment, and of the commercial interests of Ordnance Survey, which might well wish to have a say in regulating the way in which the material is used in our reading rooms.

Here is a case where digitization, which has so much to offer the historian, could actually lead to a deterioration in the nature of the source material available. At present the historical geographer, the cartographic historian, and the local historian, not to mention solicitors and property lawyers, geologists, and a host of others who need to use large-scale mapping from different dates, use the BL Map Library as the leading archive of the national topographic record. (The other copyright libraries in the UK provide a similar service, and are similarly affected.) It is, of course, essential to our readers' work to be able to compare changing patterns of land use over time, and often to be able to pinpoint a particular property for various dates during, perhaps, more than a century of the topographic record. The same will be true of readers in 200 years' time. How are we to ensure that the comparative information they need over time will be available to them, on the same comprehensive basis as before? If a reader in the year 2040, let us say, needs to see large-scale mapping of the Yorkshire Dales covering the period 1995–2040, he or she could find that that record has not been preserved in any library, because it was never required by any of the fee-paying customers of Ordnance Survey in the interim, and therefore was not downloaded from the digitized database. Suppose that what is wanted is large-scale mapping of the city of Leeds; snapshots of Ordnance Survey mapping will have been preserved far more frequently, for the practical purposes of town planners, etc., but they will have been preserved not in libraries but in planning offices; will they have been preserved after the date when they were needed there? How would a historian manage to get access, or even begin to find out where they were kept? Suppose, to take another hypothetical example, that a historian in the year 2100 is undertaking a study of that by then obsolete and quaint custom of preserving public footpaths across private land; and he or she wishes to compare the strength of the ramblers' lobby during the twenty-first century in the south-west and the north-east of England. How can we ensure that the data survive that will make these questions answerable?

The Ordnance Survey has been working with the BL, Public Record Office (PRO), and other national-library providers of mapping to produce answers to these questions. The solution that eventually emerges may involve compromises—for instance, over the frequency with which comprehensive large-scale mapping data for the whole country are preserved. We may collectively need to invoke the legal requirements of property law, and of such measures as the Contaminated Land Act, in order to persuade government that some residual legal responsibilities adhering to the function of the Ordnance Survey require support. Workable solutions which take into account the very disparate ways in which people use the original text may yet call for an interdepartmental committee to sort them out. This in itself is a measure of the scale of the problem. The basic difficulty derives from the cost of the technology. Associated with cost is the gap that has developed between the ways in which essentially the same text is used by different groups of people. In order to place great benefits of currency and flexibility in the hands of most contemporary users, there is a risk of damaging its usefulness to posterity, and of marginalizing the unfunded, non-commercial users.

From the point of view of the copyright libraries including ourselves, the case of the Ordnance Survey is also related to the thorny question of maintaining our collections in an era when digital publication is beginning to replace the printed page. This of course brings us back to the fundamental question of how to define 'publication', and to the practical and philosophical implications of the unstable text.

DIGITIZATION AND THE ENHANCEMENT OF AVAILABLE SOURCES

If the comprehensive store of published knowledge represented by the copyright libraries appears threatened in the era of digital technology, the opposite is true of unpublished and unique sources. Digitization brings with it exciting possibilities for the archival scholar. The BL is exploring collaborative programmes with other libraries in the UK and abroad, whereby we would exchange digitized copies of some of our complementary collections. The relatively cumbersome medium of microfilm has never presented the sort of opportunities now presented by digitization, for bringing together collections of complementary material which have been physically separated for decades or even centuries. Although microfilm will remain for the foreseeable future by far the more acceptable medium of preservation, as a versatile aid to the scholar the computer image is far in advance.

Computers and computer-assisted photography can also provide enhancement of the texts themselves. Although to my knowledge no digital scanner has yet succeeded in penetrating the ravages of gall, that most seductive and most lethal of enhancing media so widely used by nineteenth-century archivists, electronic cameras, and image processors are working effectively on fire damage, glue, and other forms of obliteration. The Library recently collaborated with the University of Kentucky to produce digitally enhanced images of the *Beowulf* manuscript and hence the answers to some mysteries which have long perplexed Beowulf scholars. (This highly successful collaboration was awarded a Meckler-Media award for innovation in 1995.) Similar techniques can be used on other fire-damaged medieval manuscripts of our Cotton collection. The conservation studio begins by producing a videotape from the electronic camera, which is then digitized and used on an image-processing computer to enhance the image.

Our photographic service offers readers the opportunity to order image-enhanced reproductions. Our publications now include, in addition to catalogues on CD-ROM, a CD-ROM entitled *Sources in History: The Medieval Realms* (British Library 1995), which is designed in part for students and teachers of the schools national curriculum history unit entitled 'Medieval Realms'. High-quality images have been scanned from photographic slides of medieval illuminated manuscripts to produce this publication, which is one of a programme derived from different parts of the Library's collections. Clearly there are all sorts of potential CD-ROM publications based on our manuscript holdings, including full-text reproductions of selected research texts from any and all chronological and geographical areas. The technology is also capable of delivering such material across the networks, and our Initiatives for Access programme has developed a portfolio of pictorial images which could be used in this way.

At every stage we must beware the many pitfalls. While the opportunities for creating and disseminating the 'virtual library' seem almost infinitely seductive, there are difficulties arising from costs, from relationships between the Library and publishers where rapid technological changes could outstrip contractual undertakings, and from considerations of preservation. The cost factor will always loom large in determining priorities, and even more painfully so now that the Library is subject to cuts in the region of 25 per cent from its government funding. Electronic advances have to be balanced against the priority of maintaining the necessary level of acquisitions, for instance. It is likely that most electronic publishing based on the Special Collections of the BL will be undertaken in partnership with other publishers, despite the fact that the Library is now a successful small-to-medium-sized publisher in its own right. Inevitably, therefore, commercial considerations will govern the great bulk of our electronic output. Any large-scale projects for electronic scanning which might be expected to yield high academic but low commercial benefits would need to be supported by special grants. In this area there is surely great scope for the BL to engage in joint ventures with university departments. There are good precedents for this sort of cooperation: to take a single example, the collaboration with the Institute of Historical Research and the PRO to produce part of the on-line *Eighteenth Century Short Title Catalogue*, using a grant from the US National Endowment for the Humanities. The Library would be only too pleased to explore further suggestions along similar lines.

PRESERVING THE TEXT

From the Special Collections point of view, one of the most speculative questions raised by the electronic media is that of the nature and durability of the archival text itself. The problem is both physical and intellectual. The physical survival of computer disks, and of the hardware and software appropriate to reading them, has been tackled by other organizations, including the PRO, and we are grateful to be able to draw on their experience. Our own collections as yet contain very little computer-generated material, but without any doubt they will soon do so. I take the view that a collection of material which is consonant with our acquisitions policy in other respects should be accepted on the assumption that we must find a way of preserving it and making it available.

The intellectual question of preservation is also a challenge. It is, of course, a sacred archival principle not to interfere with the original material once it has been incorporated into a collection. Best practice in the conservation studios dictates that all repairs should be clearly visible. Among archivists and manuscript curators, it is an essential principle to explain the provenance of the documentary sources and preserve their integrity in such a way that readers may draw their own conclusions with the minimum of interference. But how, with an electronic document, do you discern its origins, whether it is the work of more than one hand, how much altered from an original first draft, and so on?

From my own work, one particular parallel comes to mind. I once spent many months as a student using the papers of Francis Place, the radical reformer of early nineteenth-century Westminster. His collections, put together painstakingly over a long lifetime, and including large quantities of newscuttings, ephemera, overlapping narrative autobiography, and correspondence, came to the British Museum (as it then was) through his family. Being upright Victorians with a strong sense of family pride, they expunged a certain amount of the more salacious material from the record of Francis Place senior. He had been in his youth a bit of a tearaway; and in middle age he incurred opprobrium for his brave advocacy of contraception. He also outraged his first family by his second marriage to an actress of dubious reputation. There are, accordingly, pages of text in the surviving papers which have been mutilated: sections cut out or pasted over, and some very heavily scored through. Time and again, it appears that Place himself wrote in after-thoughts or amended text, often many years after first writing it. It is not difficult to discern where this has happened, and, frustrating though it is to have to surmise the contents of the missing portions of text, at least the historian is aware of the partial nature of the evidence. Com-pare this archive, one of the richest survivals there is on early nine-teenth-century popular politics and culture, with an acquisition now promised to the BL: the personal archive of Tony Benn MP. In many ways this huge and fascinating archive will provide for students of late-twentieth-century British politics something similar to what Francis Place has left for the historian of the early nineteenth century. It will be much richer, of course, since Tony Benn has played a more central and significant role in the national politics of his day. His diaries, written correspondence, and collections of political ephemera consti-tute a treasure trove in themselves. But where, among the computer disks and tapes, will be the evidence of his own reflections and after-thoughts, or the signs of intervention by other members of the office or household? We have also to devise a means of editing material which Mr Benn would wish to be withheld for a certain period on grounds of personal sensitivity, in such a way that it can be reinserted in the correct place (if necessary on a disk or tape) when the time comes. Historians in the future, and contemporary historians even now, will have to face numerous conundrums of this nature. For the curator of the collec-tions, it poses similar dilemmas.

CONCLUSION

The Special Collections of the BL thus confront the challenge of the electronic media with particular practical and intellectual difficulties. The blurred margin between published and unpublished materials affects all of our work. Our curators will face special challenges explain-ing and making available computer-generated materials. They will also find themselves at the centre of the debate over which sources are published and which are not. And yet, at the same time, the electronic revolution offers to the Library's Special Collections, and to our readers, great opportunities to use our unique research collections in new and enlightening ways.

References

British Academy and British Library Research and Development Department (1993), *Information Technology in Humanities Scholarship: British Achievements, Prospects, and Barriers* (London).
British Library (1992), *Catalogue of Printed Books to 1975* (Cambridge).
—— (1993), *Strategic Objectives for the Year 2000* (London).
—— (1995), *Sources in History: The Medieval Realms* (London).
—— (1997), *Catalogue of Printed Music* (Sutton).

Increasing the Value of Data

DENISE LIEVESLEY

ABSTRACT

The benefits of ensuring that data are preserved are well recognized. However, this chapter argues that it is essential to support the use of data by providing a flexible and speedy service in disseminating data. It will also consider the importance of data documentation and will discuss ways in which the value of data may be increased through, for example, integration of data sets and the compilation of teaching packages.

INTRODUCTION

This chapter examines the role of archives of machine-readable data as a resource for research and as a source of teaching material. Throughout the paper the Data Archive at the University of Essex will be used as an example.

THE DATA ARCHIVE

The Data Archive has existed for thirty years. It is based at the University of Essex and is funded mainly by the University, the Economic and Social Research Council (ESRC), and the higher education funding councils. Other funding is obtained on a project specific basis. The Archive comprises a library of computerized data on a wide range of topics mainly within the fields of social and economic research. Although the data largely result from censuses and surveys, an increasing volume of data arises from administrative processes. This is the largest collection of accessible computer-readable data in the social sciences and humanities in the UK, with over 4,500 data sets of interest to researchers from many different disciplines.

The Data Archive's *raison d'être* is to promote the widest use of the data for research and teaching by providing an efficient and flexible user service, and by sharing information and encouraging the use of the data by means of workshops, bulletins, user groups, and networks. It also has a vital role in the preservation of the data for the future. The Archive's location in a university which has a reputation for excellence in social research ensures it is perceived to be upholding high standards. It is also a politically neutral location, which is vital with respect to some of the data sets it contains. The Archive is able to service any user, unlike some data archives, which can provide services only to subscribing or member institutions or which need to impose charges for data. The Data Archive is non-profit-making and provides its services on a cost-recovery basis. When the proposed research has received some external funding, however, administrative fees are imposed. These differ according to whether the funder is a charity, a non-profit, or a commercial organization. The Archive may, in addition, collect a royalty fee for the data owner. This is discussed with the data owner at the time the data are deposited, and it forms part of the contract between the owner and the Archive.

DATA ACQUISITION AND MANAGEMENT

Benefits to depositors

In order to maintain the support of data depositors, it is essential to consider what benefits accrue to depositors as a result of the dissemination of their data. Some depositors may believe that they have an obligation to archive and make available their data by virtue of having used public funds to collect them or publicly funded time and cooperation to obtain and structure them. Other depositors may be willing to deposit data for reasons of altruism. The ethos of sharing data can be encouraged:

- by fostering communication between producers and users of data (through user group meetings, newsletters, electronic bulletin boards, or networks),
- by recognizing that data deposit involves resources, particularly in the preparation of documentation, and by supporting researchers in seeking funds to cover these costs where necessary; and

- by urging all secondary analysts to acknowledge data sources—as they would do a publication—in *all* presentations of their research and by ensuring that higher-education performance indicators incorporate information about the compilation of data sets for secondary analysis.

Access Arrangements

A critical first step in the process of establishing a data resource for research and teaching is the location and acquisition of relevant data. The process of acquisition of data is a delicate one in which both depositors' and users' needs have to be brought into balance. It is important to establish principles of data ownership. In most cases the archive does not seek to own the data but will hold and distribute them on behalf of the owners. Licences which specify the conditions under which data are provided must be drawn up.

Discussions with data owners need to address the issue of access. From the user perspective it is important that access to the data should not be unduly restricted, for instance, by the need to apply for permission for each usage of the data set. However, many important data sets would not be made available for secondary use without the archive undertaking to administer some control on behalf of the data owner.

Data Confidentiality

Since the data depositors' support and trust must be maintained, it is vital that data suppliers are sensitive to their concerns. Frequently depositors will be anxious about the confidentiality of the data. In particular, they may need to be assured that the data will not enable the identification of individuals to take place. A common strategy to minimize the possibility of identifying individuals involves the removal of variables which are specific to an individual, and the grouping of the variables which relate to geography or location. However, such processes need to take account of the diverse needs of different researchers. Although the removal of geographical information is acceptable to most contemporary researchers, those interested in conducting spatial or multi-level analyses may be prevented from doing so by this strategy. Most researchers accept these limitations as an inevitable consequence of confidentiality requirements. However, this is not an optimum strategy for historical researchers, who often do wish to identify individuals in order to link data sets. Therefore, if at all possible, the identification information should be retained to enable such linkage to take place later, since most information is confidential for a limited period. In practice this is often not possible, because the full data set is not archived or because the 'identification variables' are never included on the machine-readable version of the data set.

COST OF DATA

One of the current concerns is the pressure within many agencies—both official and private—to raise a higher proportion of their income by selling data. The 'commodification' of data may restrict access. There are particular worries about who, under the 'user-pays principle', funds the preservation of data for historical research. Archives have an important role in ensuring that strategic data sets, at the very least, continue to be deposited at low cost.

THE PRESERVATION OF DATA

Archives which contain unique and valuable collections of information must be protected in order to serve future historians. It is essential that the data are preserved in such a way that they continue to be accessible over time, despite changes to the hardware and software environments. The Data Archive guarantees future access to the material it holds by protecting its information base against technological change. In the past it has achieved this by transforming its collection to a single house standard, and by removing the software and hardware dependencies to ensure that the data remain available after the possible demise of the packages and hardware. The increase in the use of structured databases, and the demand for data to be disseminated in a way which retains the structure of the original has led us to review the preservation procedure. As a result, data are maintained in both the preservation form described above and in software-specific formats.

The Archive guarantees a secure database by a continuing programme of rigorous checks on the storage medium's physical integrity.

In many cases the Archive holds the only copies of data sets, others being unreadable due to changes in hardware or software.

User Service

The value of archives is dependent upon the breadth and quality of their holdings, but this is not sufficient to ensure that the data are used. An efficient service to users must be provided which takes account of the diversity of potential users in terms of their backgrounds, their computing and other expertise, and the resources available to them. Three aspects of this service will be discussed: location of data, dissemination methods, and data documentation.

Location of Data

An essential part of the research process is to be able to locate the data required as quickly and easily as possible. The proliferation of data, and the increasing need for multiple data sets by researchers, mean that on-line catalogues, navigation systems to link different catalogues, and software for catalogue-searching are of critical importance.

The Archive maintains a central facility for cataloguing and indexing data, using the 'standard-study-description' format to catalogue data sets, and to provide a structured format for information retrieval. Data sets are exhaustively indexed by subject, using a controlled vocabulary or thesaurus. The catalogues and indexes, known as BIRON (Bibliographic Retrieval On-line), are available to remote users (both national and international) in a variety of ways, including access via a home page on the Internet system. The associated social-science thesaurus, owned jointly by the Archive and Unesco, can be accessed by remote users. The BIRON databases enable users to retrieve information easily without needing to know the internal database language (i.e. INGRES). Work is continuing on improving the user interface. BIRON provides descriptive information about studies held, not the data sets themselves, which have to be ordered from the Archive in a separate process. Plans are in hand to extend coverage to the complete documentation for as many data sets as possible.

Searches Based on Topics

BIRON prompts the user to type in a topic for which data are sought. This term is matched against a list of several thousand descriptive terms arranged in associated groups. If an exact match is found, the user is told how many studies have been indexed with the matching term, and are offered other associated terms which might assist in focusing the search. If no exact match is found, lists of similarly spelled words are offered for selection, and the process of matching begins there. A list of titles retrieved may be viewed. The group of titles may be saved while further selections of topics are made and saved. A combined search using Boolean operators may then be carried out.

Searches Based on Bibliographic and Methodological Data

The BIRON system allows searching on the names of persons or organizations associated with particular studies, titles or part titles, dates and geographical areas of data collection, particular methodologies of data collection, and many other items of information. Information on spatial units, where relevant, are also included and may be used as search terms.

What Information is Retrieved from the System?

If the search is successful, a list of one or more study titles may be viewed at the end of the search. Users may then bring up on screen all the information recorded about that study. The information includes a list of indexing terms showing all the topics covered by the data, and a catalogue record giving the archive number, the title, access conditions, data-processing codes, the names of principal investigators, data collectors, sponsors and depositors, an abstract detailing the main purposes of the research, and main variables. Dates, geographical areas, populations, and data collection methodologies are also displayed.

Significant developments are taking place in the use of software, such as WAIS and the World Wide Web, to enable users to search multiple catalogues of holdings, thus avoiding the need for users to have a knowledge of where particular data sets might be held. Funding has been awarded by the European Commission to assist in the development of tools to permit the integration of catalogues across the European social-science archives. This should have particular relevance to researchers wishing to embark on cross-national research, and thus needing to locate data held in different national archives.

Dissemination Methods

A significant number of users are sophisticated computer-oriented quantitative social scientists. Their demands are shaped by their computing environment. For these users the desktop machine is becoming the information centre, and they require desktop access to archival material. This is having an impact on methods of data delivery.

Data are now disseminated from the Data Archive in a variety of ways according to the users' needs. Network file transfer is increasingly popular, but 8mm video tape (exabyte), digital audio tape (DAT), and transfer by portable cartridge tape drives are used, as well as the better known flexible ('floppy') diskettes for smaller amounts of data. The Archive also has facilities to write customized CD-ROMs, which has the advantage of permitting easy distribution of large amounts of data. Occasionally users still require their data on magnetic tape and so this facility remains available.

New media offer many advantages over the magnetic tapes they replaced. However, in doing so they remove magnetic tapes' greatest advantage: physical and logical standardization. This is more a problem for the Archive than for the end-user. Typically, end-users will use only one medium. The difficulty for the Archive is that there are many of these 'common' standards.

In the past a social-science environment existed in which there were (*a*) computer-users and (*b*) non-computer-users. Computer-users did quantitative analyses and specialized in using the information held by the Archive. Non-computer-users relied on printed reports, which were readily available. The implication for the Archive was that it could make sound assumptions about its users' skills. This is no longer possible; everyone now uses computers and does so with varying degrees of skill. An increasing proportion of the users of the Archive are nevertheless very naïve and need a large amount of support and assistance from Archive staff in depositing and accessing data. The difficulties for the Archive lie in trying to identify users' needs and in providing them with the appropriate service on a range from an on-line determined access (in which the Archive itself is relatively 'transparent') through to a supportive guided approach.

Of course, the implications of technological developments are not unambiguous, and it is crucial that the Archive does not run too quickly with new developments which subsequently prove to have been misguided in some respects. Our active participation in the international archiving associations such as International Federation of Data Organizations (IFDO) and Council of European Social Science Data Archives (CESSDA) is crucial in such evaluations.

Documentation

Documentation of data is essential for secondary analysis, but the quality of what is produced by the data generators is very variable. Data archives have a vital role to play in ensuring that documentation is produced which, as far as possible, satisfies user requirements. This is not an easy task when one considers the diversity of both the user base and the data sets. Consultation with secondary analysts and with the data generators is necessary in order to ensure that the documentation supports informed and responsible analysis of the data.

Data archives also have an important role to play in setting standards for the documenting of machine-readable data. Within the Data Archive we are attempting to achieve this in two ways: first, by formulating clear objectives for minimum standards, documentation creation procedures, and dissemination of documentation within the work of the Archive as a whole, and, secondly, by providing well-thought-out and constructive guidelines for documenting data collections and, if possible, documentation software. The development of documentation guidelines is a high priority and we are working with some of the major depositors of data in their production. Longer term we hope to be in a position to recommend software to researchers at the beginning of their data collection, so that documentation can be produced in standard format and in machine-readable form. Existing software which incorporates documentation procedures is being evaluated.

Until recently almost all of the documentation deposited at the Data Archive was in paper form only. Thus it had to be photocopied—an expensive and time-consuming activity—and its quality varied considerably. Paper documentation also leads to delays in servicing users, especially given that an increasing amount of data are being delivered over the network or provided on-line, whilst documentation must be photocopied and sent by post.

A major effort is underway to ensure that documentation is deposited in machine-readable form, and, since it is generally available on word-processed disks, this is proving successful. Further plans are in train to scan paper documentation for existing data sets to create machine-readable versions.

PROMOTING THE USE OF DATA

Exploiting the Potential of Data

Although the acquisition and preservation of data are laudable activities, they will not result in widespread use of the data unless the archives take an active role in promoting it. Many data sets are of complex structure, with large and sometimes complicated sets of documentation. It can be very valuable in such situations to provide opportunities for researchers to share their experience of using particular data.

Fostering Communication amongst Users and Depositors

As the holders of information on data, their origins, and their users, archives are in a unique position to promote dialogue on analytical methods and research. The sharing of expertise among users, and between data originators and secondary users, is encouraged by archives. Where participants cross disciplinary boundaries and professional backgrounds, a rich mix of ideas is fostered. User seminars can be focused upon particular data sets, particular types of data, or particular analytical methods. The archive may also provide a forum for the discussion of more general issues such as standards for the documentation of data. Conferences, workshops, electronic and printed newsletters all provide means for the exchange of information.

The Data Archive holds regular data-user seminars to facilitate the sharing of solutions to common problems encountered in analysing particular data sets or to focus on particular research applications. Formal user groups are organized around the Family Expenditure Survey, General Household Survey, the Workplace Industrial Relations Surveys, and the Labour Force Survey. Conferences and workshops discuss research on these data, newsletters are published, and a dialogue maintained between primary and secondary researchers.

A Mailbase Superlist, using the JANET mailbase facilities, enables the Archive to inform users of popular data sets of new developments, such as the arrival of a new item in a series, and relevant workshops and seminars. It allows dialogue among researchers and between researchers and the Archive, providing an immediate channel for discussion of substantive and methodological problems.

The *Data Archive Bulletin,* which appears three times each year, is available on the Internet, and is distributed to approximately 5,000 readers in the UK and beyond. It carries news about Archive staff, announcements, and news on other data organizations and archives worldwide, one or more feature articles on research carried out using data sources, full details of selected new acquisitions, as well as a complete listing with brief details of all new acquisitions, a diary of forthcoming events, and a book-review section.

In order to inform potential users of the range and type of data available, Data Archive staff frequently address academic staff and students in social sciences, humanities, statistics, and information studies departments, as well as being prominent at national and international conferences and seminars. A programme of training courses for the use of the information system was conducted over 1993 and 1994 and will be re-established if funding permits.

Specialist Data Collections

Although most archives encourage the crossing of disciplinary boundaries by researchers, it is sometimes useful to set up a specialist unit for a particular group of researchers within the umbrella of a generalist archive. The appointment of staff with a special knowledge of the research practices and needs of a particular group—e.g. historians or environmentalists—can impact favourably on research in that area.

The characteristics which are common within a specialist collection of data may relate to the subject matter (e.g. political opinion polls), to the time period (e.g. historical social and demographic records), to the geographical coverage (e.g. Northern Ireland data), to the administrative units to which they relate (e.g. New Towns' studies) or even to the type (e.g. spatially referenced data).

Specialist collections are being established where

- specialist expertise is needed to locate and identify key data sets for inclusion in the Archive, and to assist in the establishment of targeted acquisition campaigns;
- a large number of data sets exist which have not previously been brought together or documented, or the current collection tends to be patchy in coverage;
- particular or special documentation is required in order that the data may be fully exploited;
- personal contacts are needed in order to establish the Archive's credibility with depositors; and

- particular activities (such as training courses, specialist catalogues, etc.) are required in order to ensure that possible users of the data can be made aware of their potential.

Specialist data archives differ from the rest of the Archive in a few key ways:

- in almost all cases they are established in conjunction with another department or institution which has especial substantive or analytic expertise to complement the expertise of the Data Archive. We work with these 'linked' organizations on all aspects of archiving but especially with respect to developing an acquisitions policy and promoting the use of the specialist archive;
- in some cases a liaison arrangement is made with an individual who will, in addition to the responsibilities cited above, help with the training of Archive staff so that they have a better appreciation of the needs of particular users of the data. Such individuals might also help to develop relevant internal Archive procedures, such as documentation, specific to the specialist data; and,
- the Archive will not necessarily acquire all of the identified data files—a specialist archive may comprise a small number of key data sets together with a catalogue of data held elsewhere (metadata).

The Data Archive has recognized the special needs of historians by setting up a unit to encourage the deposit of machine-readable data compiled from historical sources, and to service the particular data needs of historians. It has a vital role in promoting the use of machine-readable data, particularly amongst historians who have hitherto not used this type of material. The unit, working within the existing structure of the Archive, consists of a research officer and a data-processing assistant. It was awarded support from the Arts and Humanities Data Service in 1996 to develop its History Data Unit.

Teaching Materials

There is a need for packages, or other materials which incorporate data, to be developed for use in teaching quantitative analysis in a range of different disciplines. This need exists at both school and higher-education level and is largely unmet. A few examples of projects which have taken place are described below as an illustration of what can be achieved:

- Anglia/ITV have produced a series of teaching manuals together with related data to be analysed using KEY software as a socio-economic atlas of Great Britain. The Archive has collaborated with Anglia TV in the formulation and production of this series;
- the Open University has developed two courses which incorporate socio-economic data held by the Archive; the first on family and community research in the nineteenth and twentieth centuries and the second on data analysis;
- Surrey University researchers worked with the Archive to produce a well-documented subset of the General Household Survey. This teaching package has proved to be a very popular product.

Teaching and lecturing staff rarely have the time needed to identify, obtain, understand, and analyse complex data sets such as those held at the Data Archive. The duplication of work involved if each teacher independently conducts these activities is obviously an inefficient use of resources. Thus it makes sense to share teaching resources which incorporate relatively straightforward extracts of data formatted for use with specific software, and which are documented clearly and comprehensively.

CONCLUSION

Unless data are made available for further research, materials which have often been collected at great expense, and with significant effort, may later exist only in a small number of reports, which exhaust only a fraction of the research potential of the data. Within a short space of time the data files are likely to be lost or become obsolete as the technology of the host institution changes. Data archives store, catalogue, index, and disseminate the data for further contemporary or historical research. However, this is not sufficient to ensure that the research potential of the data is fully exploited. Data archives need to be proactive in encouraging the needs of data as well as providing a flexible and supportive service to potential users. This chapter has discussed some of the key ways in which these promotional activities might be undertaken.

German Unification and Electronic Records

MICHAEL WETTENGEL

ABSTRACT

After German unification, many former East German government agencies and institutions were closed down. Archivists had to secure not only their paper records, but also a considerable number of machine-readable data holdings. Very often, however, the documentation of these electronic records proved to be incomplete or even totally missing. In these cases, different approaches were taken to identify and verify data file structures and to reconstruct missing documentation.

INTRODUCTION

The process that led to German unification was rapid and spectacular. As nobody could foresee the dynamics of change and the sudden collapse of the former German Democratic Republic (GDR), which caused the unification of the two German states, procedures to handle the various problems of this period of transition had to be improvised.

German archivists were confronted with a situation without precedent. After forty-five years of separation during which different institutional traditions had evolved, the former East German Central State Archives were merged with the West German Federal Archives in October 1990. At the same time as this reorganization took place, archivists had to face considerable challenges. When former East German government agencies and institutions were suddenly closed down, not only their paper records, but also a considerable number of machine-readable data holdings, had to be secured or rescued from possible destruction. Whereas paper records were treated according to established professional practices, the concepts and procedures for the acquisition, appraisal, description, and management of machine-readable records were lacking.

The new situation helped to bring about a change in German archivists' attitudes towards electronic records. Whereas previously little attention had been paid to machine-readable material, the need to take care of large quantities of East German data files revealed the necessity for a stronger commitment in this field.

The Federal Archives decided to establish a section for machine-readable archives, which became responsible for electronic records from former East German central agencies and institutions, as well as from federal government offices. This section was also charged with advising these federal offices on information-management issues. The section was set up in August 1991 and provided with staff and basic technical equipment by summer 1993. By then, however, a lot of precious time had already been lost.

The experience of securing East German data files showed that the creating organizations are not the best custodians of their own machine-readable data. Many data files were no longer legible, and data documentation was at best incomplete, and in most cases missing. Federal offices cared for these electronic records only in so far as they could use them for their own purposes. This experience also showed that, in a world where state and society are in constant transition, it makes sense to have archivists engaged in electronic records management, and taking into their care records of long-term value.

CONDITIONS OF ACQUISITION

In the former GDR, machine-readable data holdings had been processed by centralized mainframe systems in big data-processing centres which belonged to the State and received their commissions from government agencies and party institutions. In most cases, they were even institutionally affiliated with one or other of these agencies. Data-processing centres throughout the East German territory performed tasks and carried out orders from central government agencies.

Office automation systems were unknown in the former GDR, and the first applications for Personal Computers (PCs) with relatively small hard disks were not introduced into East German government offices until the second half of the 1980s, shortly before the collapse of the East German state. Generally speaking, the GDR had yet to begin the introduction of decentralized desktop PCs and local server networks.

With the coming of formal unification in October 1990, East German state agencies and institutions that were not taken over by federal offices, or by one of the newly established federal states (*Länder*), were either privatized or dissolved. Many data-processing centres in the former GDR suffered a similar fate. As a result, the task facing archivists who tried to secure electronic records differed, depending on what had happened to the respective data centres after unification.

Archivists working with data-processing centres still in operation and now operated by a federal government agency or one of the *Länder* had the easiest time. In such instances, sufficiently documented data holdings could be acquired, and necessary supplementary information could be easily obtained from operators and programmers, now employed by the Federal Republic or *Länder*. Frequently, however, data-processing centres had been in operation for only a short time before they were closed. In these cases, a process of organizational and operational decay was already under way whilst the various centres were still in existence. Specialists from these centres sought new jobs elsewhere and took with them both knowledge, and the relevant manuals and data documentation. They often regarded these as their personal property. Typically, only the data carriers were left for the archivists.

The situation was better in those instances where the data-processing centre was closed down immediately and the doors locked. Archivists entered sealed rooms, where they were confronted by huge piles of paper records, printouts, manuals, card indices, floppy disks, tapes, hard-disk plates, and punchcards. Data-processing centres in the former GDR were required to create and maintain sufficient documentation on every project in at least three different copies. The chances of finding enough contextual information along with the data files in order to make meaningful access to them possible were, therefore, good.

The situation was much worse in those data-processing centres that had been privatized after unification. These newly established private companies considered data holdings which had been processed for government agencies before 1990 to be part of their business capital. They did not refrain from selling former East German government data files. Even in cases where a company acknowledged that these data files had become federal property at unification, they nevertheless charged a huge fee for activities supposedly necessary for the preservation of these data.

As can be seen from these different examples, much depended on whether there was a federal or state agency to take care of East German data files. In the case of the statistical data holdings of the former GDR, these records have been secured by the Federal Office for Statistics (Statistisches Bundesamt). The former East German Central State Administration for Statistics (Staatliche Zentralverwaltung für Statistik), which had created these records, became a branch of the Federal Office for Statistics, whereas the former Data Processing Centre for Statistics (Datenverarbeitungszentrum Statistik) continued operation until the end of 1992 under the Common Office for Statistics of the New *Länder* (Gemeinsames Statistisches Amt der neuen Bundesländer). By the end of 1991, the Federal Archives and the Federal Office for Statistics agreed on formal cooperation in order to secure East German statistical data files.

Even where conditions for acquisition were good, as in the example of the statistical records, archivists could not easily take over the files. Legal obstacles, for instance, had to be overcome. The Commissioner charged with the oversight and implementation of German privacy legislation (Bundesbeauftragter für den Datenschutz) demanded that all personal identifiers in East German data files should be deleted. In addition, the Federal Office for Statistics claimed that statistical secrecy prevented the transfer of certain statistical data files to the Federal Archives.

Despite these various problems, the Federal Archives have been successful, in most cases, in acquiring East German data holdings without alteration of the data. Progress has been made with the 'Datenspeicher Gesellschaftliches Arbeitsvermögen', which contains the personal files of a high percentage of the former GDR workforce, with detailed information on education, training, and employment. This contains approximately 7.25 million personal records and 1.5 gigabyte of data. Other projects involve agricultural statistics, and files on incidents at the border between the GDR and the Federal Republic. Machine-readable records in the fields of statistics, economics, agriculture, education, penal registration, and labour have all been taken over. The Federal Archives Law, which was amended in 1990, provided the legal authority for the transfer of East German records to the Federal Archives.

MEDIA, RECORD STRUCTURES, AND CODES

Data-processing systems in the territory of the former GDR did not prove to be entirely different from those in the West. East German computer centres possessed mainframe systems for the processing of large data compilations, as had been common in Western countries about ten years earlier. East German data holdings usually had hierarchical file structures that were not very complicated. The hardware and software used by East German data-processing centres were copies of, and variations on, Western models, although naturally with different names. For instance, the so-called ESER-mainframe systems in East Germany were copies of IBM-mainframes. This, of course, greatly facilitated the work of archivists.

In the main, nine-track tapes were used as storage media, many of which had a density of only 800 bits per inch (bpi). Owing to production problems, those tapes bearing the East German trademarks ORWO or PYRAL proved to be in very poor condition. Glue and abrasion had to be removed from the tapes before they could be read. Layers of the tape sometimes separated after the first reading because inadequate binding materials had been used. In order to secure the data, the tapes had to be copied as soon as possible. In some cases whole tapes could not be read and in others too few blocks were accessible to make it possible to reconstruct the contents of the tape. Fortunately, tapes often survived in more than one copy. Data losses could, therefore, be compensated for in many cases. Magnetic hard-disk plates had also been used as a storage medium. The uneven surface on these plates sometimes damaged the reading heads. Programs and job files were usually stored on tapes, punched cards, and 5.25 or 8 inch floppies. The physical state of the data files depended on when the information was written onto the tapes and on the storage conditions in the stack area. Where these conditions were inappropriate, up to 40 per cent of the tapes were unreadable within five years.

The labelling of the tapes followed the IBM scheme, with hardly any variation. As in Western IBM-mainframe applications, Extended Binary Coded Decimal Interchange Code (EBCDIC) was used. The Russian DKOI code (also called 'ESER-Code' in the former GDR), which in translation means Binary Code for Information Interchange, was also used for some East German data files. DKOI is very similar to EBCDIC and is basically an extension of it with a few variations (see Fig. 18.1).

Hexadecimal	4A	4F	5A	5B	6A	A1	C0	D0	E0
DKOI	[	!	]	¤			—	{	}	\
EBCDIC	'			!	$					

Fig. 18.1 DKOI code and EBCDIC compared

Binary-coded numerical values, often used alternately with fields in EBCDIC-representation, were also typical features of East German data files. The frequent use of data-compression techniques presented a particular problem to archivists. The record length was generally variable—a characteristic also common to many Western IBM-mainframe applications. However, the data fields in East German records were usually not separated by delimiters.

East German holdings had been collected and processed for very specific purposes in the fields of statistics, social and economic policy-planning, personnel management, distribution of goods, labour employment, and workforce distribution. Large data collections of statistical files, goods and production files, and personnel files had been processed with the help of programs written in Assembler or PL/1, which are highly dependent on the mainframe environment of the data-processing centres. Owing to their sequential, hierarchical file structures, these machine-readable records were archived as 'flat files'—that is to say, as mere sequential bit strings.

RECONSTRUCTING DOCUMENTATION: THE *KADERDATENSPEICHER*

In order to understand the content of East German data files, it was of great importance to obtain complete documentation. Archivists were looking not only for program and data file documentation in a limited sense, but also for the relevant contextual information on the 'history' and various uses of each data file. As a minimum requirement, the Federal Archives made sure it received the data file structure, the number of data sets, the data values, complete codebooks, compression algorithms, and a list identifying the content of each tape. In spite of this general rule, it was decided in rare instances to take over data files because of their informational value, even though this basic information could not be obtained.

One of these data files, the so-called database of party functionaries or *Kaderdatenspeicher*, may serve as an example. The *Kaderdatenspeicher* contains personal data on 331,980 staff members (in 1989) of all former East German government agencies, excluding those of the Ministry of State Security (Ministerium für Staatssicherheit), the Ministry for National Defence (Ministerium für Nationale Verteidigung), and the Ministry of the Interior (Ministerium des Innern). The *Kaderdatenspeicher* had been processed using Assembler programs. One can infer from additional sources that the operating system originally used was SVS 7.1, and that the hardware was an ESER mainframe of some description. The latter were compatible with the IBM 360/370 series. The central files which have been processed so far were divided into differing annual generations (1980, 1985, 1986, 1987, 1988, 1989), each containing about 50 megabytes. It has been estimated that the whole *Kaderdatenspeicher* might contain as much as 5 gigabytes of data. These files not only provide insights into the political and professional career of officials, but they also contain information on officials' parents. Although originally there were several copies of the *Kaderdatenspeicher*, the Federal Archives has the only surviving example. In at least one case, there is sufficient evidence that a copy of the *Kaderdatenspeicher* had been deliberately deleted shortly before the German unification in order to protect cadre members. The considerable value of this database provided an incentive for the Federal Archives to invest heavily in the reconstruction of its documentation.

After the tapes of the *Kaderdatenspeicher* had been copied, the volume labels, headers, and first blocks of data of each file were printed out. The volume labels and headers followed the IBM-scheme, so were easy to understand. From these data, information on the content of each tape, and an initial idea of the different generations and applications of the *Kaderdatenspeicher*, could be derived.

However, one typical problem had already become apparent at this early stage. In the few lines of the volume label and headers, three different ways were used to express the date:

1. day, month, year (ddmmyy) in EBCDIC (e.g. 180388 translates as 18 March 1988);
2. number of year and number of the day in that year (yyddd), both in EBCDIC (e.g. 88168 translates as the 168th day in 1988, i.e. 16 June 1988);
3. number of the day (1, 2, . . . 9, A, . . . V), number of the month (1, 2, . . . 9, A, B, C), number of the year in decade (0, 1, . . . 9) (dmy), counting from 1 to 9 in numbers and from 10 onwards in letters of

the alphabet (e.g. V18 translates as the 31st day in the first month in the eighth year of the 1980s = 31 January 1988).

Of course, there are many more possibilities for expressing dates, especially considering the different ways of 'packing' dates and numbers. There is, for instance, a very common method of storing a date from the twentieth century in only two bytes—one has nine bits for the number of days in the year (0 to 511) and seven bits for the number of years (0 to 127), starting with 1900. This way of expressing the date again leaves one with two options, starting with either the days or the years, for example:

	Byte 1	Byte 2
either	yyyy yyyd	dddd dddd
or	dddd dddd	dyyy yyyy

There is also the possibility of expressing a date by counting a bit for a defined time-sequence (usually days) from a system-dependent fixed date. These so-called 'timer-tics' are extremely difficult to decipher if the fixed date is not known. Often, when the data are separated from the original system, this dating information is lost. In East German data files, many different possibilities were used to express dates or numbers.

The data sets of the *Kaderdatenspeicher* showed that only the full name, the Personal Identification Number (*Personenkennziffer*), the address, and the agency were written in plain EBCDIC. The Personal Identification Number was a unique number given to every citizen of the former GDR at birth. By this number, every East German citizen could be identified. East Germans carried this number with them in all official records through all the phases of their lives, be that a professional career or imprisonment. This Personal Identification Number was also the key to a flourishing exchange of personal data between different East German data-processing centres, a practice which was uninhibited by privacy legislation. For the structure of the Personal Identification Number, See Fig. 18.2.

All the other data fields were coded as numerical values, represented as binary figures. The record length of the *Kaderdatenspeicher* was variable. Binary codes and packing methods had been quite common in East German data files, and the methods used often varied. Fortunately, no further compression algorithms had been utilized in the case of the *Kaderdatenspeicher*.

It became clear that without a precise description of the data-file structure, there was no way to understand the meaning of the data.

ddmmyy s cccc x

6 values   date of birth (day/month/year)

1 value   sex and century of birth

        2—male born before 1900

        3—female born before 1900

        4—male born after 1900

        5—female born after 1900

4 values   location code

        for individuals born before 1970, place of residence when the *PKZ* was received

        for individuals born after 1970, birthplace

1 value   control digit for plausibility checks

Fig. 18.2 Structure of the Personal Identification Number (*Personenkennziffer (PKZ)*)

Therefore, as much information on the *Kaderdatenspeicher* as possible was needed. The orders and commissions to create and process the *Kaderdatenspeicher* had come from the Council of Ministers (Ministerrat der DDR). The vertical files of this office had been added to the collections of the Federal Archives in Potsdam after unification. These holdings were searched for references to the *Kaderdatenspeicher* project, and a series of records that contains descriptions of the *Kaderdatenspeicher*, and reports from the data-processing centres containing a substantial amount of information, were found.

These paper records provided information on the content, purpose, history, and development of the *Kaderdatenspeicher* project, in particular:

- who planned the *Kaderdatenspeicher* and who gave the orders;
- which agencies co-operated;
- what the different aims and purposes of the *Kaderdatenspeicher* were;
- what information was contained in the *Kaderdatenspeicher*;
- how information was collected;

- which versions and updates of the *Kaderdatenspeicher* existed and which computer centres processed and stored them;
- who had access to which portions of the information contained in the *Kaderdatenspeicher*; and
- how information was used.

The reports to the Council of Ministers also contained information on the data-file structure and codebooks. The *Kaderdatenspeicher* consists of annual compilations, so-called 'generations', of data files for the year 1980 and for each year from 1985 to 1989, as well as of extracts for various purposes. Almost all of these data files have at least a slightly different structure. Nevertheless, the data-file structures of all generations of the *Kaderdatenspeicher* could be identified. Much information could be inferred from so-called 'address tables' (*Adressentabellen*), which represent the record layout of a specific file. In some instances, the content of data fields could also be determined by examining the formulas for the collection of the data, of which specimens were found in paper records. Of course, comparing the items in the formulas with the content of the data fields was possible only if the data items were not expressed in a binary form.

The data flow between East German data-processing centres mentioned above proved to be another source of information in the effort to reconstruct lost documentation. This exchange of large quantities of coded data could operate only on the basis of shared codebooks. In fact, the codes used in the big East German person-related data holdings were relatively stable and were often the same. Diagrams were found in the records, where the codes of different data holdings were compared. What was meant to be a tool to facilitate data exchange has become a guide by which archivists can discover which codes of data fields in different data holdings are the same.

The data files of the *Kaderdatenspeicher* were closely linked with the so-called staff databases of ministries and separate government branches (*Arbeitskräftedatenspeicher*), containing personal data of staff members. All the data of the *Kaderdatenspeicher* were originally collected from these staff databases. The Federal Archives have been successful in acquiring the relatively comprehensive and complete documentation of the staff database of the Ministry of Public Education (Ministerium für Volksbildung). Therefore, additional information on the record layout and the data-file structure of the *Kaderdatenspeicher* could be derived from the documentation of the staff database of this ministry.

However, many questions remain unanswered. It was not possible to examine the East German programs originally used to manipulate the data, since they were written in Assembler for a specific type of mainframe. Thus, even if you know the data-file structure of a record, the address, length, and content of a specific field, you may still not be able to understand it. To take the simple example above—there are many ways to express a date and you may not know which one was used. In these cases, specific software was used to analyse sequential files.

In order to obtain background information, archivists have also made contacts with former employees of East German data-processing centres who had created or worked with the data holdings which were acquired. In rare and difficult cases, for instance, when compression algorithms had been used which could not be deciphered, programmers from former East German data-processing centres were even hired as consultants.

ACCESS FOR RESEARCHERS

As has been pointed out, different approaches had to be taken in order to identify and verify data-file structures and to reconstruct documentation:

- analysis of labels and data;
- searching for documentation in the corresponding vertical files;
- studying the original data flow in order to identify shared codebooks and similar file structures;
- obtaining information from former employees; and
- last but not least, using specific software.

In this way, much of the missing documentation of East German data holdings could be reconstructed. However, although a number of fairly well-documented data files can already be presented for research purposes, most East German data holdings still remain a problem because of the specific hardware environment in which they were created. Since the main goal of reconstructing documentation is to facilitate access to the data, additional work is still necessary.

For long-term preservation, East German data files are stored as flat files. Apart from this 'archival copy', the Federal Archives are planning to create 'research copies' with specific formats that are well suited for research purposes and easy to handle. These research copies are not meant for archival preservation. The Federal Archives have made an agreement with the Centre for Historical Social Research (Zentrum für Historische Sozialforschung) and the Data Archives for Social Research (Zentralarchiv für empirische Sozialforschung) in order to use the expertise and the technical facilities of these institutions to create research files of East German machine-readable records. The aim of this co-operation is to promote historical social research on the former GDR.

CONCLUSIONS

Taking over East German data holdings has certainly been an extreme case from which it is difficult to generalize. However, some of the attitudes and procedures in East German computer centres are probably universal. For instance, it seems that people working with computers love to play around with programs and data but are not particularly fond of documenting what they are doing. Much of the information which is important for future archivists and researchers of data holdings will be in private notebooks or in the brains of system administrators and records creators. However, preserving these archival holdings means ensuring their accessibility in the future, and reconstructing documentation may be one of the keys to this.

The situation with which archivists were confronted after German unification points to another general principle with respect to the preservation of electronic records. Securing data files cannot success-fully start when data-processing and record centres are being dissolved. Rather, archivists need to get involved at an early stage of the creation of data holdings to ensure that their disposition is planned in advance, and that archivists can get physical control of data when necessary. If that had been the case with respect to GDR data, many of the difficulties presented here could have been avoided.

The Russian Archive System under Pressure in the Information Age

TATYANA MOISEENKO

ABSTRACT

This chapter investigates archival policy in Russia relating mainly to the storage and preservation of electronic documents in the public sector: the relations between the producers of electronic records and the State Archival Service; access to machine-readable data files stored in departmental archives; criteria for digital data appraisal and selection for long-term preservation; the peculiarities of electronic records in comparison with 'traditional' paper documents, and the additional difficulties that these cause for archivists.

INTRODUCTION

The electronic medium is replacing paper in a record-keeping revolution. It will be impossible to study contemporary society without electronic records, in the same way as it is difficult to imagine the history of nineteenth-century Europe without printed materials. Most kinds of documents (data on taxation, social insurance, statistics of health and welfare, censuses and special surveys, business records, private correspondence, etc.) are available today (at least in developed countries) both on paper and in electronic form. Moreover, the second is rapidly replacing the first. In the mid-1980s only 2 per cent of information was stored on computer media. At the present rate of development (and we may expect even higher growth rates), at the beginning of the next century 50 per cent of all information will be stored electronically.

Information technology (IT) is revolutionizing the concept of record-keeping as much as did the introduction of printing, if not of writing itself. This is leading many countries to re-examine existing record-keeping practices and current archival legislation, and to elaborate strategies of appraisal, storage, long-term preservation, and dissemination for machine-readable data files (MRDFs) (Dollar 1992; Bikson and Frinking 1993; Hofman 1995).

However, the issues of long-term preservation and 'secondary use' of electronic documents have not yet become a 'live issue' in Russian historiography. Until now archivists in Russia have paid attention mainly to 'traditional' paper documents. They express almost no concern about the necessity to analyse MRDFs as a specific type of primary source, or the need to preserve them as a part of the historical heritage for future generations. Historians are mainly interested in databases created by their colleagues and practically ignore the MRDFs produced in the public sector. Furthermore, it seems that most of them do not yet realize that, unless steps are taken immediately, many electronic documents could disappear forever, or have already been lost.

The aim of this chapter is to draw attention to these acute problems. I will examine the situation in Russia with respect to electronic documents, especially those created in the public sector, and the archival policy dealing with their storage and preservation. I will discuss the following issues: the relationship between the producers of electronic records and the state archival service; where one can obtain information about electronic information resources; where and how MRDFs are stored in Russia; how to get access to electronic documents that are to be archived; what are the criteria for digital data selection and appraisal for long-term preservation; what are the peculiarities of electronic records in comparison with 'traditional' paper documents; and what additional difficulties they pose for archiving. This chapter will chiefly address the treatment of databases, since electronic mail (e-mail), multimedia, and geographical information systems (GIS) have only recently been introduced into Russia, and the preservation of their records has not yet become a matter of concern for Russian archivists.

The situation in Russia and the Commonwealth of Independent States is unique in many respects. Therefore, in addition to many of the problems found in other countries, archivists in Russia are confronted with distinct difficulties, which also need to be described.

ELECTRONIC INFORMATION RESOURCES

What electronic information resources does Russia possess? How many electronic documents have already been preserved in national archives as part of the cultural heritage? How many MRDFs are still stored in the departments and offices that generated them, and how many have been lost? Unfortunately, there are as yet no clear answers to any of these questions.

In the former USSR (as in many other totalitarian states) data on individual citizens were input, both on paper and on electronic media, by different types of organizations, such as the state administration, the KGB, the Communist Party, and state and collective enterprises. In spite of the relative backwardness in respect of computer applications in offices, there were many information systems and databases of technical and scientific information, especially in enterprises and institutions dealing with the 'high technologies'—space, defence, aircraft, and metallurgy. A considerable amount of valuable information on the social and economic development of the USSR in the 1960s to the 1980s was created in the period of the 'ASU campaign'— ASU being the Russian abbreviation for 'automation systems of management'. By the middle of the 1980s there were about 10,000 ASUs. The outputs of this activity were thousands of magnetic tapes, of which many are still stored by Central and Regional Statistical Committees, as well as in the former USSR ministries' archives (*Bulletin of the Russian Society of Computer Sciences and Computer Engineering* 1994). Most of the MRDFs were produced on mainframes, including the popular Soviet 'EC' range, which was compatible with the IBM 360. The files were usually intended for the internal needs of the staff of departments and ministries. These databases were seldom interconnected, and often duplicated, or were complementary to, each other.

According to a census carried out in 1991 by Roskominform (the Russian Committee on Information) in conjunction with Goskomstat (the State Statistical Committee), there were at that date between 25,000 and 30,000 databases. The number of organizations which possessed databases was about 10,000, of which about 70–80 per cent belonged to the public sector. Research institutions and design offices (*konstruktorskoe biuro*) comprised half of these organizations, and computer centres about 30 per cent. The largest category of databases (about 40 per cent) consisted of technical information. Over 15 per cent were reference databases; 12 per cent contained management documentation; 10 per cent of the total were composed of databases of scientific research information; 8 per cent were statistical; 5 per cent were commercial databases; and less than 0.5 per cent were labelled 'archival databases'. More than 75 per cent of the databases were located in Moscow and St Petersburg. In Moscow alone were stored 74 per cent of the data bases with scientific and technical information, 84 per cent of the reference databases, 84 per cent of the financial and statistical data banks, 87 per cent of the data sets of management documentation, and 93 per cent of the data banks with commercial information (*Bulletin of the Russian Society of Computer Sciences and Computer Engineering* 1994). All these figures are estimates, of course, and can only indicate broad tendencies.

The fast dissemination of new technologies in the 1990s, especially the 'microcomputer revolution', has resulted in an enormous increase in the number of MRDFs. Because of the economic and social reforms, and the transformation of the social structure of Russian society, new groups of producers and consumers of electronic documents appeared, first of all in the private sector—banks, stock exchanges, private firms, and the non-state mass media. From 1989 to 1991, for instance, between 400 and 500 new information organizations were set up (Ashurbeili 1994; *Bulletin of the Russian Society of Computer Sciences and Computer Engineering* 1994).

There are a number of different types of organization preserving electronic records, and which, in principle, are able to make them available for 'secondary use'. Among these are state and departmental archives, which mainly store public records; commercial information providers; and data archives, which are mainly concerned with MRDFs created in the research community.

The State Archival Service of the Russian Federation, which provides long-term preservation for records (both paper and 'non-paper'), comprises about 2,300 state archives and centres of document storage. Among these there are more than fifteen federal (all-Russian) archives and centres of document storage; more than 300 archives of the subjects of the Russian Federation (republics, districts, regions); and about 2,000 city and district archives. Before they are transferred to the state archives, documents produced in the public sector are usually kept in the departmental archives of ministries, departments, and offices (State Duma of the Russian Federation 1994: 1066, 1068).

In the mid-1990s the number of electronic documents preserved still comprises only a tiny portion of the total number of files (dossiers) in state and departmental archives. The federal archives did not (and still do not) receive MRDFs regularly from state offices, ministries, and other data producers. Unfortunately there is no precise information on the number of electronic records in national archives, because they are included in the more general category of 'non-paper' documents (magnetic and video tapes, photos, records, etc.). Moreover, the term 'file' (*delo* in Russian) is rather vague, as it may consist of a couple of pages, or a dozen documents. We have, therefore, only very rough estimates. The total number of archival files (dossiers) which were stored in state archives (on 1 January 1994) was approximately 185.5 million (All-Russian Institute of Document and Archival Studies 1994: 16–17). Within the category of 'non-paper documents', which comprises less than 4 per cent of the total amount of archival files, MRDFs form only a small fraction. Moreover, the MRDFs in archival holdings include electronic catalogues, inventories, and other heuristic tools created by the archives themselves, and digitized paper collections, as well as records originally created in electronic form.

Why is the long-term preservation of MRDFs in the national archives in Russia frequently difficult, and sometimes even impossible? In my opinion there are two types of issue here. On the one hand, we can distinguish organizational (institutional) reasons, which are related to:

- a lack of space, money, staff, computers, and other equipment in the national archives and other institutions which should provide for the collection and storage of MRDFs;
- an unclear legislative framework with regards to the tasks of archives with respect to electronic records;
- a lack of information about public and private databases;
- difficulties of access to electronic records stored in state and private organizations—archival collections of many state institutions, such as those of the former Communist Party of the Soviet Union, the KGB, the Council of Ministries, and the Central Statistical Bureau, have yet to be declassified.

On the other hand, we can distinguish factors related to the peculiarities of documents on electronic media, such as the 'non-linear' character of electronic records, the short life cycle of electronic media, and the hardware and software dependency of MRDFs.

THE PRODUCERS OF ELECTRONIC RECORDS AND ARCHIVES

Current archival legislation covers only some aspects of the links between data producers (mainly state departments and services) and national archives (State Duma of the Russian Federation 1995*b*). Many legal issues regarding the preservation of MRDFs, including copyright, privacy, confidentiality, and security matters, are still vague. Russian archival law prescribes that electronic records, produced in the public sector, should be transferred to state archives for long-term preservation five years after their creation. Scientific and technical electronic records should be transferred to national archives when they cease to be of practical use to the organization, but not later than twenty-five years after their creation (State Duma of the Russian Federation 1994).

However, most of the electronic records are still housed in the departmental archives and institutions where they were created. The 'ownership' of records, whether in machine-readable form or not, is also often vested in the departments that generated them. Many ministries and organizations which have their own information systems also preserve data which have ceased to have operational use. For instance, the Russian Parliament, the Presidential Administration, the Intelligence Service, the Ministry of Foreign Affairs, many institutions working for the Ministry of Defence, the Centre for Geological Information, the Centre for Space Documentation, the Centre for Meteorological Data, organizations of Social Security, the Information Agency ITAR-TASS, which are the largest producers of MRDFs, also deposit electronic data in their own archives (Antopol'skii 1993; Nikitov and Orlov 1994).

The economic and political reforms of the 1990s have had a considerable impact on the relations between the producers of MRDFs in the public and private sectors, and the national archives. First, after the disintegration of the USSR, many state and social institutions of the former Soviet Union which were responsible for the maintenance and storage of these databases ceased to exist. Many of these have no legatees and things have often been 'left to chance'. As a result, many of these data sets are threatened with destruction. For instance, one of the largest state databases on agriculture was created by Central Statistical Board staff and the special department of the Central Committee of the Communist Party of the Soviet Union

(CPSU), to facilitate the management of agriculture by high-ranking state and party officials. After the prohibition of the activities of the CPSU in the aftermath of the August putsch of 1992, the original users of this database have moved on. The storage of such an enormous bulk of information is expensive, and its preservation is by no means guaranteed.

Secondly, because of the privatization of former state enterprises, many databases of previously public institutions appear no longer to be within the control of the national archives. Similarly, many state departments and private enterprises do not want to transfer their documents for long-term preservation to federal archives, using considerations of state and commercial secrecy as excuses. Many former state organizations which have been privatized, and which realize the commercial value of the information that they hold, are also unwilling to transfer MRDFs to state archives. This is a time-consuming and costly operation for which they need additional labour inputs. Last, but not least, producers of MRDFs often demand compensation for the costs of the storage media of electronic records (magnetic tapes or diskettes). During the period 1985 to 1989 the number of documents which were preserved in departmental archives for longer than the time period prescribed by archival law, increased from 4.8 to 5.6 million files (dossiers) (State Archival Committee of the USSR 1990: 4). On the other hand, because of a lack of space and the rapid increase of rents for office space, many organizations constantly destroy files which have ceased to be active in operational systems.

Until the early 1990s archivists and historians did not have the appropriate means to influence creators of MRDFs. 'Mosarchiv' (Moscow city archive service comprising eleven archives and three research centres) received powers in 1993 to impose a fine on state departments and offices (and on private firms as well!), if they do not keep their records in an appropriate order, lose them, or refuse to transfer them for long-term preservation to the archives (Kiselev 1994: 5). However, it will be virtually impossible to check thousands of information systems and databases, and their producers. In Moscow alone there are more than forty united departmental archives, more than 830 archives of ministries, offices, and undertakings, and thousands of private firms, many of which have their own information systems. To exert control over their information activities is easier on paper than it is in practice.

INFORMATION ABOUT INFORMATION

It is quite understandable that in this situation there is a lack of co-ordination in the activities of the archival services and state institutions, and, as a result, a lack of information about electronic information resources. Data on the location, content, and conditions of access respecting MRDFs are being collected by different types of organizations, such as the national archive service, and public and non-government data archives and information centres.

The total corpus of archival material in the Russian Federation can be divided into documents produced in the public and private sectors. Documents from the public sector, irrespective of their place of storage, media, and means of information presentation, are required to be officially registered by the State Archival Service, state museums, libraries, or departmental archives. The State Archival Service should also register and regularly update the list of all the departments and organizations which can be considered as sources for acquisition, their functions, the types of documents which should be selected for long-term preservation, and so on. In 1994 more than 100,000 organizations were listed by the archival services—about 3,000 at the federal archives and the rest at the archives of the subjects of the Russian Federation (All-Russian Institute of Document and Archival Studies 1994: 18). However, this list is not complete—the institutions are listed in more than 100 registers, and some 60 per cent of these are out of date. As a result, the amount of duplicate and redundant information in archives is constantly increasing.

Other state institutions which play an 'intermediary' role between data producers and users also occasionally make inventories of electronic resources. I have already mentioned, for example, the census of Roskominform and Goskomstat, which covered a sample of about 30 per cent of the organizations producing electronic documents. Information about MRDFs is made available by some information centres and archives of machine-readable documents, such as the All-Russian Institute of Scientific and Technical Information (VINITI), the Institute of Scientific Information on Social Sciences (INION), and the All-Russian Sociological Data Bank.

The information centre (Informregistr), for example, has published *Databases of Russia*, which contains about 10,000 database descriptions, and 5,000 addresses of vendors and distributors. The contents of these databases cover a very broad field, from demography, trade, and the banking system, to the history of art and chemistry (Informregistr 1993;

an earlier version of this is available in English). However, these institutes are mainly concerned with 'research' data sets and receive information about public records only sporadically.

According to recently published legal guidelines, Informregistr is entitled to receive a mandatory copy of every database (State Duma of the Russian Federation 1995*a*). However, there are insufficient incentives for organizations to send information about their MRDFs to the data archives. In fact, Informregistr and similar bodies have to rely mainly on the goodwill of organizations to answer questionnaires about their databases, and to deposit the latter in data archives.

The documents produced in the 'non-state' sector by private enterprises, political parties, foundations, individuals, and so on are preserved by their owners. These institutions, if they so wish, can deposit or transfer their records to state archives, museums, and libraries for long-term preservation. The documents of the 'non-state' sector should also be deposited in the state archives in cases where these organizations are liquidated without legatees. The creators of private records should not destroy them without the approval of the State Archival Service of the Russian Federation (State Duma of the Russian Federation 1994: 1070). However, in practice the State Archival Service cannot implement control over private records, especially MRDFs.

Now that an information market is coming into existence, organizations in the private sector are paying increasing attention to the collection and selling of 'information about information'. This could be the subject of a separate study, and I will limit myself here to describing major trends. For instance, in the period 1990 to 1992 as many as 500 new information organizations were set up in Russia. One of the first attempts to collect information about electronic data sets was made in 1991 within the framework of the Mezhdunarodnoe biuro informatsii i telekommunikatsii (MBIT) (the International Bureau of Information and Telecommunications), which united several state institutions and private companies. Since 1992 MBIT has published a quarterly *Catalogue of Information Resources of Russia* (*Katalog informatsionnykh resursov Rossii*) containing information on commercial databases (Ashurbeili 1994).

ACCESS TO DATA SETS

The question of access to electronic records has two aspects. Access for researchers to electronic records preserved in national archives is problematic, but, in addition, the archives themselves have difficulty in getting access to the scattered materials stored by the data producers. In the former USSR, access to electronic documents (and paper documents as well) was restricted by state secrecy and departmental interests. For example, the statistical characteristics of economic and social development, industrial and agricultural production, national income, standards of living, and food supply were considered to be state secrets. The degree of secrecy (or restricted access) as a rule was determined not for particular documents, but for whole organizations, departments, or categories of records. For instance, documents which were produced by the Ministry of Defence, the Ministry of Foreign Affairs, the Intelligence Service, the ministries and departments dealing with nuclear energy, geology, environment, meteorology, geographical maps, state standards, and many other topics were (and still are) excluded from the coverage of the archival laws. The records of these organizations are stored in the departmental archives of these ministries for a period determined by different special agreements. According to some estimates, these organizations now preserve more than 109 million files (State Archival Committee of the USSR 1990: 3). For example, even today the bulk of statistical data (on paper and electronic media) produced by the Central Statistical Bureau, including practically all the censuses, is stored with the designation 'for internal use' and is not therefore available to researchers. Only one census of population, for 1989, is listed in the *Directory of Soviet Databases* (All-Union Institute for Inter-Industrial Information 1991).

As a result of the democratization of Russian society, some secrecy restrictions have been lifted. The Russian State Archival Service has come to an agreement on the conditions and terms of records preservation with a series of ministries and agencies (the Ministry of Defence, the Ministry of the Interior, the Ministry of Foreign Affairs, the Intelligence Service, and so on) which had previously had the right to keep their archives permanently. In accordance with these agreements, it is planned that several collections of documents of these ministries will be gradually transferred to the state archives. In 1994 the archival institutions of the State Archival Service had already declassified more than 800,000 files (Tarasov 1995). This, of course, is only a tiny fraction of the total number of unavailable files.

Electronic networks, especially the Internet, offer great opportunities for access to archival collections and databases, as far as these require no access control. However, the Russian archives have only begun to investigate the possibilities of electronic networks. For example, Rosarchiv, the Research Libraries Group (RLG), and the Hoover Institution are discussing a trilateral agreement in order to make Russian archival material, much of which has never before been available in the West, accessible, via the RLG information network (RLIN). An on-line document on 'Revelations from the Russian Archives', prepared by the Library of Congress and the Russian archives, can already be accessed via the World Wide Web on the Internet (URL: http:// sunsite. unc.edu/expo/soviet.exhibit/gifs/soviet.gif). It contains images of more than 500 primary documents from Soviet archives which cover the entire range of Soviet history from the October Revolution of 1917 to the failed *coup* of August 1991. Documents never shown anywhere before have been extracted from archives that contained key working files of the Communist rulers—the archives of the Central Committee, the Presidential Archive, and the KGB. English translations of these are also available.

APPRAISAL OF ELECTRONIC RECORDS

In modern Russian archival practice there are two main criteria used in the appraisal of documents: 'evident or absolute value' and 'informational value', referring to the expected 'secondary use' of documents. However, both of these criteria appear to be insufficient in the world of electronic records. The recommendation prevalent in the 1980s to preserve only electronic documents which do not have paper analogues has also proved unsatisfactory.

In the 1990s the new concept of 'appraisal by functions' has taken hold (State Archival Committee of the USSR and the Russian Centre of Space Documentation 1994). The advocates of this notion among Russian archivists consider it necessary to pay attention principally to the functions of electronic documents rather than to the files and series of documents themselves. Archivists will have first to identify the organization which produced an electronic record, and then examine its business or scientific functions and fields of activity. Analysis of software used in information systems is also desirable. It is intended that the selection of documents will be carried out by an expert commission, formed by producers, which should include also a representative of the State Archival Service.

However, electronic documents could eventually lose their value. The costs of storage of MRDFs and especially their 'rewriting' according to new technologies and standards may be higher than the benefits of their preservation. Therefore, some archivists suggest the need to reconsider the concept of an 'absolute' or 'eternal' value of a document, and use instead the term 'long-term value'. This will 'free' archives from a too absolute and rigid position with regard to the long-term preservation of MRDFs, which are seen as unrealistic from an economic point of view.

THE CONTEXT OF ELECTRONIC DOCUMENTS

Archival services aim to extend 'normal' procedures for paper records as far as possible to the appraisal, storage, and preservation of MRDFs. However, the dissemination of new information technologies forces archivists to reconsider many basic terms and notions of archival practice, which have been used for many decades. The new technology is changing not only the medium on which documents have been preserved, but also the whole concept of a document as an integral and independent record. One of the main peculiarities of electronic documents is their 'non-linear character'. The form and the content (logical structure, paragraphs, and chapters in a book, for example) of traditional paper documents are the same. In contrast, machine-readable or electronic documents are stored as separate elements in databases, and only after certain programs or computer commands have selected data from these database can they constitute a document, when printed or shown on the monitor (All-Russian Institute of Document and Archival Studies 1994: 94).

Under these circumstances the traditional approach to the preservation of records according to their provenance is difficult. It is likely that archivists will have to change the whole system of 'intellectual' classification of documents, which provides the maintenance of the logical connections and relations between separate documents and groups of documents. Some Russian archivists propose to consider as a basic unit of such classifications not an electronic document itself (or a separate file), but the information system, which produces these files and documents (State Archival Committee of the USSR and the Russian Centre of Space Documentation 1994).

STORAGE

It is not yet clear where is the best place to store the MRDFs that need to be archived, and who will be responsible for their storage and preservation. Should electronic records be archived centrally by national archival services, by departmental archives, in special centres of scientific and technical information, or at the institutions and computer centres which created the MRDFs?

Three main facets of the world of paper documents were favourable for the creation and development of centralized archival storage:

- the unity of archival collections of documents according to the principle of provenance;
- cheaper storage in centralized archives;
- the ability to identify important documents in state archives more easily than in organizations where data selected for long-term preservation were stored together with more ephemeral operational data.

However, with the appearance of electronic documents the role of these factors has changed. Now many archivists in Russia consider it unlikely that central archives will provide the storage and preservation of MRDFs.

One of the main reasons for this is the poor material and technological base of the Russian archives. Many of them suffer severely from a lack of money, physical storage space, personnel, and modern equipment. Thus, in 1994 the federal archives and centres of document storage (except research institutions) had a mere 108 personnel computers (PCs) at their disposal, and the 2,000 state archives of the subjects of the Russian Federation possessed only 152 (All-Russian Institute of Document and Archival Studies 1994: 20). Some archives have closed down, some are operating on a reduced scale. In order to survive some have to carry out commercial projects far removed from their main field of responsibility.

Many departmental archives, which should provide temporary storage of documents, are in an especially poor state. About half of them do not have special storage space, and in many there are no special staff responsible for these tasks. In these conditions it is extremely difficult for many archives to provide appropriate preservation conditions for documents on electronic media, especially their 'rewriting' according to new technical standards.

Therefore the authors of a new programme of computerization for the State Archival Service have come down in favour of the decentralized storage of MRDFs in the organization that generated them, or in departmental (intermediary) archives. In their view, the central state archives, which are not currently able to provide the physical conditions required for the storage of MRDFs, should reduce their task to taking stock of MRDFs, controlling their preservation at local archives and organizations, and also providing the central cataloguing of these data sets and access to them. They suggest that organizations which generate electronic records, and still use them as operational data, should also get resources and help to transfer these documents to a new standard format, with yearly maintenance routines conducted to measure the deterioration of the data. Of course, these are merely recommendations, but many archivists seem to support these notions. The question is whether the departmental archives and organizations generating electronic records will be willing to carry out this expensive labour, especially in respect of data which have already been withdrawn from operational systems. (For a general discussion of the problems associated with this strategy, see Higgs, Chapter 12, this volume).

CONCLUSION

Today the Russian archives, in common with national archives in many other countries, are confronted with a difficult choice—to begin the centralized storage and preservation of electronic records, or to let them stay in the organizations that produced them, thereby running the risk that the bulk of MRDFs may be destroyed. The federal archives in Russia have hardly begun to store digital documents. In spite of the fact that a special department of machine-readable documents was created in 1982 at the Tsentral'nyi Gosudarstvennyi Arkhiv Narodnogo Khoziaistva (Central State Archive of Economy), state archives are still mainly receiving MRDFs on an experimental base. Today the bulk of electronic records is still housed in the organizations that produced them, in departmental archives, or in special documentation centres.

The peculiarities of electronic records, such as hardware and software dependence, the short life cycle of electronic media, and rapid changes in information technologies, have caused considerable difficulties for archivists in the West, as well as in Russia, and forced them to modify existing procedures of appraisal and storage of documents. However, the State Archival Service is now confronting many difficulties which are specific to the current situation in Russia. Because of the relative backwardness of Russia with respect to computer and new information technologies compared to the West, there were restricted numbers of organizations which generated MRDFs. Moreover, the informational activity of many state departments and ministries, which are better equipped with computers and which produce the majority of electronic documents, such as research institutions of the space industry and the Ministry of Defence, the Ministry of Foreign Affairs, the Central Statistical Bureau, and others, is excluded from common archival law. So far, they mainly keep their own records. Many documents in state archives are also not accessible for research as yet because of consideration of state secrecy.

On the other hand, the national archives cannot at the moment provide for the mass storage of electronic documents, because of a lack of physical storage space, equipment, money, and technical skills amongst their staff. Therefore, they have tried to shift the responsibility for electronic records keeping to departments and offices which are producing MRDFs. The latter are often destroying electronic documents which are not in operational use. A state policy related to the long-term preservation of electronic records in state archives does not yet exist. Therefore the preservation of many MRDFs is by no means guaranteed in Russia. Many have already been destroyed, some are stored without relevant hardware and software and cannot be 'read', and some are damaged because of inadequate conditions for preservation.

Some urgent steps need to be taken immediately in order to save the electronic memory of Russian society of the last decades of the twentieth century. It is necessary to draw the attention of archivists and decision-makers to this problem, and to elaborate a state policy respecting the storage and long-term preservation of electronic resources. Existing practice and archival legislation should be revised with respect to criteria for appraisal of machine-readable documents, the physical standards of their storage, standards of cataloguing, and means of disclosure and access. Tomorrow will be too late, it is probably already too late today!

References

All-Russian Institute of Document and Archival Studies (1994), *Elaboration of the Conception of the Complex Informatization of the Archival System* (Moscow). (Всероссийский научно-исследовательский инситут документоведения и архивного дела (1994), *Разработка концепции комплексной информатизации архивного дела*) (Москва)).

All-Union Institute for Inter-Industrial Information (1991), *Directory of Soviet Databases* (Moscow).

Antopol'skii, A. B. (1993) (ed.), *The Problems of the Creation and Use of Data Banks and Databases* (Moscow). (Антопольский, А. Б. (1993) (ред.), *Проблемы создания и использования баз и банков данных* (Москва)).

Ašhurbeili, I. (1994), 'Formation of the Information Market in Russia', *Information Resources of Russia*, ns 1: 6–8. (Ашурбейли, И. (1994), 'Становление информацнонного рынка в России', *Информационные ресурсы России*, ns 1: 6–8).

Bikson, T. K., and Frinking, E. J. (1993), *Het heden onthouden / Preserving the Present: Towards Viable Electronic Records* (The Hague).

Bulletin of the Russian Society of Computer Sciences and Computer Engineering 'Automatized Information Resources of Russia: State and Tendencies of Development' ns 4–5: 7–66. (Автоматизированные информационные ресурсы России: Состояние и тенденции развития (1994), *Вестник российского общества информатки и вычислительной техники*, ns 4–5: 7–66).

Dollar, C. M. (1992), *Archival Theory and Information Technologies: The Impact of Information Technologies on Archival Principals and Methods* (Ancona).

Hofman, J. (1995) (ed.), *Het papieren tijdperk voorbij: Beleid voor een digitaal geheugen von onze samenleving* (The Hague).

Informregistr (1993), *Databases of Russia* (Moscow). (Информрегистр (1993), *Базы цанных России* (Москва)).

Kedrovskii, O. (1994) 'The Information Space of Russia', *Information Resources of Russia*, ns 4: 2–3. (Кедровский, О. (1994), 'Информационное пространство России', *Информационные ресурсы России*, ns 4: 2–3).

Kiselev, A. S. (1994), 'Moscow Archives: The Year 1993 and New Tasks', *Russian Archives*, ns 2: 3–6. (Киселев, А. С. (1994), 'Москвские архиы: год 1993 и ноые задачи', *Отечественные архивы*, ns 2: 3–6).

Nikitov, V. A., and Orlov, E. I. (1994), 'Information Provision for the Council of Federation of the Federal Assembly of the Russian Federation', *Scientific and Technical Information*, ns 9: 11–17. (Никитов, В. А., и Орлрв, Е. И. (1994), 'Информационное обеспечение Совта Федерации Федерального Собрания Российской Федерации', *Научнотехническая информация*, ns 9: 11–17).

State Archival Committee of the USSR (1990), *Main Tendencies of Improvement of Departmental Preservation of Documents: 1990–1995* (Moscow). (Главархив СССР (1990), *Основные направления совершенствования ведомственного хранения документов ГВФ СССР: 1990–1995 гг* (Москва)).

——and the Russian Centre of Space Documentation (1994), *Machine-Readable Documents: Acquisition for State Custody and Creation of Specialized Archives* (Moscow). (Главархив СССР, и Российский научно-исследовательский центр космической документации (1994), *Машиночитаемые документы: прием на государственное хранение, создание специализированных архивов* (Москва)).

State Duma of the Russian Federation (1994), 'Statute on the Archival Fund of the Russian Federation', *Gazette of the Supreme Soviet of the Russian Federation*, NS 12: 1065–1071. (Государственная Дума Российской Федерации (1994), 'Положение об Архивном Фонде Российской Федерации', *Ведомости Верховного Совета Российской Федерации*, NS 12: 1065–1071).

——(1995*a*), 'Compulsory Deposit of Documents: Federal Act of the Russian Federation of 23.09.1994', *Collection of Federal Constitutional Laws*, 18–29. (Государственная Дума Российской Федерации (1994), 'Об обязательном экземпляре документов: Федеральный закон Российской Федерации от 23.09.1994', *Сборник федеральных конституционных законов и федеральных законов*, 18–29).

——(1995*b*), *Information, Informatization and Protection of Information: Federal Act of the Russian Federation* (Moscow). (Государственная Дума Российской Федерации (1995), *Об информации, информатизации и защите информации: Федеральный закон Российской Федерации* (Москва)).

Tanonin, V. A. (1994), 'Information Society and Machine-Readable Archives', *Russian Archives*, NS 1: 14–18. (Танонин, В. А. (1994), 'Информационное общество и архивы на машинных носителях', *Отечественные архивы*, NS 1: 14–18).

Tarasov, V. P. (1995), 'Information on International Activities of Rosarchiv and its System during 1994 and the first Half of 1995', *Social History and Russia* (2 July), 6–7.

Data Conservation at a Traditional Data Archive

HANS-JØRGEN MARKER

ABSTRACT

The Danish Data Archives (DDA), founded in 1973, have recently been incorporated into the national archives of Denmark, the Statens Arkiver. The DDA holds strong views on the standard of documentation and processing needed for the long-term preservation of data. The standards employed by the DDA exceed those used by most other data archives and are most certainly beyond what is feasible for a public archive receiving masses of data from the administration. Nevertheless, the methods employed by the DDA, and the general philosophy behind them, could serve as a starting-point for a discussion on what to do with data that are so bulky that it is impossible within normal economic resources to get detailed knowledge on what they contain.

INTRODUCTION

Valuable data need to be protected from becoming unavailable. When the data in question are going to be preserved for posterity, the necessary level of protection is especially difficult to ensure. The equivalent of putting paper in boxes and boxes on shelves does not presently exist for machine-readable data, and there are no signs that such a paradigm is going to materialize in the immediate future. An important reason why means of simple and reliable storage of data materials are a thing of the future are the rapid advances in data-processing technology. Changes in technology afflict the machine-readable material in two ways. The medium—the actual physical carrier of the data—will almost certainly become obsolete within a decade or two after its creation, as other, better, media replace it. Soon after a particular medium becomes obsolete, functional machinery to read that medium becomes a rarity. Therefore, reading data stored on the medium becomes very difficult. Many of the media in use now have a very limited guaranteed life span to begin with. Moreover, data are always created by or in association with some software, and are usually dependent on that software to be read. As versions of the software involved replace each other in rapid succession, files created by superseded versions of the software may no longer be readable. In the face of these difficulties, long-term preservation of data without the continuous intervention of an archive cannot be achieved. Because of the large amount of data produced, it is, however, of prime importance that the actual intervention needed to preserve particular data is minimized.

The methodology that has been used at data archives for ensuring long-term preservation of data was essentially directed towards numerical data with a fixed and very simple format. The methodology is easily extended to structured data of the type which essentially consists of tables. The current methodology does not cope very well with data of a more complex nature (e.g. multimedia). Data archives have experience going back twenty to thirty years. Compared with the experience of paper archives, this is very short. Measured against the data-using community in general, data archives represent institutions which have been in existence from the beginning of the culture. The data-archive tradition is evolving, as is everything else in data-processing. In a discussion of proper archival procedures for machine-readable material, the data archival procedures should be of value as a guide. Below I shall give an overview of traditional data-archival procedures involved in the preservation of data.

PHYSICAL PRESERVATION

Though the hardware situation was in broad terms fairly stable in the early 1990s, there were quite a few developments in storage media. Optical storage media especially underwent development during the same period. Some optical storage media have already been scrapped, and even the most commonly available, the CD-ROM, is a target for further improvement. Even in the areas where we have relative stability of hardware, we naturally have no guarantee that it will remain this way. It is necessary, therefore, to rewrite the material to new media at reasonable intervals. Traditional good data-archival practice indicates that every three years is the optimal time-frame. As media quality improves and perhaps more stability of types and formats of media is achieved, the intervals between rewriting can possibly be prolonged. At each rewriting of the data, it is then of importance that the media chosen for the rewrite are current and common. This is the best way to ensure that the next rewrite can be achieved with minimal difficulty.

LOGICAL PRESERVATION

A very complicated threat to the readability of data is software development. If the software used for storing particular data becomes extinct, a loss of information will result. The extent and severity of the loss will, of course, depend on the nature of the data. The problem can be solved in a number of ways. Usually the preferable solution is to reduce the dependency on software by transforming the data to an ASCII character format, and then document them thoroughly. In this way, the full potential of the material can be realized, when the data are read into any appropriate software.

TABULAR-FORM DATA

Much of the data recorded and used by various software systems, such as databases, spreadsheets, and statistical analysis systems, can be considered as tabular in form. In this category I count data which consist of one or more tables. A table consists of a number of objects (rows) that all have the same set of characteristics (columns). A simple spreadsheet is a table. In data archival terminology, the rows of the table are called records and the columns are called variables. A uniform card file is a table where each card is a record and each piece of information on a card is the value of a variable. When all the variables have fixed lengths, the data file is called rectangular. The rectangular data file is a classic of statistical analysis.

For rectangular statistical data, the processes of transformation and documentation are known as 'data-processing' in data archives. Data-processing is carried out somewhat differently at different data archives. The DDA practice is outlined below. My knowledge of the procedures followed at other data archives is only patchy, so it would be most improper for me to attempt to give a comparative account. The basis for the methodology used at the DDA is the statistical software package OSIRIS, which is not really in existence any more. The OSIRIS file format was chosen at the end of the 1970s as a common file format for data-archiving by a large number of data archives. Among people with a superficial knowledge of data-archival practices, the OSIRIS file format is scorned. The prime reason for this, paradoxically, is that the systems file format is well documented and widely known. I suppose that few would consider Paradox systems files a revelation of beauty if they were handling them on a character level. The facility to handle OSIRIS files without access to the software, using only knowledge of the file definition, is a feature that makes OSIRIS files suitable for data-archival purposes. The better described and the less complex the OSIRIS file format is, the easier it is to access with procedures written in other languages. Another important feature of OSIRIS files is that they contain only letters and numbers in character format. There is nothing binary in the files. Thus an OSIRIS file can be created and deciphered with only a text editor and knowledge of the format. This is not, however, the way it is usually done. At the DDA we have a set of programs used for manipulating the OSIRIS files, and for converting OSIRIS files to and from Statistical Analysis System (SAS). Thus actual data manipulation is done in SAS, while OSIRIS remains the basis of the archive file format. OSIRIS data files are rectangular character files. Each line of the file is called a record, all records are of equal length. As the format deals with tabular data from only one table, each record has the same number of variables. All variables must have a fixed width. Variables can be alphabetic or numeric. In numerical variables only the integers 0–9 are allowed.

To read an OSIRIS data file you need a formal description, which is found in the data dictionary. The minimal OSIRIS dictionary would consist of a header line and a line for each variable. The header line gives essential information, such as the type of dictionary, the number of variables, etc. A line describing a variable gives the variable's position in the data record, the variable's label, the variable's type, and, if the variable is numeric, the number of decimal places. In addition to the types used in the minimal data dictionary, a number of other line types are defined and used. These line types convey background information on the variables and structural information.

On the basis of the dictionary and the data, printed documentation, the codebook, can be produced. This document consists of the information found in the dictionary combined with one-way frequency tables of the variables. The codebook is a very formal document. In the original OSIRIS format, everything had to be upper case, so an original OSIRIS codebook would be extremely ugly. One of the DDA extensions to the OSIRIS format is to allow mixed case. Besides making a codebook for data material, the DDA produces a study description (SD). The SD is a formal document consisting of a number of elements. Among the elements found in the SD are bibliographical citations, information used for version control, background on the creation of the data material, information on the contents of the data material, and other essential background material. At the DDA, it is an ongoing development process to identify types of important information on the data materials processed by the DDA, which have a proper place in neither the codebook nor the SD. When such types of information are identified, one of the two documentation media is expanded to accommodate the information. As both the SD and the codebook are essentially international standards, international agreement is sought, where possible, before the data structure is expanded. The SD and the codebook are amalgamated and printed together in a document which is called the data documentation publication (DDP). If data material consists of more than one table, the DDP can contain more than one codebook. To conform with the codebook format, relations between the tables must be reduced to variables.

NON-TABULAR CHARACTER DATA

Text files can be documented using the Text Encoding Initiative (TEI) standard (Sperberg-McQueen and Burnard 1994). The TEI is an SGML2 document-type declaration. SGML is a language for formally describing mark-up languages (ISO 1986). A mark-up language is a set of mark-ups which are used for marking certain features of texts. Mark-up can be used to describe the appearance of a text, much like the text is seen in the display feature under WordPerfect. The appearance of a text should, however, have a consistent relationship with its interpretation. If all foreign-language quotations in a text are typeset in italic, you would accomplish this in a word processor by marking all the quotations and then selecting an italic typeface for them. In a generalized mark-up language, you would, however, not necessarily mark the quotations italic, another possibility would be to mark them as quotations.

The latter option leaves the decision about the physical representation of quotations to printing time, and maintains a distinction between foreign-language quotations and, say, authors' names, which might be lost in traditional word-processor treatment of the text. Essentially, a TEI representation of a document consists of a header at the front of the actual text of the document and a mark-up of the text itself. The header gives the background information to the document, such as information used for bibliographical and version control.

OTHER TYPES OF DATA

For complex databases, hypertexts, etc., it is extremely difficult (bordering on the impossible) to define an equivalent to the data-processing methods used for tabular data. Naturally it should be the responsibility of the software producer to include facilities for writing out data representations created in their software in an archive format. By an archive format I understand a format which is commonly recognized and independent of any particular software. Unfortunately, software producers' interest in proper archive formats seems to be minimal. This is especially disappointing when the software producers have ties to the historical research community.

Very large corpora of items differ from the data types already mentioned. The items could each be either tabular or textual, but the large number of items in the collection makes the methods described above inappropriate. An example of this could be the correspondence between a major government agency and the rest of the world. Such material can be embedded in an office automation system. Information on and when a particular item was sent and to whom would be part of the overall system. Furthermore, many of the interesting features of such material are features of the entity not of its items. Many of the items are probably not particularly interesting in themselves, but, taken as a whole, they can shed light on governmental thinking and procedures which is not easily obtained from other sources. As an example of this one could easily analyse differences in the vocabulary used by different departments of the agency or by different levels of authority within the agency. Many other examples could be mentioned. Unfortunately, in spite of the fact that the data-archival procedures mentioned above could probably cope quite well with the items of such a corpora of data, they are not well adjusted to deal with the entity. The large number, and relative low value, of the individual items make it very cost ineffective to treat the single item with TEI-mark-up, or create a DDP for it. A proper archive format for large corpora is very desirable.

When an archive format does not exist, the only way to maintain access to a data collection is to keep migrating the data to new software environments as the old ones become obsolete, much in the same way as the problem of hardware development is handled. The expenses involved in providing this type of data preservation are naturally enormous.

REUSE OF THE DATA

For data archives, the holdings are mostly composed of research materials which are expected to be immediately reusable for further research. It is one of the primary justifications for collecting research data that they will be valuable for other research projects. This value can be derived either by asking new questions of existing data or by combining data materials to provide insights in areas which are not covered by the specific data materials. Furthermore, data material which has been an integral part of an academic publication needs to be available to provide documentation for that publication and to provide a means of rechecking the conclusions presented therein. Finally, data sets can be scientific achievements in themselves. The data archives serve as a means of publication for such works. When data produced in a research process is used again for research purposes this is called secondary analysis. The data archives regard it as a prime responsibility to provide data in a format well suited for secondary analysis. Usually this means providing them in a format which is well suited to current analysis software. This is somewhat different from putting data in an adequate archive format, a task which often includes providing conversion tools between the archive format and formats supported by popular analysis software systems.

Secondary analysis is not of the same immediate importance for traditional archives. The machine-readable files which are archived in traditional archives are usually produced too recently to be available for the research community. The problems will, however, become of interest in the not too distant future. When the logical originals are over thirty years old, their file formats will be very archaic. Then it will become of immense importance to have well-described archive formats and reasonable tools to provide conversions from them.

THE DATA ARCHIVES

Data archives in Europe are institutions with national responsibilities. The paradigm on which most of them are founded is the International Consortium for Political and Social Research (ICPSR) in Ann Arbor, Michigan, USA. In the beginning, data archives were considered part of the research infrastructure for the social sciences. A result of this is that most of them have 'Social Science' in their name—e.g. *Norsk Sosjalvitenskaplig Datatjenst*. The DDA differs somewhat from the other national data archives in that it was understood from the planning phase that the DDA was also supposed to be of use for historical research. Thus the decision of the founding fathers was to create a data archive which collected data 'which describes society'. The data archives were very much influenced by library rather than archival tradition. Much emphasis is put on correct bibliographic citation, much less on provenance. In the early stages of the formation of data archives, the exchange of views between paper archivists and data archivists was somewhat difficult because a common vocabulary was absent. For instance, it makes no sense to try to preserve the physical original of a data file, if the medium it is held on will inevitably crumble. The preservable original of a given data file is the logical original. Distinctions such as this had to be discovered by the data archivist before they could be communicated to the paper archivists. Because of the relative lack of communication between data and paper archivists, the former still have much to learn from a closer study of the paper archive tradition.

The discussions on establishing a Danish data archive started in 1967, the decision was taken in 1972, and the DDA was set in motion in 1973. The DDA went through an experimental phase in the years 1973 to 1978. In the experimental phase the DDA was located in rooms which belonged to *Rigsarkivet*, the Danish National Archives. In 1978 the DDA became a permanent institute with nationwide responsibilities located at Odense University. In 1992 a reorganization of the governmental archival system in Denmark took place. As a result of this reorganization, the DDA, together with the *Rigsarkivet*, the four *Landsarkiver* (regional archives), and the '*Erhvervsarkivet*' (business archive), now form the *Statens Arkiver*, the archives of the government. The DDA joined the *Statens Arkiver* on 1 January 1993.

DATA ARCHIVES AND NATIONAL ARCHIVES

Data archives concern themselves with data from only a minority of the data producers in a country, the research community. The national archives have to serve a much larger community of data producers, the government. National archives across Europe are working to establish procedures to deal in an assured manner with publicly produced data. In traditional archives it is often believed that the really important stuff will always be on paper, and thus, as long as proper procedures for preserving paper material exist, the major sources for future historical studies will be secured. Naturally it is a self-fulfilling prophecy that future historical studies will have to be conducted on whatever is preserved. Unfortunately this does not guarantee that the sources we choose to preserve are the sources that will best illuminate our own time. The ratio of material found only in machine-readable form is likely to increase.

The methodology needed to deal with governmental data in a secure way is just being developed. Data archival procedures can perhaps serve as an inspiration during this development, but clearly they do not offer the solution to the problem that is facing paper archives. The resources necessary for running an operation such as the DDA, which processes a couple of hundred new data materials per annum and maintains a couple of thousand, is on the level of fifteen staff. The amount of material that a national data archives will need to concern itself with is ten or perhaps a hundred times that of the DDA. Although some economies of scale would be expected and access to archived governmental material is restrictive when compared to research materials, we are still talking about a large demand for manpower. These requirements are totally out of proportion to what is available at the machine-readable files divisions, which the national archives are running today. In the *Statens Arkiver*, the machine-readable files division consists of fifteen staff, and the division also serves as computer centre for the institution.

What is needed is not only the development of a methodology for dealing with machine-readable products of government but also an increase in the resources set aside for such activities. Machine-readable data differ from traditional archival material to such an extent that it is inconceivable that archives will be able to deal with this kind of material without receiving a considerable increase in resources.

References

ISO (1986): International Organization for Standardization, *ISO 8879: Information processing—Text and office systems—Standard Generalized Markup Language (SGML)* (Geneva: ISO).

Sperberg-McQueen, C. M., and Burnard, L. D. (1994) (eds.), *Guidelines for the Encoding and Interchange of Machine-Readable Texts*, edn. P3 (Oxford).

Electronic Records and Historians in the Netherlands

PETER DOORN

ABSTRACT

The preservation of electronic records has become an important issue during the last few years in the Netherlands. The Dutch General State Archives are carrying out research and pilot projects in order to develop a policy of electronic data-archiving. Archiving and access to data files in public and private institutions are of great concern to research data archives such as the Netherlands Historical Data Archive (NHDA) and the Steinmetz Data Archive (STAR) for the social sciences. The tasks of these data archives are primarily oriented to computer files created for scientific purposes. Experience gained from the treatment of research files can be of use for 'traditional' archives which are confronted with masses of institutional files. The aspects of electronic data archiving covered in this chapter include the size of the problem, financial aspects, centralized versus decentralized storage, criteria for selection of files, documentation and cataloguing standards, the problem of hardware and software dependence, and juridical aspects (privacy, confidentiality, copyright).

INTRODUCTION

The preservation of electronic records has become an important issue in the Netherlands. The General Audit Office (Algemene Rekenkamer) called for attention to be paid to the problem for the first time in a report published in 1988. It warned that a policy for the storage and destruction of computer files had yet to be developed. After a second report published in 1991, the issue became politically more relevant and the National Archive Service started research and pilot projects in order to develop a policy for electronic data-archiving (Doorn and Matthezing 1992). The Rijksarchiefdienst (RAD) or State Archival Service comprises twelve archives in each of the provinces of the Netherlands. In The Hague, the capital of the province of South-Holland, the archives of the province and of the National government form the Algemeen Rijksarchief (ARA) or General State Archives. Other public archives include municipal and town archives (*gemeente-en stadsarchieven*), district archives (*streekarchieven*), and archives of polder districts (*waterschapsarchieven*).

The NHDA and the STAR for the social sciences are at this moment only tangentially involved in this field. The work of these data archives is primarily oriented to computer files created for scientific purposes. On the other hand, the topics of archiving and access to data files in public and private institutions are of great concern to these research data archives. Experience gained with the treatment of research files can be of use for 'traditional' archives which are confronted with masses of 'process-produced files'.

Moreover, social scientists and historians are important users of public records for research purposes. Some computer files that are considered relevant for social-science research are now acquired, documented, stored, and made available to researchers by the Steinmetz Archive. These are mainly statistical files based on surveys and censuses by the Netherlands Central Bureau of Statistics (CBS). In addition to the services of the Steinmetz Archives, a 'Statistical Data Agency' has been created which acts as an intermediary between the producers and users of statistical files (De Guchteneire 1993). As a data intermediary, the NHDA provides services to both archivists and historians for the preservation and access to machine-readable records kept in archives.

In the long term, according to the Dutch archive law, public archives will be responsible for preserving and disseminating data produced in state organizations. A problem in this respect is the time period before records have to be handed over by the record producers to the archives. According to the Archive Law of 1962, files should be transferred to the record office within ten years after the documents have become fifty years old. From 1 January 1996 onwards, the revised Archive Law reduced the time limit for the transfer of records to twenty years for most classes of records. For many electronic records, this time period may still be much too long, unless the archiving procedures in the producers' institutions can be guaranteed.

THE SIZE OF THE PROBLEM

The central difficulty with the archiving of institutional computer files is the sheer quantity of material involved. Research data archives are dealing with small numbers of files (and suppliers/users of data) in comparison to the vast numbers of files stored on hundreds of thousands of personal computers (PCs), minis, and mainframes in public and private institutions. For example, the National Audit Office mentioned a number of about 100,000 files (or computer systems) in the state sector of the Netherlands in 1991 (Algemene Rekenkamer 1991); in reality, there is not even the inkling of an idea how many electronic records are being produced (see also Hofman 1995). As the research data archives already face capacity problems archiving a few hundreds or thousands of research data sets, the archiving of these hundreds or thousands of files will really be an immense task, which the available current resources could not accommodate.

At this stage nobody really knows how to handle the problem within the presently available budgets. There is a tendency among archivists to shift archival action to ever earlier stages in the 'life cycle' of electronic records. Preservation is to begin not after the records are twenty years old, not after they have gone out of use (death?), not when they are produced (birth?), but when they are conceived (impregnation?). In a way, the situation can be compared to the problem of environmental pollution: extra investment is needed in the conception and production phase of databases for proper documentation and archiving, in the same way as extra overhead costs for pollution control must be made at the time of industrial production or in planning new plant development. The axiomatic belief that the 'polluter has to pay' could be translated as 'the record-creator has to archive'. Whether such an approach is practically feasible, and whether there are means to force the record-creator to take archival action, remains to be seen.

CENTRAL OR DISTRIBUTED STORAGE?

A basic question is where to store the files that need to be archived: should they be archived centrally at the public records offices or decentrally at the computer centres of the institutions that created them (see Higgs, Chapter 12, this volume)? There have been ideas about a National Computer Archives as a massive concrete bunker somewhere in the polder of the Ijsselmeer, but it is not realistic to aim at archiving everything centrally. Distributed storage with a central catalogue and guidelines on how to store data will have to be combined with some central storage. The possibilities for archives to prescribe documentation and cataloguing rules need to be extended. Also, they should be able to inspect and verify data-archiving procedures of data collectors which fall under the archiving responsibility of the public record offices. A network needs to be created, comparable to the library networks that already exist in many countries. In similar ways as title descriptions of printed materials are fed into central catalogues by participating organizations in library networks, data descriptions will have to be entered by institutions participating in national archiving networks. Standards and tools for the documentation and cataloguing of files need to be established and prescribed for database creators.

ARCHIVAL METHODOLOGY

In principle, archives are aiming to extend 'normal' procedures for paper archives to electronic archives as broadly as possible, taking into account the difference in the medium on which the data is stored. Access to and use of electronic data are always dependent on machines and software. Worse, it is often dependent on specific machines and specific software. In principle, we should aim to minimize such dependence, although fast technological developments are making this practically unfeasible. Research data archives have been using and promoting the strategy of storage in a uniform format for over twenty-five years. From this standard format, they can be transported to other formats or upgraded to new software relatively easily (see Marker, Chapter 20, this volume). For instance, the Steinmetz Archives are converting their holdings to SPSS system files. The NHDA stores data as plain ASCII files. With the increasing complexity of data sets (multimedia and hypertext, geographical information systems, etc.), it is not likely that such practices will be feasible in the long run.

Where software-independent storage of data is impossible, it is vital that software or special applications are archived together with the data. It is inevitable that many of these data sets will become technologically outdated. If this is the case, saving a hard copy of the data (by printing it on paper or microfilm) must be considered (Morelli, Chapter 11, this volume). We need criteria to determine which medium is most appropriate for the preservation of which information in the long run. A mixed policy of preservation is inevitable: some data files can be saved independently of software (or in a standard format), other files will be meaningless without the software, and again other files will have to be converted to other media, maybe even to paper or microfilm (Morris 1992). More research is needed into the possibilities of special programs which emulate the functionality and database environment of outdated computer systems, in order to keep application software running and databases accessible in their original context (Swade, Chapter 13, this volume; Rothenberg 1995).

Copyright, privacy, confidentiality, and security matters regarding electronic information should be dealt with in the same way as paper information. Catalogues of data should be freely accessible, the data themselves should be protected. Distinctions between 'public-domain' data and restricted data should be drawn according to existing practices applied to paper information. Although existing legislation makes no fundamental difference in this respect between electronic and paper information, the ease of copying of electronic data without noticeable distinction between original and copy apparently makes both archivists and the public, in general, more nervous about digital data than about paper-based information.

Special attention is required for the anonymization procedures currently being used by statistical bureaux such as the Dutch CBS. In order to protect the privacy of respondents, the name and address information is removed from all statistical files. For the sake of future historical research, it is essential that these procedures be made reversible, so that in due course (after, for instance, fifty or 100 years) individualized research will be possible.

Criteria used for the selection of computer files to be archived should be as similar as possible to those used for paper archives. Additional criteria are needed with regard to the technical quality of the data (e.g. software independence) and of the documentation. For large files of vital national interest (e.g. the computerized population register of the Netherlands), special data-archiving arrangements have to be made.

Although extending existing archival methods for paper to computer files is possible and recommended, it is clear that archival theory also needs to be adapted to meet the newer demands information technology (IT) poses (Dollar 1992). There is a considerable gap between IT and the activities carried out by archivists. Instruction in computer techniques will have to become a part of the training of archivists.

The Archive School in the Netherlands has recently been reorganized and now includes a special programme in IT, which is carried out in collaboration with the department for library science and documentary information of Amsterdam University.

SOFTWARE DEPENDENCY, CONTEXT, AND DOCUMENTATION

The software that is or was used for database creation and retrieval will be vital for the investigation of the context in which data were used. What tools were available to decision-makers to evaluate data? How much effort had to be invested to extract information from a database? Questions such as these can be answered only if future researchers know what software was available in the past and can access it.

The complete description and accurate documenting of data sets are labour-intensive and time-consuming tasks for social-science and historical data archives. Most research data archives use a standard description scheme for documenting data sets deposited by researchers. The information about the data sets supplied by depositors is often incomplete or vague. Data-archive staff put a lot of effort into checking, completing, and correcting the data documentation.

Describing and cataloguing a data set will probably always cost more time than cataloguing a printed publication. This is due to the fact that the printed publication is a much clearer and a more coherent unit than a computer file. A book, report, or article exists as a physical unit, and usually has a title, author, publisher, date, and place of publication, etc. No special equipment is needed to access the information that is in it. A computer file is in principle a virtual unit which cannot be read without hardware and software. Especially if we are dealing with complex data structures, ranging from coded numerical and hypertext files, to relational databases to image data and multimedia, the records will not have any meaning without software and proper documentation.

It is the structured, coded, numerical, hypertextual, relational, and multimedia data sets that create most of the problems, because it will not be possible to get the information out if we do not know what the structural relationships or links are, what the codes mean, and what the numbers stand for.

From an archivist's point of view, it is convenient if electronic text is marked up in a systematic way, but, given the speed of technological development, one may doubt the longevity of any computer standard in any field (hardware, data communication, and software). Gone are punched cards, 8-inch floppies, and many tape formats. For how long will CD-ROMs continue to exist? New video CDs with a much higher capacity will soon be on the market. Will there always be ASCII? Multiple octet coding schemes for character repertoires will soon supersede ASCII. Will SQL (Standard Query Language) prevail as a query language for relational databases? Will the relational model itself continue to exist? Will mark-up systems for texts such as SGML (Standard Generalized Markup Language), or tagging instructions such as the TEI (Text Encoding Initiative) guidelines (Burnard 1993), survive in the long run? Will OSI (Open Systems Interconnection) be the model for open systems in the future? After how many years will MS-DOS be as forgotten as CP/M (Control Program for Microcomputers) is already?

TOWARDS A DATA-ARCHIVING POLICY FOR THE NETHERLANDS

In June 1993 the State Archive Service of the Netherlands presented a report and recommendations concerning the policy on machine-readable files (Project MLG 1993). It noted that the archives are as yet insufficiently equipped to accept machine-readable files for storage. However, plans are being developed to create the technical infrastructure necessary to archive such files. The electronic files, or at least catalogues of them, should become available to the public in the study rooms of the archives. The report mentions the need for a central repository for the five largest archival services (the General State Archives and the municipal archives of the four largest cities), which are to provide services to other, smaller archives.

A splitting-up of technical and 'intellectual' management tasks is proposed. The 'intellectual' management, which includes the documentation of files, should be carried out by the archives, whereas the technical management (physical storage) should be carried out at a central repository. Standards for the way in which electronic files must be deposited by state services have to be prescribed by the archival inspectorate. It should be noted that in this respect the public archives have more power than research data archives, which rely merely on moral arguments to encourage researchers to deposit their data in a specific form.

It is proposed to store electronic files in a comparable way as paper records are stored. Paper files are stored in cardboard boxes according to their provenance, and the State Archives Service would like to put electronic files in 'electronic boxes', although it is not yet clear how this could be achieved. The policy report mentions a 'standard infrastructure', which implies conversion to a certain standard format. Whether such a treatment will allow the preservation of the context of data files remains as yet unanswered. In fact, a fundamental paradox presents itself here: on the one hand, there is a plea to preserve files in their original context; on the other, it is desirable to develop a standard infrastructure, to which various formats have to be converted. However, the original software which forms part of the context of data will be lost when the data are converted to a standard format!

In *Preserving the Present,* a report for the State Archive Service published late in 1993, Bikson and Frinking shed light on the problem of electronic records from three points of view: organizational context, technological vantage, and archival management. From the organizational point of view, the researchers notice that decentralization in organizations is accompanied by a shift of responsibility for IT and archiving. Where in the past one electronic monster of a mainframe computer was fed with punched cards by operators in white coats, we now find a network of PCs where everybody is more or less his own systems manager. In the distributed organization, it is much more difficult to impose standards for record-keeping.

The central message is that the top management of the ministries ought to care more about the management and administration of electronic information in their organizations, because it is in the interest of the organizations that the information is well administered and controlled. A second important recommendation is that the juridical status of electronic information needs to be more clearly described. This is, however, easier said than done. Archiving has a low administrative priority, and it is questionable whether the leadership of ministries will be interested in what will happen to the files that are out of use. The importance of the records for the cultural heritage and for historical research will hardly make much difference. The possibilities for democratic control might even be experienced more as a threat than as a blessing, because everything that is in your files might be used against you.

From the point of view of the technology, the report stresses the importance of paying attention to good documentation practices in an early stage in the life cycle of electronic records, because they are a precondition for long-term archiving. Good software tools have to become available to facilitate this. The report also stresses the need for standardization and open systems. Without these the consultation of files in the future will be impossible. OSI standards are seen as a panacea for preventing the rapid technological ageing of files.

With respect to archival management, the report recommends that guidelines be formulated for electronic record-keeping, although central directions are considered less effective. The conclusions consist mainly of questions; to answer these further research is needed.

In a report edited by Hans Hofman (1995), leader of the project on machine-readable records of the State Archive Service, computer files are described as a time bomb for the democratic functioning of society and for the possibilities of auditing and monitoring government. Data that are now being used in computer systems will have to be transferred to a public archive after twenty years. Printing the data on paper/microfilm is not a viable means to preserve the digital information: it is too expensive, analog media cannot represent the internal structure of computer files, and the access to the data will be poor.

The second part of the report presents a survey of machine-readable records in several government institutions. Databases appear to constitute the largest group of records that will need to be preserved, followed by text files and financial/administrative systems. The percentage of the digital material that deserves consideration for long-term preservation from the total of all records produced appears to be much higher than is the case with paper records, namely 20–40 per cent. Administrative bodies do not have complete and up-to-date lists of their own files at their disposal. One of the conclusions is that database management and administration in the public sector does not observe the existing rules (including the Archive Law) very well in this respect. As a result, electronic records are disappearing or are being destroyed imperceptibly. The final conclusion of the report is, therefore, that measures need to be taken in order to prevent the explosion of the 'ticking time bomb' and the irretrievable loss of our past.

THE ROLE OF RESEARCH DATA ARCHIVES

Several of the social-science data archives are more than twenty-five years old. Their archiving methods were developed in the 1970s, when punched cards, mainframe computers, and statistical packages such as SPSS dominated the quantitative scene. Their experience is at the same time an asset and a burden, because it is not easy to change your archiving strategy when you are managing thousands of files.

Typically, the data sets stored in these research data archives are based on interviews and surveys. The answers of respondents are either written down on paper interview forms or, when computer-aided interviewing is used, directly typed into a database. The central problem in archiving this material is establishing the context of the survey—how was the data collection designed in terms of sampling strategies, interview lay-outs, and coding schemes? The structure of the files is often in a relatively straightforward form as tables. The content consists of answers to interview questions, which are often coded. This is a simplification which does not take into account spatial information embedded in geographical information systems, but one look at the catalogue of ICPSR, the Data Archive at Essex University, or the Zentral Archiv will show that most studies take this general format. Therefore, practices central to the archiving methods of the social-science data archives include:

- the separation of data from hard- and software in an attempt to make the data as transportable as possible;
- the preservation of all data in a standard format, which may be pure ASCII, but also the internal format of system files of a standard statistical package (SPSS) may be used;
- bibliographic description of studies according to a standard description scheme.

The archiving routines in historical data archives are borrowed or adapted from social-science data archives. Although the NHDA's experience indicates that the majority of the research files created by historians still have a tabular structure, the numbers of (hyper)texts and multimedia applications continue to increase.

A characteristic of historical research files is that they are based on historical sources which have been converted in one way or another (typing, scanning) into electronic form. The paper source is the original, which forms the context of the historical data and which needs to be described in detail. A central archiving problem for the historical data archives is therefore: how does the computer file relate to the paper original? If the database was created to solve a particular historical problem, the answer may be quite different from cases where the aim was to represent a source as well as possible in electronic form (problem-oriented versus source-oriented computing). Which selections were made, whether spelling was standardized, how completely the source is covered, which other interpretations crept in: these are the issues at stake here.

Both the structure and the contents of historical research data sets largely depend on the structure and contents of the original source and can be either textual or tabular in form. Other, hybrid and multimedia data formats also occur.

The archiving process starts with finding out who has which data where. Historians are encouraged to complete a data registration card to provide a general idea concerning the creator, contents, and technical properties of existing data sets. A digital version of the form is available through the World Wide Web. The NHDA can establish the priority for acquisition of the data on the basis of the information supplied.

In a second phase, owners of data sets are requested to supply more detailed documentation about their data. A do-it-yourself data documentation program called DOCIT! was developed to assist data-creators in providing documentation in a standard format. In a third stage, those who are willing to deposit a copy of their data are invited to do so. An agreement signed by creator and the NHDA stipulates the conditions for access to the data. The NHDA completes the data documentation using a system called DOCUSYS. The data collections are described in a standard way according to our Historical Data Set Description Scheme, which is derived from the Standard Study Description Scheme used by most European social-science data archives. Data sets free of depositor-imposed restrictions are made available over the Internet together with associated documentation (URL: http: // oasis. leidenuniv.nl/nhda/nhda-welcome-uk.html).

The NHDA is seeking closer collaboration with the State Archive Service for several reasons. As mentioned before, files based on historical research can be seen as a drop in the ocean of official, 'process-produced' files. Secondly, the NHDA might offer an interface for users of electronic data resources and the national archives. The NHDA may offer support in locating, retrieving, processing, and analysing data. Data archives such as NHDA and Steinmetz Archives can make the following contributions in the field of 'electronic records for historians':

- providing technical and substantial expertise (consultancy) with regard to selection, documentation, cataloguing, storage, and dissemination of computer files;
- developing special courses in data-archiving for archivists;
- setting up and carrying out research/pilot projects;
- providing the scientific community with information about computer files kept elsewhere (data intermediary); and,
- representing the scientific interest with regard to the storage and access to institutional data files (including PR-work and increasing the awareness amongst the public/scientific community/policy-makers of the importance of the problem).

In summary, future historical research is in imminent danger of massive digital amnesia. Practically all government information is now stored in electronic form. Municipal population registers, police archives, trade statistics, juridical data, correspondence of ministries, practically all important sources for historical research are now digital. Research data archives and public records offices should unite in order to preserve and make accessible electronic information resources that matter for history.

References

Algemene Rekenkamer (1991), *Machineleesbare gegevensbestanden: Archivering en beheer bij het Rijk* (The Hague).

Bikson, T. K. and Frinking, E. J. (1993), *Het heden onthouden/Preserving the Present: Towards Viable Electronic records* (The Hague).

Burnard, L. D. (1993), 'The Text Encoding Initiative: Towards an Extensible Standard for the Encoding of Texts', in Ross and Higgs (1993), 105–18.

Clubb, J. M., and Scheuch, E. K. (1980) (eds.), *Historical Social Research: The Use of Historical and Process-Produced Data* (Stuttgart).

De Guchteneire, P. F. A. (1993) (ed.), *Data-infrastructuur; bundel ter gelegenheid van het 25-jarig bestaan van het Steinmetzarchief* (Amsterdam).

Dollar, C. M. (1992), *Archival Theory and Information Technologies: The Impact of Information Technologies on Archival Principles and Methods* (Macerata, Italy).

Doorn, P., and Matthezing, H. (1992), 'After the Flood: Archiving Electronic Records in the Netherlands', *History and Computing*, 4/3: 197–200.

Hofman, J. (1995) (ed.), *Up-to-date/Het papieren tijdperk voorbij: beleid voor een digitaal geheugen van onze samenleving* (The Hague).

Morris, R. J. (1992), 'The Historian at Belshazzar's Feast: A Data Archive for the Year 2001', *Cahier VGI*, 5: 42–51.

Project MLG (1993), *Documenten uit de tijd: Behoud en beheer van digitale informatie,* (The Hague).

Ross, S., and Higgs, E. (1993) (eds.), *Electronic Information Resources and Historians: European Perspectives* (St Katharinen).

Rothenberg, J. (1995), 'Ensuring the Longevity of Digital Documents', *Scientific American,* 272/1 (Jan.), 24–9.

22

Swedish Society and Electronic Data

CLAES GRÄNSTRÖM

ABSTRACT

In Sweden the legal structure has a major impact on the issues surrounding electronic data. The most important legislation here is the Freedom of the Press Act, which, amongst other things, states that every Swedish citizen shall have free access to official records (documents) in order to encourage the free exchange of opinion and the enlightenment of the public. Electronic data are equated with records in the traditional sense. When a piece of information becomes an official record is also defined in the Act. Other acts, such as those relating to privacy, data protection, and archives, will be described, since they are all interrelated. How different directives of the European Union will affect this legislation will be described, as well as the intense discussion in Sweden on these matters. As the universities in Sweden are state agencies, these acts are relevant to their activities. University researchers have taken advantage of these acts to obtain information from other agencies. This, and the fact that Swedish society uses electronic data-processing (EDP) in conjunction with a personal identification number unique to each individual extensively, is important for the Swedish social sciences.

FREEDOM OF INFORMATION LEGISLATION

The status of electronic records under Swedish law is a matter of current interest in Sweden, reflecting the country's strong tradition of open government (Bohlin 1988; Seipel 1988; Gränström 1990, 1993*a*, 1993*b*; Gränström *et al.* 1993; Swedish Data Protection Board 1995).

Sweden received its first 'Freedom-of-Information Act' (the Freedom of the Press Act) in 1766. This became part of the constitution of the

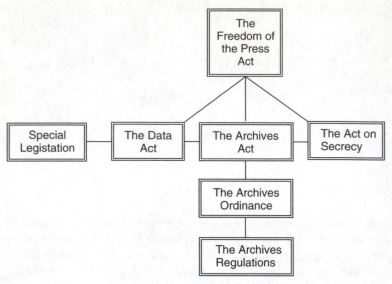

Fig. 22.1 Computer records and Swedish (archival) legislation

State, and amendments to it required two decisions in Parliament with an election in between. The most recent change of a substantive nature was enacted in 1949. This revised Act was very elaborate, since it had proved possible to circumvent the previous Act which had been less precise (Fig. 22.1).

The Freedom of the Press Act affords protection to the press in four main spheres:

- it provides protection against action by the authorities which raises obstacles to the printing, publication, or dissemination of printed matter;
- it promotes the supply of information;
- it defines, in essential respects, the boundary between what may, and what may not, be stated or published in print; and
- it provides guarantees on penal or bureaucratic forms of action against abuses of the freedom of the press.

The second sphere, the promotion of the supply of information, is the most important. The principle that records of public authorities shall be accessible to all citizens is of utmost significance. This legislation applies to all records, wherever they are in their record life cycle. Thus, there is no difference between live records and archives in Sweden within the public sector, since they are all considered official records. The Act states that every Swedish citizen—and this right extends to foreign citizens—shall have free access to official records in order to encourage the free exchange of opinions and to inform the public. The principle of the public nature of official records extends to both central and local state agencies, and to local communes and municipalities. Sound recordings and electronic data-processing (EDP) records, including materials from electronic mail (e-mail), geographical information systems (GIS), graphics systems, etc., are equated with documents in the traditional sense. Records within a public authority are official as soon as they have been received by, or drawn up at, the agency. Any official record which may be made accessible to the public shall be produced forthwith or as quickly as possible and free of charge. No public authority may enquire into a person's identity in respect of his or her request for an official record, or seek to know the reason why the request is being made.

A consequence of these principles is that any party concerned in a particular matter is free to study the material which constitutes the basis for an authority's actions. He or she is also entitled to have access to the records in similar cases to enable him or her to establish the common practices of the authority. Another important consequence is that the press, radio, and television also have access to, and may examine, the records of public authorities. The knowledge that files and records are accessible to everybody is supposed to make the authorities more careful, and reduce the risk of arbitrary action. Under certain circumstances this principle is, of course, subject to restrictions. These restrictions were grouped together and laid down in the Official Secrets Act.

The growth of communications, and the increasing use of EDP in society, made it necessary to strengthen the right of public access. After some debate it was agreed that this should be done via two measures. The first step was to require that every agency create without delay a register or similar journal of all records received and drawn up by that agency. The second step was to stipulate that the agencies should organize their EDP systems with due consideration to the right of free access as stipulated in the Freedom of the Press Act. Also, the agencies should, if possible, give the public access to a computer monitor or other access device. It is also prescribed that the agencies should have a minimum level of documentation for their EDP systems. The required documentation includes:

- the title of the EDP system;
- the purpose of the EDP system;
- the type of information in the EDP system;
- the names of other agencies at which the information is available in readable form;
- terminals and other equipment that the public can use at the agency;
- information about the regulations governing secrecy that the agency can apply to the records in the EDP system;
- details of the staff at the agency who can advise on the EDP system and how it is used; and,
- the specification of appraisal regulations—the Parliamentary Standing Committee on the Constitution has stated that a piece of information in an official document may in principle never be erased. If an item is amended, the altered (e.g. incorrect or updated) item must still be readable.

These regulations constitute a new chapter in the Official Secrets Act. It was suggested that a new law to be called the 'Law on Public Documents' should be drafted, but after deliberation Parliament decided to limit new legislation to the additional chapter in the Official Secrets Act. This information on EDP systems is of great value for the archival authorities in their supervisory work.

SECRECY LEGISLATION

The Official Secrets Act regulates the restrictions governing access, and follows the form of the relevant part of the Freedom of the Press Act. The right of access to official records may be restricted only if the restrictions are shown to be necessary. Grounds for limiting access include, for example, national defence, and the personal and financial affairs of private individuals. Any restrictions on the right of access are scrupulously specified in this Act. It is possible to appeal in court against the decision by an agency to withhold information. Each denial of access must be supported by a reference to a specific section in the Official Secrets Act.

My experience is that the courts are more inclined to give access to official records than the agencies (state government and municipal). Awareness of this tendency makes the agencies more liberal in their approach. Consequently, the decisions of the courts play an important role in the application of the legislation.

DATA-PROTECTION LEGISLATION

According to the Data Act, which came into force in 1973, all automatic processing of personal data required the permission of a new agency, the Data Inspection Board. By the beginning of the 1980s the number of EDP systems had grown to such an extent that it was not possible to treat each system individually and grant each one an individual licence. In 1982 it was decided that it was sufficient for the responsible custodian to have a licence for those kinds of personal files not considered personally sensitive. The responsible custodian could keep several personal files under one licence. For some files, however, special permission was still required.

Certain personal files have potential value to future researchers, and the conditions and guidelines for their preservation were laid down. The principle that all data should be removed from the personal file when they were no longer needed for the purpose for which the file had been created was considered inappropriate. For example, data concerning taxation would be removed after six years, if the data, after being used for its primary purpose, were on electronic media. The solution was that data in electronic form, which would be kept for posterity if they were in the corresponding paper records, are to be transferred to the National Archives, which are also an archival authority and thus exempt from some of the regulations in the Data Act. The most important of these exemptions was from the requirement that, on request, persons be notified as soon as possible of the personal data recorded, and if no data had been recorded that such data did not exist.

With respect to personal data held in the public sector, it is necessary in some cases to have a special permit from the Data Inspection Board, which decides on the appraisal and preservation of this material after consultation with the National Archives. In the case of other personal files, the file controller must have a licence, and the National Archives come to a decision on appraisal on their own authority. All personal data in the private sector must be destroyed after being used for the purpose for which the data were created.

ARCHIVAL LEGISLATION

Although it was soon realized that the fulfilment of the Freedom of Information Act required the listing and preservation of records, there was no Archives Act to provide a mechanism for this. In the state sector the government issued regulations, and in the growing municipal sector (the communes) there were a few short and inadequate municipal laws. When records consisted mainly of paper documents in long series, it was, generally speaking, not very difficult for agencies to describe what kind of information they kept. As the public sector grew and produced greater and greater quantities and varieties of information, and as information was stored on computerized media, with attendant problems of access, it became necessary to draft an Archives Act and to consider other acts and regulations. As a result, Parliament passed an Archives Act, which came into force in 1991. Parliament has defined the concepts of an archive, a record/document, and the interpretation of the principle of provenance.

In the 1991 Archives Act, the goals of archival management are stated as facilitating:

- the right of access to official documents;
- the provision of information for the administration of justice and public administration; and
- research.

Archives play a crucial role in preserving Swedish cultural heritage.

The Archives Act indicates that the archives of every public authority comprise those official records that relate to the authority's operations, and other records mentioned in the Freedom of the Press Act. The Act regulates which public authority shall be the responsible custodian of computer records when they are accessible to, or created by, several public authorities. In the first instance this will be the authority that is responsible for the greater portion of the records.

The Act lays down, among other things, that the public authority shall:

- pay attention to the importance of registration for long-term accessibility;
- choose suitable materials and methods for the creation of records in order to guarantee that information is accessible and can be preserved as long as it is not appraised/destroyed;

- organize the departmental archives to facilitate the right of public access;
- draw up a description of the departmental archives which provides both an introduction to the archive and also a systematic, archival inventory (finding aid);
- protect the departmental archives from damage, theft, and unauthorized access;
- clearly define the archives by deciding which records belong there; and
- carry out appropriate appraisal (and subsequent disposition) of official documents.

In accordance with the Archives Act, the government has issued an Archival Ordinance. The National Archives have been given delegated responsibility to issue regulations about materials and methods of document creation. The National Archives can also issue regulations to the state authorities on, for example:

- the use of writing material and storage facilities (cartridge cases, boxes, etc.); writing materials can be defined in terms of the base (e.g. paper, film), the writing medium (e.g. ink, pencils, printing), as well as different combinations of these (e.g. special ink on maps), and different technologies (e.g. copying machines);
- the maintenance of departmental archives, including:
  - how the archives should be structured (organized so that the right of public access will be facilitated),
  - the description of the archives,
  - the systematic archival inventory,
  - the demarcation of the archives,
  - the protection of the archives,
  - the carrying-out of appraisal;
  - the transfer of the whole departmental archive, or part of it, to another agency or to an archival authority; and
  - the conservation of records.

The National Archives may also issue regulations on appraisal and destruction of records in departments.

In accordance with the Archival Ordinance the National Archives has issued many regulations. These can be divided into four groups:

- general regulations;
- regulations concerning different media such as computer records, micrographics, and paper records;

- regulations concerning archival storage facilities, the selection of appropriate products and the quality of systems, and appraisal; and
- regulations concerning technical requirements with regard to materials and methods.

THE PHASES OF REGULATION

The regulation of computer records can be seen in terms of the three phases in the life cycle of computer records. During each of these phases there are different requirements placed on the public authority. These are summarized in Fig. 22.2.

Electronic Data-processing Systems in Development and Use

The first phase is when the EDP system is under development or in use, and no computer records have been moved from active use to long-term storage. During this period certain documentation should be assembled, or created if it does not already exist. The degree of detail required of the documentation is in some part determined by the complexity of the system. This means that the amount of effort needed to write the documentation is hopefully not disproportionate to the effort involved in developing the system in the first place. However, this may not always be the case, since the regulations are the same whatever the size of the system.

Documentation can be broken down into that relating to:

- the system/application (in the form, more or less, of a relatively short description);
- input and output (forms, reports, etc.);
- manual routines and how they relate to the system/application (i.e. access control systems and how these relate to the organization);

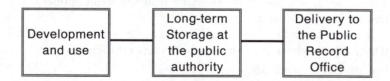

Fig. 22.2 Three phases in the life cycle of computer records

- regular/automatic routines (i.e. consistency checks, rules in expert systems);
- descriptions and definitions of data elements, records, relations, etc. (preferably written in Structured Query Language (SQL)) and,
- details of changes in functionality.

At the moment the only requirement is that applicable standards and technical norms, as well as directions given by the manufacturer, are followed. No specific standards and norms are listed at present, but the areas to which they will primarily apply are data carriers, data representation, data organization, and methods of documentation.

Long-Term Storage at the Public Authority

The second phase is when computer records are moved to long-term storage within the public authority. At this stage there are additional requirements as to the data carrier which may be used, such as half-inch magnetic tape, magnetic tape cassettes/cartridges, or optical disc. The first regulations concerning technical requirements came into force in 1992. Ongoing research into storage media is being carried out.

Most importantly, at this stage the agency is responsible for ensuring that it is possible to transfer the computer records to new data-carrier formats when required, without incurring the loss of any information. There are also rules regarding how the transfer of the computer records to data carriers for long-term storage, handling, etc., should be planned and documented.

Delivery to the Public Record Office

The third phase in the life cycle begins when the computer records are delivered to the National Archives, or another archival authority. In principle, all previously mentioned regulations continue to apply, but the National Archives when receiving the records may make additions, and/or changes, to previous choices of data carrier, data representation, and data organization. These are laid down in the transfer document on delivery rather than being explicitly stated in the archives regulations. This makes it easy to make changes whenever new equipment or software is acquired. The National Archives issued regulations in late 1994 regarding the delivery of EDP records from agencies to the National and Regional Archives.

The National Archives regularly receives personal and other data stored on magnetic tapes. It holds approximately 20,000 tapes (10,000 originals and 10,000 back-ups), and the work of preserving and making these available is very demanding.

These data can, in principle, be divided into five main categories:

- nationwide systems
  - systems for taxation,
  - systems for VAT,
  - systems for the registration of people,
  - systems for recording real property from county administration boards and county taxation boards;
- National Bureau of Statistics
  - quinquennial censuses from 1960 to 1990
  - yearly ongoing surveys,
  - special surveys/investigations;
- central/regional/local state agencies
  - Labour Market Board,
  - National Board of Health and Welfare,
  - National Social Insurance Board, etc.;
- 'System S'—the centralized accounting system for all state agencies (1968–);
- universities—all kinds of scientific data from various research projects.

Developments in Other Scandinavian Countries

Developments in Denmark, Finland, and Norway have been very similar to those in Sweden. The legal framework differs, however, because of the different traditions in each country. In all three countries the preservation of records on electronic media is regarded as normal, and each of the National Archives has received and stored electronic records.

Co-operation between the Scandinavian countries in this field includes all aspects of archival/records administration, such as inventorying, appraisal, storage, standards, and accessibility. With regard to accessibility, although the legal frameworks differ somewhat, the principle of an open society is evident in each of these countries. Discussions about archival theory and the principle of provenance are promoted by this co-operation. The fact that three of the Scandinavian countries have joined the European Union also promotes close contacts.

RECENT DEVELOPMENTS

The use of EDP has grown rapidly, and the widespread use of personal computers (PCs) has made existing legislation inadequate. In the beginning of the 1990s a committee discussed the current system of permissions and licences for the most sensitive personal files, the status of personal files, appraisal, co-ordination with other legislation, and changing terminology. Whether the current Swedish Freedom of the Press Act can be restricted by the rules proposed by the then European Community was also discussed. The report from this committee was forwarded to the government in 1993, but the latter decided to wait until the Directive on the Protection of Individuals with Regard to Processing of Personal Data and on the Movement of such Data was adopted by the European Union. For the National Archives the most interesting issue is perhaps whether personal confidentiality, on the one hand, or freedom of access and research, on the other, will prevail. Up till now considerations of personal confidentiality have taken precedence, and, as a consequence, the Data Inspection Board has taken decisions with respect to more important information.

A fact which cannot be ignored is that the borders between the public and private sectors are now tending to disappear. This is especially true in an electronic society, where data are rapidly transferred through different networks between separate databases. Also in Sweden, as in many other countries, important functions have been and will continue to be transferred from the public authorities to private bodies. The problem of access to these important data is now being investigated by government committees.

Since the adoption of the Directive from the European Union in October 1995, new government committees have been appointed to consider how to adapt the current legislation to changed circumstances. One committee had the task of examining if the concept of the record, as defined in the Freedom of the Press Act, can be used in the electronic environment. Another committee was set to work to adapt the legal framework to take account of the use of electronic records in administration and business, and the use of bulletin-board systems.

The National Archives are, of course, deeply involved in the process of establishing laws, ordinances, regulations, and standards for appraisal, choice of media, inventorying, and taking care of electronic records, amongst other matters.

CERTAIN ARCHIVAL PROBLEMS

What constitutes a record in electronic systems has been the subject of intense debate. It was not difficult to determine what paper material could be considered official documents according to the established rules. In the mid-1970s a debate began as to what records in a database, for example, could be considered official documents. There was, moreover, the question as to what combinations of information should be made available to the public, since technology had made it easy to vary and combine data almost unendingly. At this date the guiding principle adopted by the legislature was that access should not be diminished but enhanced and facilitated. It was decided, therefore, that even so-called 'potential' or 'virtual' records made possible by the computer's ability to combine and search information were official records. It was even stated that the public could furnish the agency with computer programs in order to facilitate the creation of new combinations of data, although this right has since been abolished.

This problematizes the relationship between official records and archival records. Information was fixed in paper records and could not generally be changed. Official records and archival records were in principal equivalent, and were both classified in archival finding aids according to a system adapted to the requirements of freedom of information as well as archival legislation. It is, of course, virtually impossible to define or describe in an archival finding aid all the possible combinations of data that can be generated from automated systems. It is possible, however, to describe data elements and how the agency has used these documents in its activities. Consequently, the definition of an official record and that of an archival record will drift apart.

Also, it is stated in the Freedom of the Press Act that official records are those electronic records maintained by a government agency, or which are available to the agency for transcription in such a way that they can be read or listened to, or otherwise rendered comprehensible. This means that, if a data element from a database produced by another agency or private institution is available on screen in an agency via the Internet, this element is considered an official record. In archival legislation, these kinds of official records are generally not considered archival records outside the originating body, and are consequently inventoried only in the latter body's finding aids.

CONCLUSIONS

The principles of freedom of information and of provenance have been put to the test in a new environment, the complexities of which were not foreseen at the outset. Technological developments have meant that the nature of documents/records has become more complicated. In Sweden, fortunately, the Freedom of the Press Act and the principle of provenance fit very well together. In order to maintain the access granted by the freedom-of-information principle, it is necessary to adhere to the principle of provenance, which assumes that the original order (context) is preserved.

This is shown by the linkage between the Freedom of the Press Act and the Archives Act. The meaning of the concept 'freedom of information' has also evolved from a level of access to records in a certain case/matter (level 1), to access to information on a certain activity—that is, to records with no connection to a case specified by the applicant (level 2), to access to the mass of information controlled by the agency in all its different permutations and formats (level 3). The Swedish concept of freedom of information lies between levels 2 and 3. Only the principle of provenance will allow such access by preserving both the text/information and context/surrounding. Research is required, therefore, to integrate this principle into information management, and thus provide adequate facilities for obtaining information in both the long and the short term.

Harmonization between differing legislation is very important. The existing legislation is now, in principal, uniform, and is equally applicable to all official documents, regardless of whether they are in the custody of the originating agency or have been delivered to an archival authority. In the explanatory statements in the Archives Bill of 1990, its linkage to the Freedom of the Press Act was stated to be of utmost importance. Therefore the discussion as to what constitutes an official record is relevant to deciding what constitutes an archival record. Also the need to maintain a balance between protecting personal confidentiality, and meeting the demands of scholars for research materials and journalists for the free interchange of information, has put archives in the public spotlight.

One common difficulty is that, if these general goals are to be met in a high-technology society, archivists or persons working in records management must have the requisite knowledge and skills. It has been stressed that in a society like Sweden every official must have adequate knowledge of the current legislation on freedom of information, and implement it in his or her work. The international influences are also much more important in the 1990s than previously. One thing is certain; we are going through exciting times, where the position of our archival institutions depends on our competence and ability to perform the tasks placed on us by society.

References

Bohlin, A. (1988), *Allmanna handlingar* (Stockholm).
—— (1994), *Offentlighetsprincipen* (Stockholm).
Gränström, C. (1990), *The Evolution of Tools and Techniques for the Management of Machine-Readable Data: Management of Recorded Information* (Munich).
—— Lundquist, L., and Fredriksson, K. (1992), *Arkivlagen. Bakgrund och kommentarer* (Goteborg).
—— (1993a), *Will Archival Theory be Sufficient in the Future? Information Handling in Offices and Archives* (Munich).
—— (1993b), 'The Impact of Information Technology on Legislation', *Janus*, 2.
Seipel, P. (1988), *ADB-upptagningars offentlighet* (Stockholm).
Swedish Data Inspection Board (1995), *IT 2005 LEXIT Pre-Study* (Stockholm).

Towards a United but Distributed Archives of Europe?

HANS HOFMAN

ABSTRACT

This chapter examines the position within European archives in the late 1990s with respect to the preservation of electronic records and the use of computers. It then discusses possible future developments in these fields, and the prospects for the creation of an integrated archival network in the European Union.

INTRODUCTION

The increasing use of information technology (IT) has had a substantial impact within the archival world, as in society as a whole. IT not only provides new tools to pursue the traditional goals of archives, but also changes the nature of the object they preserve—the record. It is forcing archivists to rethink their methods and to adapt archival principles to the electronic environment. In almost every European country, archives are developing programmes and planning new strategies to meet these new challenges. There are significant differences in pace and proposed strategies, but these are partly a consequence of the different legal contexts in which archives work. Although each European country has its own archival tradition, the continued growth of the European Union is exerting a unifying force.

This chapter sketches out the state of affairs in the late 1990s, and indicates the issues which need to be addressed in order to be able to present researchers and historians working in a global environment with an instrument for access to archives based on digital communications. In doing so, I will try to give an impression of the situation regarding automation within European archives, and, closely related to this, their involvement in electronic records. This should provide an answer to the question as to whether or not cooperation is possible, and what benefits users and researchers could gain from it.

WHAT IS GOING ON IN EUROPE IN THE MID-1990S

Two surveys conducted in 1994 provide an overview of what national archives in Europe have done in the field of electronic records (Hofman and Wettengel 1994; Higgs 1995). The results show that they have barely entered the Information Age. This does not mean that nothing is happening—on the contrary there is a lot going on—but that the activity can be characterized as extremely scattered, tentative, and narrow in scope and perspective. These surveys found that:

- the differences between countries in their approach to the hand-ling/managing of electronic records are quite large. A very import-ant reason for this is the differing legal contexts in which they work (Bikson and Frinking 1993);
- experience in the field of electronic records is mainly based on (flat) data files and statistical databases, specifically in Sweden, Denmark, Germany, France, and Norway. This is mainly due to the fact that these datasets are the sorts of electronic records currently transferred to the archives (Hofman and Wettengel 1994; Higgs 1995); and,
- there is a generally accepted need for co-operation.

Preceding these surveys, a report was published by the Group of Experts on the Coordination of Archives (1994) which described the work of the national archives of all the member states of the European Union. Two chapters were devoted to electronic or digital archives. One related to the preservation of such archives, and the other to data communication between European archival institutions. The first focused on records created electronically, and the second on paper archives that have been digitized and information about archives such as finding aids and guides. Both chapters contain suggestions/proposals for co-opera-tion. The Council of Ministers of the EU indicated by a resolution of 17 June 1994 that one of its priorities should be the preservation of digital archives.

Some of the most interesting developments in the field of electronic records are taking place in northern Europe. The Nordic countries (Sweden, Norway, Denmark, Finland, and Iceland) have worked together in the Tools for Electronic Archives Management (TEAM) project on the preservation, accessibility, and availability of electronic data files. The project is limited to mainframe database records. Important components of the research being done here are investigations into the possibility of making departmental registers of electronic records accessible to researchers (Denmark), and of departments creating registered files according to a model available from the archives and transferring metadata on these files to the latter (Norway). The legal context of these countries gives the archives more authority to issue guidelines to agencies than in the case of other European countries. The Swedish National Archives are looking at the implications of their very liberal freedom-of-information legislation for the handling of electronic records (see Gränström, Chapter 22, this volume). The Bundesarchiv in Koblenz (Germany) has been concerned with similar issues since reunion with East Germany confronted it with the many data files of the former Communist regime (see Wettengel, Chapter 18, this volume).

The Swiss Bundesarchiv is developing a central repository for electronic text documents (ARELDA) as a means of preserving them. Another important initiative is the development of a strategy for guaranteeing the metadata of electronic records (GEVER = *Geschäftsverwaltung*). As a last example of current initiatives, the archival institutions in the Netherlands are co-operating in a project which has developed a strategy for dealing with electronic records, and are now developing functional requirements for an appropriate infrastructure with applications, procedures, and equipment to manage and preserve electronic records in general (Doorn, Chapter 21, this volume).

Whether or not electronic records should be transferred to the archival institution, or stay with the agency that created them, has become a major issue of debate. In the latter case, electronic records will not be physically transferred to the custody of an archive but remain in the possession of the creating organization. Archives will still need to have intellectual control over these records, so that they can fulfil their function of facilitating access to them, or of providing historical information. Whether these 'non-custodial' or 'distributed' archives, where the records are physically at different places but are controlled intellectually by the archives, will become widely adopted is unclear.

In general most archives still tend to have records transferred, because things have always been done that way. They also fear that they would lose their grip on electronic records if they are not transferred, a concern not without some substance (see Higgs, Chapter 12, this volume). The only example so far in which the national archives have decided to leave electronic records with the government agencies which created them is that of Australia (Stuckey 1995). From the point of view of researchers this is perhaps not an issue, because for them it does not matter where the records are held, as long as they can have access to them.

The situation with respect to automation within archives is less clear, but the general impression is that it is still in its early stages. In several European countries, systems have been built automating traditional archival tasks such as accessioning, repository management, and the creation of finding aids (Group of Experts on the Coordination of Archives 1994: ch. 6; Hannigan 1995). In the field of new services, experiments are being carried out on imaging important archival paper records, as in the case of the Archivos de los Indias in Spain. Furthermore, plans are being made to establish a network linking archival institutions.

The work being done in most European archives is very piecemeal and *ad hoc*, and there is hardly any co-ordination between archival institutions. This is another potential obstacle to the exchange of archival information on a European level, and to making it available on a network. This would cease to be a problem only if archivists develop one interface instead of confronting them with as many different interfaces as there are countries in Europe, or, worse still, as there are archival institutions.

WHAT FUTURE DEVELOPMENTS CAN WE EXPECT?

Archives in Europe have a long way to go before they will be able to co-operate in offering researchers, historians, and others new services based on modern IT. First of all, archives need to grasp that the Information Age requires a fundamentally different approach. What is their mission and how should this be accomplished in this new environment? Existing methods and activities need to be reviewed in order to establish whether or not they are adequate in this respect (Bearman and Hedstrom 1993).

Furthermore, archives have to organize and update their internal electronic infrastructure before they can effectively offer services on the electronic highway. Only in France with its Minitel video-text system can archives actually be accessed electronically. In other European countries, such as Spain and the Netherlands, plans exist, or are being drawn up. In the case of Sweden there is a legal problem, in that their freedom-of-information legislation implies that, if they are connected to the Internet, all information thereby communicated will become records of the Swedish archives. List servers for archives, such as those in North America, do not yet exist in Europe. Also, in the 1990s the most used network facility, the Internet, is still in its pioneering phase, with all the usual problems this brings. Obtaining information can still be difficult on the Net, in spite of the development of search engines. Furthermore, if one wants to use the Internet in order to disseminate archival information, this assumes the ownership of a personal computer (PC). And last, but not least, there is a lot of 'non-information' provided on the system. The more serious information is almost completely buried, unless one knows where to look for it.

Nevertheless, in view of the emergence of, and rapid developments in, information and communication technology, some co-operation between archival institutions in the different European states, and elsewhere, needs to be considered and realized. It would be a waste of energy and resources to invent the wheel afresh in different locations. Information and communication technology offers new opportunities for archives, and also makes it possible to realize co-operation. The 'global village' also includes the archival and historical community.

In the above-mentioned Report of the Group of Experts on the Coordination of Archives in the European Union, one gets a sense of the obstacles that obstruct the road towards co-operation. One way or another on its way towards a joint policy/approach, the archival community in Europe has to deal with linguistic barriers, different legal contexts which determine the way archives work, and different privacy regulations and rules relating to access and security, all reflecting cultural differences between the member states. In the field of archival theory itself there is, for instance, no universally accepted standard of archival description, although this is a field, as in the area of technology, where the basis for a common approach is present.

Yet the opportunities offered by a worldwide communication medium such as the Internet are promising. Archives are more and more aware of the possibilities which this rather informal but very powerful tool offers them. The arrival of 'global archives' is just a matter of time, but only if the archival world seizes its opportunities. What role should archives play in this respect and how can they use worldwide networks? As an example of what could be done, archives within Europe could develop a form of common gateway for access, with a common interface and retrieval function. This interface should give, amongst other things, an overview as to what archives are available in Europe, and allow researchers to gain access to historical sources in the differing European countries.

To achieve such new initiatives in IT, archives can and should use the several programs which the EU has established to stimulate these developments, such as INFO2000 or Raphael. INFO2000 was set up under a proposal of the European Commission to the European Council in 1995 and has a budget of 100 million ECU for the period 1996–2000 (see INFO2000 website at URL: http://www2.echo.lu/info2000). This has as its objective the stimulation of the production, development, and distribution of electronic publishing and interactive multimedia services. It is meant to contribute to the solution of structural problems in this field. Part of this program is, for instance, the exploitation of government information in Europe, and the development of multimedia information in the field of European cultural heritage. Raphael is part of the cultural policy of the EU and as such attempts to facilitate access to European cultural heritage. The activities of international bodies such as the International Council on Archives (ICA) and its committees, especially those on archival automation and electronic records, could also play an useful role in this respect.

CONCLUSION

The questions to be answered are no longer how, on the one hand, archives should implement new IT, or, on the other, how they should deal with electronic records, but how an archival institution can survive in the rapidly developing Information Age. In other words, how can archives best position themselves, and develop an integrated approach to meet both challenges? Co-operation or co-ordination of the various attempts within Europe to deal with these challenges is an important step in this process, which could stimulate and accelerate the use of IT in archives. The knowledge and experience within archives in different countries, and in different fields of IT, need to be brought together.

To take advantage of the new opportunities offered by IT, new approaches, skills, and expertise are required. Training and education are necessary to change the traditional world of archives. Only when archives succeed in this will they be able to meet the needs of users, researchers, and historians, reveal new perspectives and opportunities, and deliver new services.

References

Bearman, D., and Hedstrom, M. (1993), 'Reinventing Archives for Electronic Archives: Alternative Service Delivery Options', in Hedstrom (1993), 82–98.

Bikson, T. K., and Frinking, E. J. (1993), *Het heden onthouden/Preserving the Present* (The Hague).

Group of Experts on the Coordination of Archives (1994), *Archives in the European Union* (Brussels).

Hannigan, K. (1995), 'Sober Ways, Politic Drifts and Amiable Persuasions: Approaching the Information Highway from the Dusty Trail', *IASSIST Quarterly*, 19/2: 110–21.

Hedstrom, M. (1993) (ed.), *Electronic Records Management Program Strategies* (Archives and Museums Informatics Technical Reports No. 18, Pittsburgh).

Higgs, E. (1995), 'Information Superhighways or Quiet Country Lanes? Accessing Electronic Archives in the United Kingdom', in Yorke (1995), 52–67.

Hofman, J., and Wettengel, M. (1994), 'Electronic Records: The European Scene' (unpublished report).

Stuckey, S. (1995), 'The Australian Archives Policy on Electronic Records—the Technical Issues', in Yorke (1995): 121–32.

Yorke, S. (1995) (ed.), *Playing for Keeps: The Proceedings of an Electronic Records Management Conference hosted by the Australian Archives, Canberra, Australia, 8–10 November 1994* (Canberra).

INDEX